Elementary
School

Physical Education
LESSON PLANS

Guy C. Le Masurier

Charles B. Corbin

Meg Greiner

Dolly D. Lambdin

Human Kinetics

Library of Congress Cataloging-in-Publication Data

Fitness for life : elementary school physical education lesson plans / Guy C. Le Masurier . . . [et al.].
   p. cm.
  Includes bibliographical references.
  ISBN-13: 978-0-7360-8719-3 (soft cover)
  ISBN-10: 0-7360-8719-2 (soft cover)
1. Physical fitness for children--Curricula.   I. Le Masurier, Guy C.
  GV443.F529 2010
  613.7'042--dc22

                        2009043018

ISBN-10: 0-7360-8719-2 (print)
ISBN-13: 978-0-7360-8719-3 (print)

The Web addresses cited in this text were current as of December 2009, unless otherwise noted.

Acquisitions Editor: Scott Wikgren
Developmental Editor: Ray Vallese
Assistant Editor: Derek Campbell
Copyeditor: Alisha Jeddeloh
Permission Manager: Dalene Reeder
Graphic Designer: Fred Starbird
Graphic Artist: Angela K. Snyder
Cover Designer: Keith Blomberg
Photographer (cover): © Human Kinetics
Photographer (interior): Neil Bernstein, unless otherwise specified; photos on pp. 1, 27, 38, 54, 59, 65, 68, 75, 88, 95, 114, 129, 131, 134, 140, 144, 162, 172, 182, 201, 206, and 216 © Human Kinetics
Photo Asset Manager: Laura Fitch
Visual Production Assistant: Joyce Brumfield
Photo Production Manager: Jason Allen
Art Manager: Kelly Hendren
Associate Art Manager: Alan L. Wilborn
Illustrator: Keri Evans, unless otherwise specified
Printer: Versa Press

Printed in the United States of America

10 9 8 7 6 5 4 3 2 1

The paper in this book is certified under a sustainable forestry program.

Human Kinetics
Web site: www.HumanKinetics.com

United States: Human Kinetics
P.O. Box 5076
Champaign, IL 61825-5076
800-747-4457
e-mail: humank@hkusa.com

Canada: Human Kinetics
475 Devonshire Road Unit 100
Windsor, ON N8Y 2L5
800-465-7301 (in Canada only)
e-mail: info@hkcanada.com

Europe: Human Kinetics
107 Bradford Road
Stanningley
Leeds LS28 6AT, United Kingdom
+44 (0) 113 255 5665
e-mail: hk@hkeurope.com

Australia: Human Kinetics
57A Price Avenue
Lower Mitcham, South Australia 5062
08 8372 0999
e-mail: info@hkaustralia.com

New Zealand: Human Kinetics
P.O. Box 80
Torrens Park, South Australia 5062
0800 222 062
e-mail: info@hknewzealand.com

E4966

CONTENTS

P A R T
I

GETTING STARTED
1

P A R T
II

LESSON PLANS FOR
GRADES K-2
27

PART III

LESSON PLANS FOR GRADES 3-6
131

LESSON FINDER

This guide provides 32 lesson plans—4 for each Wellness Week for grades K-2 and 4 for each Wellness Week for grades 3-6. There are four Wellness Weeks that will be conducted throughout the school year. This Lesson Finder will help you easily locate each lesson plan as you conduct the activities throughout the year.

Week	Lesson Plan	K-2	3-6
1	Warm-Up 1	page 31	page 135
		Instant Activity: Move and Freeze	Instant Activity: Move and Freeze
		Fitness Activity: Animal Antics	Fitness Activity: Physical Activity Pyramid for Kids Circuit
		Lesson Focus: Video Routine Practice	Lesson Focus: Video Routine Practice
		Culminating Activity: Fruits and Veggies Tag	Culminating Activity: Fruits and Veggies Tag
	1.1	page 36	page 141
		Instant Activity: Move and Freeze	Instant Activity: Move and Freeze
		Fitness Activity: Animal Antics	Fitness Activity: Physical Activity Pyramid for Kids Circuit
		Lesson Focus: Video Routine Variations	Lesson Focus: Video Routine Variations
		Culminating Activity: Fruits and Veggies Tag	Culminating Activity: Fruits and Veggies Tag
	1.2	page 41	page 147
		Instant Activity: Move and Freeze	Instant Activity: Move and Freeze
		Fitness Activity: Animal Antics	Fitness Activity: Physical Activity Pyramid for Kids Circuit
		Lesson Focus: Jumping for Joy	Lesson Focus: Jump Squad
		Culminating Activity: Fruits and Veggies Tag	Culminating Activity: Safety Scramble
	1.3	page 47	page 154
		Instant Activity: Move and Freeze	Instant Activity: Move and Freeze
		Fitness Activity: Animal Antics	Fitness Activity: Physical Activity Pyramid for Kids Circuit
		Lesson Focus: Tossing and Catching Skills	Lesson Focus: What's the Catch?
		Culminating Activity: Fruits and Veggies Tag	Culminating Activity: Safety Scramble

Week	Lesson Plan	K-2	3-6
2	**Warm-Up 2**	**page 55**	**page 163**
		Instant Activity: Athletes in Motion	Instant Activity: Athletes in Motion
		Fitness Activity: Grab Bag	Fitness Activity: Moving to Music
		Lesson Focus: Video Routine Practice	Lesson Focus: Video Routine Practice
		Culminating Activity: Cardio Caper	Culminating Activity: Soda Swarm
	2.1	**page 60**	**page 169**
		Instant Activity: Athletes in Motion	Instant Activity: Athletes in Motion
		Fitness Activity: Grab Bag	Fitness Activity: Moving to Music
		Lesson Focus: Video Routine Variations	Lesson Focus: Video Routine Variations
		Culminating Activity: Cardio Caper	Culminating Activity: Soda Swarm
	2.2	**page 66**	**page 176**
		Instant Activity: Athletes in Motion	Instant Activity: Tempo Tag
		Fitness Activity: Grab Bag	Fitness Activity: Moving to Music
		Lesson Focus: Ready, Set, Run	Lesson Focus: PACER Practice
		Culminating Activity: Cardio Caper	Culminating Activity: Small-Sided Sports
	2.3	**page 72**	**page 183**
		Instant Activity: Athletes in Motion	Instant Activity: Tempo Tag
		Fitness Activity: Grab Bag	Fitness Activity: Moving to Music
		Lesson Focus: Sport Centers	Lesson Focus: Sport Skills Circuit
		Culminating Activity: Cardio Caper	Culminating Activity: Small-Sided Sports

Week	Lesson Plan	K-2	3-6
4	**Warm-Up 4**	page 105	page 217
		Instant Activity: Healthy Body Tag	Instant Activity: Pirate Fitness
		Fitness Activity: Olympic Athlete Workout	Fitness Activity: Sensational Circuit
		Lesson Focus: Video Routine Practice	Lesson Focus: Video Routine Practice
		Culminating Activity: Veggie Medley	Culminating Activity: Water Fight
	4.1	page 111	page 223
		Instant Activity: Healthy Body Tag	Instant Activity: Pirate Fitness
		Fitness Activity: Olympic Athlete Workout	Fitness Activity: Sensational Circuit
		Lesson Focus: Video Routine Variations	Lesson Focus: Video Routine Variations
		Culminating Activity: Veggie Medley	Culminating Activity: Water Fight
	4.2	page 118	page 230
		Instant Activity: Healthy Body Tag	Instant Activity: Pirate Fitness
		Fitness Activity: Olympic Athlete Workout	Fitness Activity: Sensational Circuit
		Lesson Focus: Are You Balanced?	Lesson Focus: BMI Practice
		Culminating Activity: Healthy Food Medley	Culminating Activity: Water Fight
	4.3	page 124	page 237
		Instant Activity: Healthy Body Tag	Instant Activity: Pirate Fitness
		Fitness Activity: Olympic Athlete Workout	Fitness Activity: Sensational Circuit
		Lesson Focus: Kick It!	Lesson Focus: Sensational Small-Sided Games
		Culminating Activity: Fruit Salad	Culminating Activity: Water Fight

PREFACE

Fitness for Life: Elementary School is a unique program that focuses attention on schoolwide wellness during four weeks of the school year. A primary objective of the program is to help schools incorporate coordinated activities that will enable them to meet national standards and guidelines for physical activity and nutrition as part of their school wellness policy. The program promotes healthy lifestyles in physical education and classrooms as well as in the entire school and community. Featured components of healthy lifestyles are sound nutrition and regular physical activity. The program is designed specifically for elementary school students and provides lesson plans for physical education, physical activities for the classroom (including video-led routines and afternoon activity breaks), and whole-school events and activities. The program is designed to be easy to use, engaging, and fun for teachers and students. More complete details are included in part I of this book.

Fitness for Life: Elementary School is the result of a team effort. Scott Wikgren, director of the Health, Physical Education, Recreation, and Dance division of Human Kinetics, was the driving force behind this project. He was responsible for bringing the successful and award-winning **Fitness for Life: High School** program to Human Kinetics and also was the driving force behind the award-winning **Fitness for Life: Middle School** program. With Scott's assistance, an author team and a team of expert consultants were assembled. Together, Scott and I chose Guy Le Masurier, Dolly Lambdin, and Meg Greiner as coauthors for the project. Ellen Abbadessa and Jeff Walkuski were chosen as consulting authors. Guy contributes youthful enthusiasm, an excellent ability to put words on paper in a meaningful way, and a practical understanding of the needs of school-age youth. Dolly, former President of the National Association for Sport and Physi-

cal Education (NASPE) and recipient of the University of Texas' Massey Award for Excellence in Teacher Education, also brings years of practical experience working with both students and teachers, an understanding of pedagogical principles and curriculum planning, and sound leadership. Meg has been honored as a NASPE Elementary Physical Educator of the Year, Disney Outstanding Specialist Teacher, and a *USA Today* All-Star Teacher. She has years of practical experience and is known for her innovative methods of promoting physical activity for all children. Ellen, an elementary physical education teacher and supervisor, helped with all aspects of the program but particularly with the teacher resources. Jeff, known for his years as a professor of physical education pedagogy, also contributed to all aspects of the program but primarily contributed to the afternoon activities in the classroom guides and related teacher information in each classroom lesson.

Other consultants who contributed to the project are listed on the acknowledgments page (p. xi). The consultants provided field testing, critiques of activities and book content, and suggestions for revisions and improvement. Special thanks go out to Linda Coyle, the social studies, physical education, and health specialist for the Paradise Valley, Arizona, schools. We also thank her excellent physical education advisory committee members for their input at all stages of program development and for their help in field testing the program. Many of the **Fitness for Life** instructors who participate in a program jointly sponsored by Physical Best and Human Kinetics also provided input.

Finally, I (and my coauthors) cannot say enough about the excellent work done by our editors, Ray Vallese and Derek Campbell, and our video and audio production partners, Doug Fink, Chris Johns, and Roger Francisco. In many ways Ray was really a coauthor of the program; not only did he do excellent development work and project coordination, but he also contributed many ideas and excellent content. Derek contributed in many similar ways. Both editors worked long hours and were diligent far beyond the call of duty. Doug and Chris were the creative minds behind the video productions and deserve Oscars for their work. Roger is the real pro who provided us with the music and other audio resources necessary for making the project a success. We cannot thank these people enough for their hard work and attention to detail. We would also like to thank all of the other people at Human Kinetics who contributed to this team effort.

Charles B. "Chuck" Corbin

ACKNOWLEDGMENTS

Many people played a role in the development of **Fitness for Life: Elementary School**. The following list credits the people who made this program possible. As noted in the preface, many others at Human Kinetics also contributed, and we acknowledge them all.

Video (Human Kinetics)

- Doug Fink, producer/director
- Roger Francisco, audio director
- Gregg Henness, camera operator/production assistant/teleprompter operator/Avid editor/DVD programmer
- Bill Yauch, camera operator
- Dan Walker, location audio
- Mark Herman, Avid editor/DVD programmer
- Chris Clark, Avid editor
- Sean Roosevelt, computer graphics art designer
- Stuart Cartwright, computer graphics art designer
- Amy Rose, production coordinator
- Chris Johns, scripts

Video Production (Camera Originals, Oak Brook, Illinois)

- Caren Cosby, producer/assistant director
- David Pierro, director of photography
- Dave Cosby, camera operator
- Tom McCosky, camera operator
- Ian Vacek, camera assistant
- Mark Markley, lighting
- Peter Horowitz, grip
- E.J. Huntemann, grip
- Dave Jack, audio technician
- Jackie Florczak, makeup/wardrobe
- Sarah Murphy, production coordinator
- Lauryn Kardatzke, production assistant
- Casey Lock, production assistant
- Kim Williams, O'Connor Casting

Video Hosts (K-2)

- David Goodloe
- Britni Tozzi

Video Hosts (3-6)

- Akula Lyman
- Laura Ball

Video Messages (authors)

- Chuck Corbin
- Guy Le Masurier
- Dolly Lambdin
- Meg Greiner
- Ellen Abbadessa (contributor)
- Jodi Le Masurier (contributor)

Audio/Music (Human Kinetics)

- Roger Francisco

Music Lyrics

- Chuck Corbin

Lyrics Advisors

- Cathie Corbin
- Dave Corbin
- Kris Youngkin
- Joan Milligan
- Dolly Lambdin

All About Dance Studio

- Jessica Goldman

Dance Consultants

- Josie Metal-Corbin
- Cathie Corbin
- Katie Corbin

- Julia Corbin
- Molly Corbin
- Suzi Corbin
- Joan Milligan

Performers (K-2)

- Christopher Chu
- Rohan Jain
- Carlton Jenkins
- Alex Rich
- Hayden Whitley
- Vincent Wilkinson
- Princess Jenkins
- Olivia Klein
- Brooke Kolker
- Claire Seymour
- Mollie Smithson
- Emma Weiss
- Chloe Zoller

Performers (3-6)

- Krystal Anderson
- Nair Banks
- Allie Bensinger
- Lauren Borg
- Caroline Chu
- Courtney Cosby
- Emily Schwartz
- Ashlyn Wiebe
- Aram Wilkinson
- Benjie Barclay
- Travis Little
- Kyle Birnbaum
- Nick Lucero
- Robert Banks

Performers (Guide for Wellness Coordinators DVD)

- Mollee Carter
- Ana Martinez
- Jose Quiroz

- Heaven Reed
- Rufina Reutov
- Rolando Sifuentez

Teacher Consultants

Paradise Valley, Arizona

- Linda Coyle, social studies, physical education & health, curriculum specialist
- Jay Thomas, Pinnacle High School
- Tonya Schwailler, Horizon High School
- Tammy Butler, Mountain Trail Middle School
- Craig Vogenson, Explorer Middle School
- Michael Wooldridge, Village Vista Elementary School
- Michele Popa, Desert Springs Elementary School
- Becki Griffen, Copper Canyon Elementary School
- George Mang, Pinnacle Peak Elementary School
- Susie Etchenbarren, PVUSD Adaptive Physical Education

Austin, Texas

- Laura Mikulencak, Pillow Elementary School
- Courtney Perry, Barton Hills Elementary School
- Tammy Arredondo, Graham Elementary School

Phoenix, Arizona

- Suzi Corbin

Contributing Authors

- Ellen Abbadessa
- Jeff Walkuski

Physical Best Authors

- Laura Borsdorf
- Lois Boeyink
- NASPE in association with AAHPERD

Dance Credits

- Harvest Time: movements adapted, with permission, from a video of a traditional African harvest dance (Djole) by Charles Ahovissi.

- Tinikling: movements adapted from Corbin, C.B. (1969), *Becoming physically educated in the elementary school*, Philadelphia: Lea & Febiger, used by permission of author and copyright owner, pages 323-329.

- Jumpnastics: movements adapted from Corbin, C.B. & Corbin, D.E. (1972), *Inexpensive equipment for games, play and physical activity*, Dubuque, IA: Brown, used by permission of authors and copyright owners, pages 49-50.

- Stomp and Balance: adapted from the Danish dance Seven Jumps as described by Corbin, C.B. (1969), *Becoming physically educated in the elementary school*, Philadelphia: Lea & Febiger, used by permission of author and copyright owner, pages 308-309, credit to RCA records, 1958 for original permission (now out of print).

- Hip Hop 5: adapted from a routine created by Mychal Taylor, Cecily Taylor, and Josie Metal-Corbin, used by permission.

- Keep on Clapping: adapted from a routine created by Mychal Taylor, Cecily Taylor, and Josie Metal-Corbin, used by permission.

PART

I

GETTING STARTED

• •

Part I of this guide provides a general introduction to the **Fitness for Life: Elementary School** program and a more detailed section on using the physical education lesson plans.

• **Program Introduction** (page 3): This section introduces the **FFL: Elementary** program, discussing its rationale, organization, components, responsibilities, educational foundations, and overall philosophy. It also includes an executive summary (page 8) that distills the ratio-

nale and main components into a single page. This program introduction is similar to those found in the classroom guides and the *Guide for Wellness Coordinators*.

• **Using the Lesson Plans** (page 15): This section outlines the role of the physical educator, presents delivery options for the **FFL: Elementary** physical education lessons, describes the lesson plan structure, and provides tips for successful delivery of the lesson plans.

PROGRAM INTRODUCTION

Fitness for Life
Elementary School

Fitness for Life: Elementary School (FFL: Elementary) is a unique program that focuses on schoolwide wellness. It provides curriculum materials for the classroom and physical education classes, as well as school-wide activities and take-home information that promote healthy lifestyles in the school and the community. The healthy lifestyles components feature sound nutrition and regular physical activity. The program is designed specifically for elementary school students and involves the entire school, including teachers, administrators, and staff.

Program Rationale

Every school that receives federal school lunch program money must develop and carry out a school wellness policy. **FFL: Elementary** helps schools carry out a wellness plan. It supplements other school programs, such as physical education, health curricula, and school cafeteria programs. It provides a focal point for healthy lifestyle promotion on a schoolwide basis. Some important outcomes of **FFL: Elementary** include the following:

- **Helping children meet national physical activity guidelines**. National physical activity guidelines call for 60 minutes of physical activity each day for every child. Many youth do not get the recommended amount of activity (United States Department of Health and Human Services [USDHHS], 2008). **FFL: Elementary** helps students meet the guidelines and is especially important to children whose daily activity outside of school is low.

- **Helping children avoid becoming overweight or obese**. Childhood obesity has tripled since the 1980s. Today, more than 15 percent of children are classified

Some of the information provided in this section is similar to information provided in the introduction to the classroom guides and the *Guide for Wellness Coordinators*. This overlap is intentional. Not all teachers will read the same books, and it is important for everyone to get similar information. The *Guide for Wellness Coordinators* includes more detail about the **Fitness for Life: Elementary School** program and its educational foundations. Wellness coordinators may want to lend their guide to classroom teachers, physical education teachers, and others who want more information about the program.

as obese, and an additional 15 percent or more are classified as overweight (Ogden et al., 2008). Regular physical activity and sound nutrition can contribute significantly to solving the problem.

- **Helping children avoid long periods of inactivity.** National guidelines indicate that children should not be inactive for long periods of time. We often condemn television watching and excessive use of computer games by children because they promote inactivity, yet schools often do the same thing—keep children inactive for long periods of time. Providing activity breaks and teaching children about physical activity and nutrition are good educational policies.
- **Helping children eat well.** Reinforcing sound nutrition in **FFL: Elementary** programs can help children improve nutrition habits, help prevent obesity, and improve general health.
- **Enhancing academic achievement.** Recent evidence clearly shows that time taken during the school day to involve children in physical activity does not decrease academic learning. In fact, there is ample evidence that physical activity breaks during the day enhance academic learning (Hillman et al., 2009a; Hillman et al., 2009b; Le Masurier & Corbin, 2006; Ratey, 2008; Smith & Lounsbery, 2009).
- **Stimulating cognitive function.** Benefits of regular physical activity include improved blood flow and vascular supply to the brain and increased production of brain-derived neurotrophic factor (BDNF) that supports neural connections (Ratey, 2008).
- **Helping your school fulfill its wellness plan.** All schools receiving federal funding for school meal programs must have a school wellness policy and comply with it (Le Masurier & Corbin, 2006). Taking the time to include **FFL: Elementary** in your program will help you and your school meet the school wellness policy requirement.

Program Organization

Fitness for Life: Elementary School focuses attention on physical activity and nutrition during four weeks of the school year. One week out of every nine weeks of school is designated a Wellness Week. During each Wellness Week, the entire school focuses on wellness, emphasizing sound nutrition and regular physical activity. The exact dates of each Wellness Week are determined by the school staff. A wellness coordinator will be chosen to help coordinate the week's activities. In many cases, the physical education teacher will serve as wellness coordinator; however, the coordinator could be a classroom teacher, a nurse, a school staff member, or even a parent.

You may find the **FFL: Elementary** format so engaging and helpful that you want to include the activities every week, which would be great. But the basic program involves classroom activities during one week of every nine weeks of school.

Each Wellness Week has two themes, one for physical activity and one for nutrition. Daily wellness messages are emphasized during the Wellness Weeks. Table 1.1 illustrates the themes and messages for each Wellness Week. Special schoolwide nutrition activities are planned every Wednesday (Eat Well Wednesday), and schoolwide physical activities are planned every Friday (Get Fit Friday). You and your students will participate in these activities, which are organized by the wellness coordinator.

Program Components

The components of Wellness Week include the following:

- **Special physical education lessons.** The program provides one physical education lesson plan to be used the week before each Wellness Week (a warm-up lesson) and three lesson plans for use during each Wellness Week. Part II of this book includes the lesson plans for kindergarten through grade 2, and part III includes the plans for grades 3 through 6.

Table 1.1 Messages for Each Wellness Week

Wellness Week	Activity theme	Nutrition theme	Daily messages for K-2	Daily messages for 3-5	Daily messages for 6
Week 1 (held in fall, or during the first 9 weeks of the school year)	Moderate physical activity	Fruits and vegetables	1: Be active every day. 2: Keep on trying. 3: Fitness foods 4: Play safely. 5: I can, you can, we all can.	1: 60 minutes every day 2: The more you practice, the better you get. 3: Eat 5 a day. 4: Start with safety. 5: Fun for me, fun for you, fun for all.	1: There are lots of fun physical activities. 2: Practice builds skills. 3: You are what you eat. 4: Safety is key for staying healthy. 5: I can!
Week 2 (held in fall/winter, or during the second 9 weeks of the school year)	Vigorous physical activity (vigorous aerobics, sports, and recreation)	Grains and high-calorie foods	1: Get your body moving! 2: Get better with practice. 3: Foods with fats 4: Exercise your heart. 5: Never, ever give up!	1: Play for a good day. 2: Build skills, have more fun. 3: Avoid empty calories. 4: Aerobic activity every day 5: Show respect.	1: Active all day 2: Start with the basics. 3: High-calorie foods 4: Heartbeats for health 5: Self-respect
Week 3 (held in winter/spring, or during the third 9 weeks of the school year)	Muscle fitness and flexibility exercises	Protein	1: Get your muscles ready. 2: Move your body. 3: Food for strong bones and muscles 4: You have only one body; make it fit! 5: If it is to be, it's up to me.	1: Take care of your muscles. 2: Practice for fitness. 3: Protein power 4: Be specific; look terrific. 5: Don't be a character—have character.	1: There is no "I" in "team". 2: Feedback to improve 3: Protein is important. 4: You get what you train for. 5: Rules rule!
Week 4 (held in spring, or during the fourth 9 weeks of the school year)	Integration (energy balance)	Energy balance	1: Get off your seat and move your feet. 2: Play lots, learn lots. 3: Healthy food helps us move. 4: Be water wise. 5: Plan to get better.	1: Brain and body exercise 2: Combine skills just for the fun of it. 3: Balance energy in (food) with energy out (exercise). 4: Water, water, before I get hotter! 5: Personal fitness starts with you.	1: Build a healthy body; build a healthy mind. 2: One step at a time 3: Balance calories. 4: Hit the water. 5: SMART goals

This table presents the overall nutrition theme for each Wellness Week; each grade range has a more specific variation of that theme. For example, the K-2 nutrition theme for Wellness Week 1 is "Fruits and vegetables (fitness foods)."

WHAT IS WELLNESS?

The **Fitness for Life: Elementary School** program focuses on wellness for school children. It includes Wellness Week activities that can be used to implement wellness policy as mandated by federal law. To implement an effective wellness program, it is helpful to have a clear understanding of the meaning of the word *wellness*. Many years ago, the World Health Organization defined health as being more than absence of disease (WHO, 1947). It was agreed that wellness, not just sickness, should be included in a definition of good health. The characteristics of wellness include the following:

* Wellness is part of good health.
* Wellness is a state of being exemplified by quality of life and a sense of well-being. Examples of quality of life and a sense of well-being from the health goals for our nation include the ability to perform activities of daily life without restriction, happiness, satisfaction with our lives, self-esteem, and a positive outlook on life.
* Wellness is considered the positive component of good health (more than freedom from illness).

* Health and its positive component (wellness) are integrated; each interacts with the other, and if one is influenced, both are influenced.
* Both health and wellness are multidimensional. The most commonly described dimensions are physical, social, intellectual, emotional (mental), and spiritual.

Two healthy lifestyles prominent in **FFL: Elementary** are regular physical activity and sound nutrition. These two lifestyles have been shown to have a positive impact on wellness and to reduce the risk of chronic diseases. Especially important is the fact that regular physical activity and sound nutrition are factors in life over which people have control. For this reason, these two behaviors are considered to be high-priority lifestyles. They can be changed with the help of educators and sound educational programs such as **FFL: Elementary**. Those who adopt healthy lifestyles will have improved health and wellness. Wellness programs typically include an emphasis on physical activity and nutrition because of their known benefits to personal wellness.

Adapted from Corbin, C.B., & Pangrazi, R.P. 2001. Toward a uniform definition of wellness: A commentary. *President's Council on Physical Fitness and Sports Research Digest, 3*(15), 1-8. Available at www.fitness.gov/publications/digests/pcpfs_research_digs.html.

* **Classroom activity breaks using video routines** created especially for **FFL: Elementary**. The lesson plans for using these routines are provided in the classroom guide for each grade, and the routines are included on the DVD in each guide.
* **Classroom activity breaks using additional activities** that reinforce academic concepts in subjects such as math, science, and language arts. Plans for these breaks are included in the classroom guide for each grade.

* **Conceptual learning** related to wellness (focusing on nutrition and physical activity) using messages on the DVD video routines. These are done in the classroom and in physical education class.
* **Signs** for the classroom, the gym, the cafeteria, and school bulletin boards promoting sound nutrition and regular physical activity. These are provided on the CD-ROM in this book, as well as in the resource materials available to classroom teachers and wellness coordinators.

- **Chants** to reinforce the major messages of each lesson.
- **Eat Well Wednesdays** that feature schoolwide nutrition activities (involving the cafeteria). The general nutrition themes for each Wellness Week are shown in table 1.1. The wellness coordinator works with the cafeteria staff to conduct the special nutrition activities.
- **Get Fit Fridays** that feature schoolwide physical activities called TEAM Time; TEAM stands for "Together Everyone Achieves More." The TEAM Time activities are organized by the wellness coordinator with the help of all school staff.
- **Other schoolwide events** (celebration activities) promoting sound nutrition and regular physical activity. These are coordinated by the wellness coordinator with the help of all school staff.
- **Newsletters** for distribution to families during Wellness Week. It is recommended that these be printed by the wellness coordinator and administrative staff and distributed to teachers for distribution to parents. However, they can also be printed at the classroom level or sent to parents by e-mail. Newsletters are provided among the resource materials for each book and can be customized to suit local needs.
- **Worksheets** for use in promoting sound nutrition and physical activity. Worksheets are used in the classroom and in physical education, and they are provided among the resource materials for each book.
- **FFL: Elementary Web site**. A Web site dedicated to **FFL: Elementary** is available at www.fitnessforlife.org. This site provides information for teachers, students, and parents.

Program Responsibilities

A general overview of the **FFL: Elementary** program is provided in the Executive Summary on the next page. This summary will help school staff better understand the components of the program. The summary (also available on the CD-ROM for distribution to school staff) provides a section to help classroom teachers fit the program into their daily routine.

Responsibilities for school staff are listed below. Duties for the physical education teacher are given first.

Physical Education Teacher

- Teaches the warm-up lesson the week before each Wellness Week. This includes teaching the video routine to be performed in the classroom during Wellness Week.
- Teaches lessons during Wellness Week.
- Posts Wellness Week signs in the gym.
- Assists with schoolwide events planned by the wellness coordinator (e.g., Eat Well Wednesday, Get Fit Friday, celebration activities).
- May serve as the wellness coordinator—if so, performs the coordinator duties listed below. For more details, refer to the *Guide for Wellness Coordinators*.

Classroom Teacher

- Conducts activity breaks in the classroom using video routines on the DVD included with the classroom guides.
- Conducts discussions about wellness messages included on the videos.
- Conducts integrated activities in math, science, and other academic content areas as activity breaks (as outlined in the lesson plans in the classroom guides).
- Conducts the classroom discussion for Eat Well Wednesday.
- Posts the Wellness Week signs (from the classroom guide DVD) in the classroom.
- Sends home the Wellness Week newsletter (provided by the wellness coordinator or printed from the classroom guide DVD).
- Uses classroom worksheets (on the classroom guide DVD) as appropriate.
- Assists with schoolwide events planned by the wellness coordinator (e.g., Eat Well Wednesday, Get Fit Friday, celebration activities).

School Principal

- Appoints or aids in selection of the wellness coordinator.
- Provides enthusiastic support for the **FFL: Elementary** program.
- Participates in schoolwide Wellness Week activities.

EXECUTIVE SUMMARY

What Is Fitness for Life: Elementary School?

Fitness for Life: Elementary School (FFL: Elementary) is a program designed to promote wellness, physical activity, sound nutrition, and healthy lifestyles throughout the entire school.

Why Should I Do the Program?

Some of the principal benefits of **FFL: Elementary** are as follows:

* Helps your students meet national physical activity guidelines.
* Helps your school implement a wellness policy as required by law.
* Helps prevent childhood obesity by teaching about expending calories and limiting caloric intake.
* Helps build youth fitness.
* Helps children eat a healthy diet and meet national nutrition goals.
* Promotes academic achievement.
* Stimulates activity that increases blood flow to the brain.

What Are the Basic Components of the Program?

FFL: Elementary is a schoolwide wellness program that requires participation by all school employees and students. Once every nine weeks, the entire school conducts a Wellness Week (four each year). Major activities of each Wellness Week include the following:

* **Classroom activity breaks** that use teacher-friendly DVD videos and lesson plans
* **Physical education activities** that use provided lesson plans

* **Schoolwide special events** with plans for Eat Well Wednesday (a day of nutrition activities), Get Fit Friday (a day of TEAM Time physical activities), and celebration activities
* **School signs** promoting wellness to be posted throughout the school
* **Educational video messages** that teach children about wellness, sound nutrition, and physical activity
* **Worksheets** to reinforce learning about sound nutrition and physical activity
* **Newsletters** to help families get involved in Wellness Week
* A **Web site** to help students and families learn more about important wellness concepts

How Do I Find Time for the Program?

Time is at a premium in elementary school, and there are many educational goals to be met. So how can you find the time for **FFL: Elementary**? The program is conducted during four weeks each year so that a concentrated effort can be placed on wellness during these specific weeks. The classroom activity breaks can be done in 5 to 6 minutes. The total time for **FFL: Elementary** is 10 to 15 minutes per day. Research shows that time in physical activity can promote learning in the classroom, so the time is well spent. The breaks also promote fitness, health, and wellness. Taking 2 to 3 minutes from each hour of the school day will provide the time to conduct classroom activity breaks. The physical education lessons can be conducted in regular physical education classes and can be integrated with the regular physical education program.

Wellness Coordinator

- Conducts faculty–staff meeting to explain Wellness Week (uses PowerPoint® file on the *Guide for Wellness Coordinators* DVD).
- Coordinates Wellness Week activities.
- Oversees schoolwide events such as Eat Well Wednesday and Get Fit Friday activities.
- Distributes materials to teachers and staff (e.g., Wellness Week newsletters, plans for Wellness Week schoolwide events).
- Provides in-service as necessary.

Art Teacher

- Works with the wellness coordinator and classroom teachers to promote wellness, physical activity, and nutrition during each Wellness Week.
- Has students create art related to wellness for posting on school walls (or as part of a wellness art show).

Music Teacher

- Works with classroom and physical education teachers to promote wellness during Wellness Week.

- Helps students learn songs from the video routines (on the classroom guide DVDs) to be performed in the classroom.

Librarian/Computer Teacher

- Identifies books on wellness, nutrition, and physical activity and encourages students to read them during Wellness Week.
- Supports computer activities related to Wellness Week (e.g., MyPyramid Tracker, Activitygram).

Nutrition Staff

- Conducts schoolwide nutrition activities on Eat Well Wednesday.
- Posts Wellness Week nutrition signs in the school and cafeteria.

Other Staff

- Assist the wellness coordinator with schoolwide events.
- Assist in printing and posting Wellness Week signs.

Parents

- Help with schoolwide events.
- Encourage children to be active and eat well, especially during Wellness Week.

The physical education teacher helps students learn the routines that they perform during their classroom activity breaks.

HELP TEACHERS FIND THE TIME FOR CLASSROOM ACTIVITIES

Classroom teachers have many subjects to cover during the school day. Some may feel that they do not have time for classroom physical activities during Wellness Week. Help these teachers understand that the time taken for Wellness Week activities will not only improve student health and fitness but will also contribute to achievement in the classroom and to better test performance (Hillman et al., 2009a; Hillman et al., 2009b; Le Masurier & Corbin, 2006; Ratey, 2008; Smith & Lounsbery, 2009). Taking just 1 to 3 minutes from each hour of the school day (or 1 to 3 minutes from five activities during the day) will provide the time needed for classroom Wellness Week activities. You can also remind teachers that Wellness Week occurs only four times a year.

Educational Foundations

Fitness for Life: Elementary School is based on sound educational foundations. Some of the key information that was considered in building the program is summarized in this section. More comprehensive coverage of the educational foundations for **FFL: Elementary** is available in part III of the *Guide for Wellness Coordinators*. If you are interested in learning more about these foundations, borrow the guide from your wellness coordinator (if you are not serving as the coordinator).

Child Nutrition and WIC Reauthorization Act

In 2004, the U.S. Congress passed the Child Nutrition and WIC (Women, Infants, and Children) Reauthorization Act, and it was signed into law (Public Law 108-265). As a result of the act, all states, school districts, and schools receiving funding for school lunch programs must have a policy (a plan) designed to encourage total school wellness. Central to a sound wellness policy is the notion that the primary mission of schools is to promote optimal learning for all children, and this cannot be achieved if students are not fit, healthy, and well. **FFL: Elementary** helps schools meet key guidelines of the legislation and can help your school meet wellness planning guidelines. Action for Healthy Kids is a group dedicated to promoting school wellness and has many online tools to help implement school wellness plans. For more information, visit www.actionforhealthykids.org.

USDHHS National Physical Activity Guidelines for Children

In October of 2008, the U.S. Department of Health and Human Services (USDHHS) published national physical activity guidelines for children. These guidelines, as abstracted below, were used in developing the **FFL: Elementary** program. For more details, visit www.health.gov/paguidelines.

- Children should perform physical activity at least 60 minutes each day. Choose from either moderate activity (equal in intensity to brisk walking) or vigorous activity (elevates heart rate).
- Children should perform vigorous activity at least 3 days per week.
- Children should perform stretching and muscle fitness activities that build muscles and bones at least 3 days per week.
- Activities should be age appropriate, enjoyable, and varied.

USDA National Nutrition Guidelines

Every five years, a committee of the U.S. Department of Agriculture (USDA) revises the national nutrition guidelines. A recent revision resulted in the development of MyPyramid (see figure 1.1). The nutrition component of the **FFL: Elementary** program relies heavily on information associated with MyPyramid. The steps on the side of the pyramid represent the various forms of physical activity that are also depicted in the Physical Activity Pyramid for Kids (see figure 1.2). The USDA nutrition guidelines emphasize the importance of physical activity and sound nutrition in promoting health and wellness.

Physical Activity Pyramid for Kids

The Physical Activity Pyramid for Kids (see figure 1.2) illustrates the different types of physical activity that can be used to promote good health, fitness, and wellness. The basic pyramid is used in all **Fitness for Life** programs, but there is a special version just for young children; the upper-level programs use the Physical Activity Pyramid for Teens. The Physical Activity Pyramid for Kids helps children better understand the benefits of the different types of activity. As noted earlier, each of the four Wellness Weeks focuses on a different type of physical activity from the pyramid.

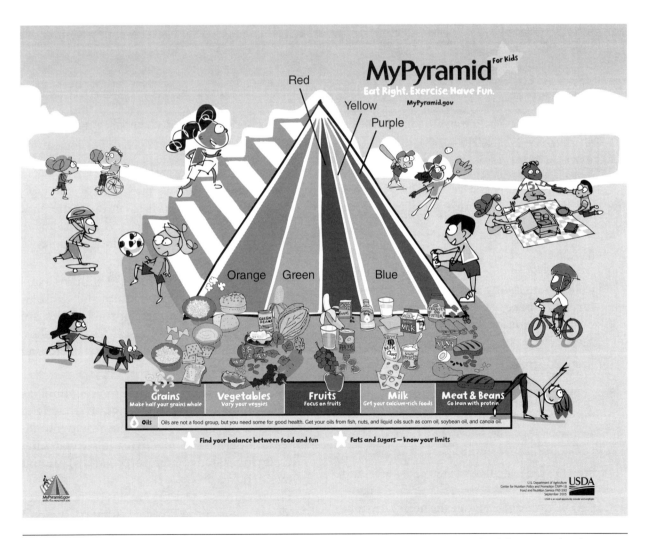

Figure 1.1 MyPyramid is a visual model designed to help children learn about each of the major food groups. MyPyramid is used extensively in the **FFL: Elementary** program. For more information, go to www.mypyramid.gov.

Adapted from U.S. Department of Agriculture.

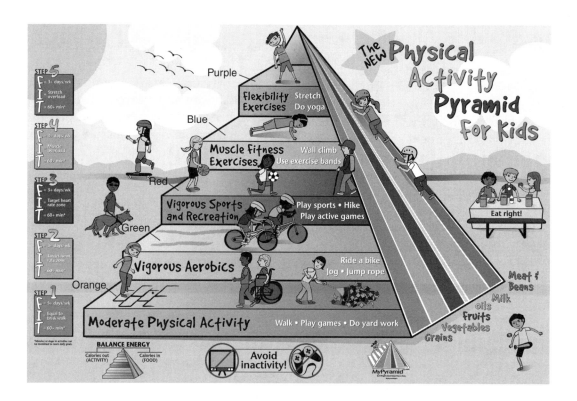

Figure 1.2   The Physical Activity Pyramid for Kids is a visual model designed to help children learn about the five major physical activity types.

© 2010 Charles B. Corbin

The Physical Activity Pyramid for Kids has five colored steps that represent different types of activity.

- Moderate activity is represented by step 1 (orange). It includes activities equal to brisk walking, including active play for children. It is at the base of the pyramid because it is the most commonly performed activity and can be done regularly by all people.

- Step 2 (green) includes vigorous aerobics. Activities that are vigorous enough to elevate the heart rate in the heart rate target zone are considered to be vigorous aerobics. Jogging, biking at a relatively fast pace, and lap swimming are examples.

- Step 3 (red) includes vigorous sports and recreation such as tennis, soccer, and hiking. Only activities that elevate the heart rate sufficiently are considered to be vigorous in nature. Some sports and recreational activities such as bowling are classified as moderate (step 1).

- Step 4 (blue) includes exercises for muscle fitness. Climbing on a climbing structure,

calisthenics such as push-ups or curl-ups, elastic band exercises, and stunts that require the use of arms and legs to move the body (e.g., crab walk) are examples of muscle fitness exercises.

- Step 5 (purple) includes flexibility exercises. Activities that require the muscles to stretch beyond their normal length are called flexibility exercises. Examples are gymnastics stunts, yoga, and stretching calisthenics (e.g., sit and reach).

National guidelines for children recommend activity from all steps of the pyramid. Inactivity or sedentary living is shown below the pyramid. Extended periods of inactivity (e.g., watching TV, playing inactive computer games) should be avoided.

The resources CD-ROM in this book includes a color version of the Physical Activity Pyramid for Kids. The pyramid is provided as one of the general signs for use during any Wellness Week (see pages 21-22 for details about the general signs). Part III of the *Guide for Wellness Coordinators* provides more details on the pyramid.

EAT 5 TO 9 A DAY

To encourage consumption of a variety of fruits and vegetables, the **FFL: Elementary** program uses the simple "5 to 9 servings a day" message that is designed to help children meet national recommendations. For cooked vegetables, 1/2 cup equals one serving, and for leafy vegetables, 1 cup equals one serving. One medium apple, banana, or pear equals one fruit serving. The Centers for Disease Control and Pre-vention (CDC) uses the "Fruits & Veggies— More Matters" campaign to encourage more fruits and veggies in the diet. For more information, visit the following Web sites:

* www.fruitsandveggiesmatter.gov
* www.mypyramid.gov/pyramid/fruits_counts.html
* www.mypyramid.gov/pyramid/vegetables_counts.html

NASPE Physical Education Curriculum Standards

The National Association for Sport and Physical Education (NASPE) has developed standards for the physical education curriculum (NASPE, 2004). These standards have been used by 48 of the 50 states in developing state standards and physical education curricula. The NASPE standards define the content needed to help children develop the knowledge, skills, and confidence to enjoy a lifetime of healthy physical activity. The lesson plans in this book identify NASPE standards associated with each educational activity. A description of the six primary NASPE standards and the performance outcomes used to build the **FFL: Elementary** program are included in appendix B.

Integrating Other Languages and Sensations

The physical education lesson plans in this book provide several ideas for integrating other languages into activities. Integrating languages other than English into your lessons can be an enjoyable learning experience and will allow children to learn from others and about other cultures. In addition to integrating other languages, there are ideas for introducing and reinforcing students' understanding of sensations (touch, hearing, sight, smell, and taste). Movement forces us to use sensations in different ways and in unique settings. The sensations require interpretation by our brain. When we expose young people to movement, we are challenging them physically and mentally. We have provided some basic ideas for integrating languages and sensations into your lessons. We are sure that you and your students will have many more ideas for integrating language and sensations into your lessons.

Fitness for Life Philosophy

Fitness for Life: Elementary School is part of a comprehensive K-12 program. In addition to **FFL: Elementary,** there are **Fitness for Life** programs for middle school and high school (see www.fitnessforlife.org for details). All **Fitness for Life** programs are based on the **HELP** philosophy. The first letters in four key words form the **HELP** acronym.

* **H**ealth. The program is designed to help elementary school students learn about health-related physical fitness and the benefits of healthy lifestyles, including regular physical activity and sound nutrition.
* **E**veryone. The program is designed for everyone (all elementary school students), not just those with physical talents.
* **L**ifetime. The activities included in **Fitness for Life** were chosen to get kids active now as well as build habits that will last a lifetime.
* **P**ersonal. All lessons are designed to help each student learn personally appropriate physical activity and nutrition information.

USING THE LESSON PLANS

Fitness for Life Elementary School

This section outlines the role of the physical educator, presents delivery options for the **FFL: Elementary** physical education lessons, describes the lesson plan structure, and provides tips for the successful delivery of the lesson plans.

The **FFL: Elementary** physical education lesson plans were created to meet three main criteria:

1. To provide students with a variety of movement experiences that meet NASPE standards and reinforce key physical activity and nutrition concepts

2. To provide teachers with a consistent lesson plan structure that is easy to use, is flexible, and takes into consideration the equipment demands of delivering physical education lessons to a variety of grade groups throughout the school day

By design, the lesson plans for each Wellness Week have some common components. Plans for each week are comprehensive so that you will not have to refer back to previous lessons to find information. Each set of lesson plans provides everything that you will need for each Wellness Week.

3. To provide teachers with numerous pedagogical strategies for challenging students, providing feedback to students, incorporating other academic areas into physical education, reviewing key physical activity and nutrition concepts, checking for student understanding, and encouraging healthy lifestyles outside of school

Taking the time to read this information before going into the actual lesson plans will help you understand how to deliver the lesson plans efficiently and effectively.

Role of the Physical Education Teacher

The duties of the physical education teacher include the following:

- Teach one physical education lesson during the week before Wellness Week. This warm-up lesson teaches students how to perform the video routines that will be used for classroom activity breaks during Wellness Week. This increases the likelihood that the classroom teacher will conduct an activity break using the video routine.

- Teach several Wellness Week physical education lessons during Wellness Week. Use the lesson plans in this book, and teach as many during the week as the schedule allows.

- Print and post signs that promote wellness. The signs are provided on the resources CD-ROM in this book.
- Conduct discussions of wellness messages featured in lesson plans.
- Assist with schoolwide wellness activities (such as Eat Well Wednesday and Get Fit Friday) as requested by the wellness coordinator.

In many cases, the physical education teacher will serve as the wellness coordinator for the **FFL: Elementary** program. The coordinator's duties are described in the *Guide for Wellness Coordinators*.

Physical Education Lesson Plans

The **FFL: Elementary** base plan assumes that a school has physical education three times per week. In this case, you would deliver the warm-up lesson during the last class before Wellness Week. During Wellness Week, you would deliver the three lesson plans for the appropriate grade. Part II of this book includes the lesson plans for the four Wellness Weeks for kindergarten through grade 2. Part III includes the lesson plans for the four Wellness Weeks for grades 3 through 6.

Table 1.2 provides suggestions for delivering the lessons when you have a different number of classes per week. For schools lucky enough to have physical education scheduled more than three times per week, appendix A provides sources where you can find extra activities.

Lesson Plan Structure

The **FFL: Elementary** physical education lesson plans are structured in a unique way. They have been developed for grade groups. K-2 lesson plans are used with kindergarten, grade 1, and grade 2, and 3-6 lesson plans are used with grades 3, 4, 5, and 6.

Before we run through all the parts of a lesson plan, let's look at the four main components. Each lesson plan is built around an instant activity, a fitness activity, a lesson focus, and a culminating activity. Figure 1.3 illustrates how these components fit together.

During each Wellness Week, the lesson focus changes from day to day. The instant activity, fitness activity, and culminating activity are usually the same each day, but you can keep them fresh by using the provided refinements and extensions.

- Refinements are suggestions for helping students improve their movement skills. This will require close observation of students and the delivery of feedback that will help students work on a specific element of the skill.
- Extensions provide ideas for challenging students or incorporating new ideas into an activity for the purpose of improving motor skills.

During some Wellness Weeks, the instant activity, fitness activity, or culminating activity are not the same each day. For example, the K-2 lesson plans for Wellness Week 3 use two instant activities (Warm It Up and Active Every Day) and three culminating activities (Cool It Down, Flexibility Tag, and Muscle-Builder Tag). This approach offers additional variety that goes beyond refinements and extensions.

Table 1.2 Physical Education Lesson Plan Schedule for Base Plan* and Other Plans

PE schedule	Week before Wellness Week	Wellness Week
Day 1	Regular curriculum	Wellness Week Lesson Plan 1
Day 2	Regular curriculum	Wellness Week Lesson Plan 2
Day 3	Wellness Week Warm-Up Lesson	Wellness Week Lesson Plan 3
Days 4 and 5	Regular curriculum	Repeat a Wellness Week lesson plan or choose a lesson from appendix A

*Assumes physical education three days per week.

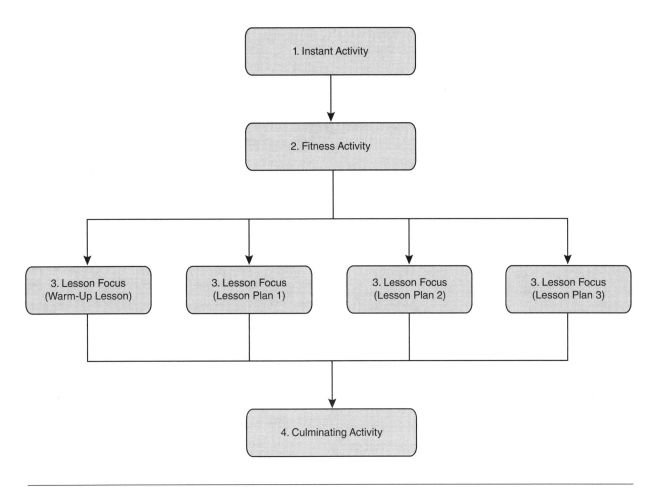

Figure 1.3 Most parts of the warm-up and Wellness Week physical education lesson plans remain the same from day to day, but the lesson focus shifts every day.

Now, let's take a closer look at all the parts of a lesson plan.

Overview

This section provides a brief description of the lesson plan. It usually notes the activities performed by students or opportunities for learning.

NASPE Standards

This section provides a list of student-centered learning outcomes. The relationship of objectives to selected NASPE standards is coded using numbers and letters to identify the standards addressed by each lesson plan. We identify many standards that could be met using each lesson plan; however, the lessons are written to meet a few specific objectives based on these standards. You may decide to alter the lesson to focus on different standards and objectives. Appendix B provides a written description of selected standards for K-6 students that are targeted by **FFL: Elementary**.

Objectives

This section lists the objectives for the lesson (based on NASPE standards). The general objective "Students are active for at least 50 percent of the class" is an important objective for every lesson, although it is usually not included in the list. Please read "Tips for Using the Lesson Plans" (page 24) to maximize activity time during your physical education lessons.

Equipment

This part of the lesson plan provides a list of the equipment that you'll need to conduct the lesson. For many lessons, you will need a CD player so that you can play tracks from the music CD in this book, and you'll need a DVD player and TV so that you can play videos from the two DVDs in this book. (For more details about the CD and DVDs, see "Using the Discs" on page 21.)

We know that your daily schedule might require that you teach students in different grade levels in a random order. Thus, we have designed the lesson plans to minimize the amount of equipment you need each day regardless of the order of your classes. For example, the K-2 lesson plan for week 1, lesson 1, requires similar equipment as the 3-6 lesson plan for week 1, lesson 1.

Resources

This section lists the resources to be printed from the resources CD-ROM in this book. In addition to printing activity cards, task cards, and worksheets to use during the lesson, you'll print Wellness Week signs to post in your gym or activity room, and you'll reinforce the signs' messages in your classes. The physical education lesson plans mention only a few specific signs, but the CD-ROM includes many more Wellness Week signs (which match signs used by the classroom teachers) that you can use if you wish.

Every lesson also includes the At-a-Glance PE Lesson Plan card. For each lesson, print a copy of the At-a-Glance card, cut it into smaller cards, and write notes on them about each part of the lesson. You can use the At-a-Glance card with the lesson plans provided in this book or with other lesson plans that you create.

For more details about the CD-ROM, see "Using the Discs" on page 21.

Chants

This section lists one or more chants to use in class. These chants serve several purposes, including creating a fun learning environment, reinforcing key physical activity and nutrition concepts, and assessing the level of student engagement. You can decide where you want to insert the chants in the lesson plan, and you can use the chants in several ways:

- Start each chant by saying the first part and have the students respond with the second part. This will require a quick practice.
- Have one group of students start the chant (on your signal) and have another group of students respond.
- Students and teachers can say the whole chant together.

Delivering the Lesson

This section provides the four main components mentioned previously: an instant activity, a fitness activity, a lesson focus, and a culminating activity. Selected parts of the lesson include text in quotation marks that is meant to be communicated to students. You can read this text out loud directly from the book, or you can paraphrase the quoted text using your own words.

Instant Activity

As the name implies, this part of the lesson gets students moving as soon as they enter the activity area. The main purpose of the instant activity is to progressively warm up students for activity. Thus, these activities start slow, focus on controlled movements, and are modified by the physical educator to increase in intensity. Each instant activity is designed to be brief and should take no more than 5 minutes of class time.

If necessary, you can take roll during the instant activity. Unfortunately, many teachers spend a lot of time at the beginning of physical education taking roll. When students come to physical education, they want to be active and they need activity. Don't waste valuable class time taking roll when you can multitask.

Keep the instant activities simple. If you introduce too much equipment, lots of rules, or complicated instructions, instant activities become instruction time and management time. Instant activities should begin immediately, require little to no equipment, and require little organization.

Fitness Activity

This part of the lesson provides students with an opportunity to participate in fun activities that can improve components of their health-related fitness and help them learn about basic fitness concepts. Most fitness activities are teacher-led or use stations. In order to improve fitness, students will need to spend some time working at these fitness activities. By keeping the instant activity brief, you can dedicate time to the fitness activity.

Lesson Focus

This part of the lesson is adapted to each grade level and is the featured activity of the day. Although the other main components (instant activities, fitness activities, and culminating activities) for a given Wellness Week usually stay the same, this part of the lesson always changes to engage students in the following:

© John Birdsall/age fotostock

The **Fitness for Life: Elementary School** program provides activity for all children.

- Warm-Up Lesson: Teaches the video routine that students will perform in the classroom during Wellness Week.
- Lesson 1: Focuses on students working together to create new moves to music. Students review the video routines taught during the warm-up and create new routines in small groups using the music from the video routines.
- Lesson 2: Focuses on fundamental movement skills, fitness, Fitnessgram self-assessments for grades 3 through 6, and some Fitnessgram activities for kindergarten through grade 2.
- Lesson 3: Focuses on motor skill activities for all grades.

Culminating Activity

This part of the lesson provides an opportunity for students to play a game that will integrate movements and knowledge from the preceding activities. Culminating activities should be fun

for students. If you have your own culminating activities that students love, we encourage you to use them in the lesson plans, but be sure to integrate the given physical activity, fitness, or nutrition concepts.

Closure Routine

This part of the lesson is called a *routine* because there is an intentional sequence we encourage you to follow.

- Compliments: Ask students to share compliments about individuals, groups, or teams.
- Reflection and Review: Ask students to respond to questions and reflect on their experience in the class. This is an excellent opportunity to review key concepts from the lesson. We have placed an emphasis on students reflecting on the sensations they get from participating in activity.
- Take It Home: These are simple activities students can do with friends and family, at home and in the community.

Assessment

This section provides selected strategies for determining whether the objectives for the class have been met. Observation is a critical tool for assessment in movement settings and is recommended in many of the lesson plans. Student observation is also a skill that takes time to develop. Use the observation icons (see "Icons for Effective Teaching Practices" on page 20) in the lesson plans to practice and develop your observation skills.

Using Lesson Plans Multiple Times

Each grade group (K-2 and 3-6) has one warm-up lesson plan and three standard lesson plans for each Wellness Week, which should provide you with plenty of material. However, you can go through many of the lesson plans more than once and have enough refinements and extensions to keep the activities engaging and interesting for students. Many lesson plans have specific instructions for teaching part of the lesson plan a second time through. There are many good reasons for teaching a lesson more than once:

- It takes time for you to establish protocols, organize students, and deliver the lesson content efficiently so that students can move through an entire lesson and spend a large proportion of class time (more than 50 percent) engaged in physical activity.

- It takes time for students to learn the lesson content and the protocols for moving through the lesson.

- It takes time for you to provide feedback and help students refine their movement skills.

- It takes time to provide interesting variations and challenges for lesson activities.

- It takes time to incorporate creative activity variations and challenges provided by students.

Icons for Effective Teaching Practices

Throughout the lesson plans, you will encounter icons that signal opportunities to enhance your teaching of the lesson. You can use these strategies for assessing student learning and student participation. You may want to come up with a system on your roll sheet for identifying student understanding and student behavior for assessment purposes.

(⭐) **Teacher Tip:** This icon is accompanied by a suggestion that you may want to consider when delivering the lesson.

(↻) **Review:** Whenever you encounter this icon in the lesson plans, we have provided suggestions for reviewing key lesson concepts or concepts from a previous lesson. As you deliver the lessons, you may find that there are many more situations where reviewing key concepts or class protocols would enhance the lesson.

(?) **Comprehension Check:** Whenever you encounter this icon in the lesson plans, we have provided suggestions for checking students' understanding of the class content, instructions, or demonstrations. You may find many

more opportunities during the lessons where a check for student understanding would be helpful. In his textbook, *Teaching Children Physical Education, Third Edition,* George Graham (2008) outlines five approaches to checking for understanding:

- *Recognition check:* A quick way to check for student understanding is to ask students to raise their hands, give a thumbs up or down, or hold up a response card (e.g., A, B, C, or D) to indicate that the concept, instruction, or demonstration was understood.

- *Verbal check:* Ask students to tell you the concept or cue you are teaching.

- *Comprehension check:* Ask students to explain the concept. This shows a deeper understanding than a verbal check.

- *Performance check:* Ask the students to demonstrate the activity, skill, principle, and so on. This approach is especially effective in physical education because you can see whether students understand the concept through physical demonstrations.

- *Closure:* At the end of the lesson, you can use a short closure session to get an idea of how well students have learned lesson concepts. During the one- to two-minute closure session, bring students together to review key points, get student comments, or prepare for assignments or the next class.

(👁) **Observation:** This icon identifies a point in the lesson plans where observation of student behavior may be appropriate. By looking around the room, you can easily determine if students are on task, working together, performing movements correctly, and following instructions. You will often see this icon when students are asked to work cooperatively in group settings. We believe it is important to celebrate respectful communication (listening and talking) and inclusion of different points of view in physical education.

(✖) **Interdisciplinary:** This icon identifies a point in the lesson where other academic subjects could be integrated with the activity.

Using the Discs

Four discs are bound into the back of this book: instructional physical activity routines (DVD 1), physical activity routines with messages (DVD 2), a CD-ROM of printable resources, and a CD of music to be used with physical education lessons. The last page of the book provides the technical details for accessing the discs. This section discusses the contents of the discs.

The contents of all discs are intended for use only by instructors and agencies that have purchased this book. The reproduction of the contents of the discs is otherwise forbidden according to the terms stated on the copyright page of this book.

DVD Video Routines

When you insert either DVD in a DVD player, the TV screen will display a menu of video routines to use during class. The main menu offers a choice of grades. Select any grade to see the specific routines for that grade. The lesson plans will direct you to play the correct video for each lesson. Videos are closed captioned.

Each Wellness Week, each grade will perform a different physical activity routine using the videos during classroom activity breaks. The routines are designed to reinforce the weekly physical activity theme. Table 1.3 shows the routines for all grades.

You can help the classroom teachers by teaching the routines to the students as part of your physical education lessons. In the warm-up lesson (the week before each Wellness Week), use the instructional version of that week's physical activity routine, found on DVD 1, to help students learn the movements. In the first lesson of each Wellness Week, use the physical activity routine with a message, found on DVD 2, which reinforces the weekly themes.

Resources CD-ROM

When you access the resources CD-ROM through your computer's CD-ROM or DVD-ROM drive, you will see five folders of resources: General, Wellness Week 1, Wellness Week 2, Wellness Week 3, and Wellness Week 4.

General

This folder contains general **Fitness for Life: Elementary School** signs related to physical activity and nutrition. The messages and concepts in these signs are discussed in classrooms and in physical education classes and are included in video routines. Posting the general signs in the location where you have physical education classes will help reinforce what students are learning in program activities. Review the general signs and choose several to post during each Wellness Week. This folder also includes the At-a-Glance PE Lesson Plan card and a printable version of the Executive Summary (page 8).

Table 1.3 Routines by Grade Level

Grade	Week 1 Theme: Moderate physical activity	Week 2 Theme: Vigorous physical activity	Week 3 Theme: Muscle fitness and flexibility exercises	Week 4 Theme: Integration (energy balance)
K	Exercise on the Farm	Frank and Franny Fitness	We Get Fit	Shake It
1	Some More	I Can	CYIM Fit	Stomp and Balance
2	Get Fit	La Raspa	Wave It	It's the One
3	It's Our Plan	Go Aerobics Go	Tic Tac Toe 3	Jumpnastics
4	Robot	Latin Aerobics	Tic Tac Toe 4	Keep on Clapping
5	Hip Hop 5	Tinikling	Tic Tac Toe 5	Fit Funk
6	Hip Hop 6	Salsaerobics	Tic Tac Toe 6	Harvest Time

At-a-Glance Card

Blank horizontal

Blank vertical

Executive Summary

G1: Fitness for Life: Elementary School

G2: Wellness Week

G3: Physical Activity Pyramid for Kids

G4: MyPyramid for Kids

G5: Eat Well Wednesday

G6: TEAM Time: Together Everyone Achieves More

G7: Get Fit Friday

G8: Healthy mind, healthy body, healthy heart . . . let's start!

G9: ABCs of Physical Activity (signs for each letter of the alphabet, including two signs for the letter M)

G10: ABCs of Nutrition (signs for each letter of the alphabet)

When using the general signs, consider printing them all at once and saving them to reuse during future Wellness Weeks. Also, you can put students in charge of managing special bulletin boards where the signs are posted each week.

The signs are PDF files and can be printed but not edited. For this reason, we have provided two blank signs that feature the **Fitness for Life: Elementary School** design but that have no message content. You can print these blank signs and customize them as desired, either by hand or by feeding the signs back through your printer.

Throughout this book, references to general signs are accompanied by the following icon to remind you of where to find the signs on the CD-ROM:

 General

Wellness Week Resources

The CD-ROM includes one folder of resources for each Wellness Week. Each of these folders contains three subfolders:

- K-2 Resources: This folder contains activity cards, task cards, signs, and worksheets to be used for grades K-2 during that Wellness Week.
- 3-6 Resources: This folder contains activity cards, task cards, signs, and worksheets to be used for grades 3-6 during that Wellness Week.
- Newsletter: This folder contains the newsletter to be used during that Wellness Week.

Like the lesson plans, the resources are designed to meet the standards associated with the separate grade ranges. Thus, grades K-2 share the same resources, and grades 3-6 share the same resources.

The resources are presented as complete PDF files to make it easy for you to print them all at once. For example, the file called "Animal Antics cards" contains the entire set of cards used in the Animal Antics activity. Similarly, all signs for a week are grouped into one PDF file.

Each week, all grades use the same newsletter, found in the Newsletter folder. Each newsletter is a document, not a PDF file, so that you can customize it using your favorite word processing software. Ideally, your school's wellness coordinator will customize the newsletter and distribute copies to teachers to send home with students. Alternatively, you (or the classroom teachers) can prepare and distribute the newsletters.

PRINTING THE RESOURCES

Because the cards and signs are intended to be engaging, they are presented in color, but they will print normally to black-and-white printers as well. If you have a color printer but wish to conserve your color ink, you can print the resources in grayscale. (Every printer is different, so for details on how to do this, check your printer's instruction manual, or click the Help or Properties button in your Print window.)

Throughout this guide, references to Wellness Week resources are accompanied by icons to remind you of where to find the resources on the CD-ROM. For example, the icons for Wellness Week 1 are as follows:

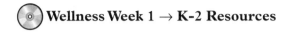 **Wellness Week 1 → K-2 Resources**

Wellness Week 1 → 3-6 Resources

Wellness Week 1 → Newsletter

Music CD

The music CD contains 15 tracks for you to use during the physical education lesson plans. The lesson plans direct you when to play each track.

The music CD has a total running time of 72 minutes, 21 seconds. Table 1.4 provides the number, description, and running time of each track.

The CD has three kinds of music: interval tracks, continuous tracks, and fitness assessment tracks. The interval music tracks have periods of music followed by periods of silence. For example, an interval track labeled 45/15 has music for 45 seconds and silence for 15 seconds. These tracks are recommended for circuits or station activities where students work continuously for a period of time and then move to another station. The silence portion allows time for students to move to the next station and receive instruction from the teacher. In addition, this intermittent type of activity (stopping and starting) matches the nature of children's movement.

Table 1.4 Description of Music CD Tracks

Track number	Description	Running time
1	30/5 interval track alternating between electronic groove and world music	5:45
2	30/10 interval track alternating between Latin groove and soul	5:57
3	30/15 interval track with ethereal music for yoga and stretching activities	6:01
4	30/30 interval track alternating between electronic groove and world music	4:59
5	45/15 interval track alternating between three mellow drum rhythms	3:00
6	45/15 interval track alternating between pop music, Latin groove, hard rock, and reggae	4:00
7	45/15 interval track alternating between electronic dance grooves	6:00
8	45/15 interval track repeating an upbeat electronic funk groove	6:01
9	Continuous track of upbeat electronic funk	2:03
10	Continuous track of electronic dance music with a strong beat	2:04
11	Continuous track of electronic dance music with a strong beat	2:03
12	Continuous track of synthesizer pop music with a strong beat	3:04
13	Continuous track of electronic trance music with a strong beat	5:02
14	Fitness assessment track: PACER test (includes instructions for starting, buzzer noises for pacing, and stage announcements)	10:48
15	Fitness assessment track: push-up/curl-up (includes "up" and "down" cadence at 50 beats per minute)	5:34

Continuous music tracks have music playing for the specified length. These tracks add some excitement to a movement setting and are recommended when you want children moving continuously during activities.

Finally, the fitness assessment tracks are provided to guide the Fitnessgram Progressive Aerobic Cardiovascular Endurance Run (PACER) and Fitnessgram tests of muscular endurance (that is, the push-up and curl-up tests). The PACER track lets students know when to start the test, provides intermittent buzzer sounds that keep students on pace, and announces the stage of the test. The muscular endurance track has a cadence of 50 beats per minute with alternating "up" and "down" signals. Students raise up with the "up" signal and move down with the "down" signal. Thus, students conducting these tests will perform 25 push-ups or curl-ups each minute.

Tips for Using the Lesson Plans

Our goal was to make the lesson plans in this book as user-friendly as possible by providing engaging and manageable content, consistent formatting and structure, ideas for reinforcing and extending the content, and strategies for assessment. As many experienced physical educators already know, delivering successful lessons largely depends on establishing effective protocols. For example, starting and stopping students, grouping and pairing students, and having students get and put away equipment help make a lesson plan run smoothly and provide students with the maximum time to be active and practice their skills.

Some tips for lesson preparation and protocols are provided below.

- Before conducting each lesson, review the overview and objectives.
- Assemble any equipment that you will need (such as a TV and DVD player) and print resources that will be used that day (such as activity cards).
- Review the signs and chants. Print and post signs at the beginning of the week before

Wellness Week and keep them posted through Wellness Week. Use them to foster discussion and to reinforce classroom messages.

- Review the icons, which identify opportunities in the lesson plan to assess student learning and participation.
- Review the four parts of the lesson prior to each lesson.
- Teach the warm-up lesson the week before Wellness Week to become familiar with the lesson format and give students a chance to try the video routine that they will do in classroom activity breaks. See the sidebar on page 25 for tips on teaching the routines.
- For each lesson, print an At-a-Glance PE Lesson Plan card, cut it into smaller cards, and write reminder notes for yourself about each part of the lesson.

Keeping Students Active

Although NASPE outlines several important standards for physical education, helping children become regularly physically active may be the most important. Physical education is one place where we can provide all children with health-enhancing physical activity. By employing a few basic strategies described in this section, you will increase the amount of physical activity you provide children in physical education.

Establish Protocols

For the first few weeks of the year, work on protocols with your students, such as entering the activity area, stopping and starting, getting into groups, getting equipment, stopping with equipment, putting equipment away, and asking questions. Protocols can also be taught in relation to specific activities. For example, teach students the protocols for activity stations early in the year. Protocols are skills and, just like skills, they need to be practiced.

Two protocols that will have a big impact on your activity time are grouping students and instant activities. Specific examples of these protocols are provided next.

Grouping Students

If you don't have a plan for grouping students, you don't have a plan for maximizing activity time. Becoming skilled at grouping will save you management time and boost your activity time. Try the following basic strategies.

Toe to Toe (Partners)

Have students get toe to toe with the person closest to them. If students run across the area to get with their friends, have all students move around the area again, freeze them, and ask them to get toe to toe again. Be sure to identify a place for students to come to if they don't have a partner. Move to that place yourself and quickly find a partner or group for those students. Take the time to switch partners so that students get a chance to work with a number of classmates. One simple strategy is to freeze the students, have one partner in each pair put up a hand, and have those students move clockwise.

Toe to Toe (Teams)

Have students get toe to toe with the person closest to them. Have one partner in each pair put up a hand and move to an area (line). The other partners in the pairs move to another area (line). You now have two teams.

Signals for Small Groups

After stopping all students in the area, use a signal to make small groups quickly. You can verbally instruct them to get into groups of four,

USING THE VIDEO ACTIVITIES

During each Wellness Week, you will play two activity videos for use with each grade. Play the instructional routine in the warm-up lesson, and play the activity routine (with conceptual messages embedded) in the first lesson of each Wellness Week.

K-2 Routines

In the instructional routines for grades K-2, the instructor faces away from your students for some of the left–right movements. Explain that students should do those movements the same way the instructor does them—when the instructor moves to the right, students should also move to the right. However, in the activity routine, leaders face forward, so their left–right movements are reversed. While performing the activity routine, your students should move in the opposite direction of the leaders for left–right movements.

3-6 Routines

The instructional routines for grades 3-6 use the whole–part–whole learning method.

* First, leaders present the whole routine to show your students what they will be performing. The leaders face your students.

* Next, an instructor demonstrates the parts of the routine. The instructor faces away from your students for some of the left–right movements. Explain that students should do those movements the same way the instructor does them—when the instructor moves to the right, they should also move to the right.

* Finally, leaders present the whole routine again, and your students follow along and perform the routine. The leaders face your students. Explain that students should move in the opposite direction for left–right movements—if the leaders move to their right, your students should move to their left.

Keep Kids Moving

Although moving in the correct direction is desirable, the key is to get all kids moving regardless of the direction. If your students have a hard time performing the activity, feel free to replay the instructional routine.

or you can use a signal (e.g., four hand claps). Be sure to identify a place for students to come to if they don't have a group. Move to that place yourself and quickly find a group for them.

Squads

A squad system allows you to group students in various ways. In a squad system, students wear the color of their squad. In addition, each squad member is identified by a number. For example, in a class of 30 students, you could have six squads (identified by color) of five members (numbered 1 through 5).

- To form six groups of five, group by squad.
- To form five groups of six, group by number.
- To break the class in half, group evens together and odds together.

Instant Activities

Have you ever noticed how much time teachers spend managing students when attendance is taken at the beginning of class? It is not uncommon to witness physical education classes where attendance takes more than 7 minutes! This wastes almost 25 percent of a 30-minute class on a simple task. Students generally enjoy moving and expect to move in physical education. As soon as they enter the activity area, get them moving with low-organization activities, strategies such as Move and Freeze, or posted instructions.

Move and Freeze

Specify a locomotor movement and a freeze position. Start the lesson by moving and freezing students several times. Use a variety of locomotor movements and freeze postures to keep it novel. Most of the instant activities in the **FFL: Elementary** physical education lesson plans are Move and Freeze activities.

Posting Instructions

Post activity instructions on the wall or write them on a chalkboard before class. Establish a protocol early in the year that students should look at the wall or board as they enter the area. As students filter into the activity area, they start performing the activity. On your signal, they put any equipment away and meet near you. Music works well with this strategy.

Establish a Consistent Format

By keeping the sequence and structure of your lesson plans consistent, students will learn the sequence and the protocols that will reduce time spent on management and instruction. All **FFL: Elementary** physical education lesson plans have the same structure.

Repeat Lesson Plans

When you repeat lesson plans, you become more efficient at setting up the activity area, delivering instruction, and transitioning students. Meanwhile, students are learning how to perform the activities and transition between activities. Both of these processes increase activity time in physical education.

Keep Instructions Brief

Although it is important to provide instructions in physical education, there are many instances where we spend too much time talking and students spend too little time moving. Challenge yourself to become more efficient with your instructions by trying the following:

- **Time your talk:** Use your stopwatch and see if you can give all of your instructions in two minutes or less. Practice improving the length of your instruction.

- **Instruction construction:** Try giving your instructions in small chunks. For example, start a game with very few rules, then stop after a few minutes and add a new rule. This approach allows you to get creative with ideas, allows children to recover, and prompts student questions that can lead to teachable moments.

- **Quick demonstrations:** Avoid long demonstrations of an activity. Perform a correct but efficient (less than one minute) demonstration at full speed where all students can see. Focus on one idea or cue. Send the students off to try the activity. Move around the area and provide feedback, extra instruction, or challenges to students in need.

PART II

LESSON PLANS FOR GRADES K-2

· ·

Part II contains the **Fitness for Life: Elementary School** physical education lesson plans for kindergarten, first grade, and second grade, organized by Wellness Week. Before you start using the lesson plans, be sure to read part I of this book (especially "Using the Lesson Plans" on page 15) and familiarize yourself with the DVDs, resources CD-ROM, and music CD bound into the back of the book.

WELLNESS WEEK 1

Fitness for Life
Elementary School

These lesson plans provide students with a variety of experiences, including locomotor and animal movements, moving to music, jumping movements, rope jumping, and tossing and catching skills. In Wellness Week 1, the activity theme is "moderate physical activity," and the nutrition theme is "fruits and vegetables (fitness foods)." These themes are reinforced through activities, signs, and chants. Take time to look through the lesson plans for Wellness Week 1 and determine which objectives are most important and which activities you will use to meet those objectives. Table 2.1 summarizes the Wellness Week 1 activities for the physical education lesson plans.

For Wellness Week 1, the lesson plans include the following:

- A warm-up lesson plan to be used during the week before Wellness Week 1. The same basic warm-up lesson plan is used for kindergarten through grade 2, but the Lesson Focus (practicing the video routine) is different for each grade.
- Three lesson plans (1.1, 1.2, and 1.3) to be used during Wellness Week 1. The same basic lesson plan is used for kindergarten through grade 2, with grade-specific variations, refinements, and extensions for some of the activities.
- Extra activity ideas for schools that have physical education class more than three days a week are provided in appendix A.

Table 2.1 Summary of Wellness Week 1 Activities

Lesson Plan	Instant Activity	Fitness Activity	Lesson Focus	Culminating Activity
Warm-Up 1 (week before Wellness Week 1)	Move and Freeze	Animal Antics	Video Routine Practice: K: Exercise on the Farm 1: Some More 2: Get Fit	Fruits and Veggies Tag
1.1	Move and Freeze	Animal Antics	Video Routine Variations: K: Exercise on the Farm 1: Some More 2: Get Fit	Fruits and Veggies Tag
1.2	Move and Freeze	Animal Antics	Jumping for Joy	Fruits and Veggies Tag
1.3	Move and Freeze	Animal Antics	Tossing and Catching Skills	Fruits and Veggies Tag

Moderate physical activity (step 1 of the Physical Activity Pyramid for Kids) is the activity theme for Wellness Week 1.

Eat Well Wednesday

Each Wednesday, known as Eat Well Wednesday, all teachers and staff are encouraged to emphasize nutrition. The wellness coordinator might plan special schoolwide events. During Wellness Week 1, the nutrition event is a fruit and vegetable bar in the cafeteria. If you have a physical education lesson on Eat Well Wednesday, place an emphasis on nutrition signs and messages.

Get Fit Friday

Each Friday, known as Get Fit Friday, a schoolwide event focusing on physical activity will be planned. (If your school participates in this event, your wellness coordinator will provide you with more details.) The Get Fit Friday activities are called TEAM Time activities (TEAM stands for Together Everyone Achieves More). During Wellness Week 1, this activity will be the School Walk. All students gather in the gym, in the multipurpose room, or outside before beginning the School Walk. Your wellness coordinator will set up and lead the activity.

Newsletter

The CD-ROM contains a newsletter for use during Wellness Week 1. It is recommended that your school's wellness coordinator edit and distribute the newsletter. Alternatively, you (or the classroom teachers) can do it. Just open the appropriate file, follow the instructions to edit and customize the newsletter, and send printed copies home with students or send them electronically via e-mail. Remind students to talk to their families about Wellness Week and the information in the newsletter.

 **Wellness Week 1 → Newsletter**

Warm-Up Lesson Plan 1

OVERVIEW

In this lesson, conducted during the week before Wellness Week 1, students will learn the grade-specific video routine that they will perform in their classroom during Wellness Week 1. You can aid the classroom teachers by teaching these routines in advance to make it easier for both students and teachers and to increase the chances that the classroom teachers will do the video routines in their classrooms.

NASPE STANDARDS

1A, 3A, 3B, 4A, 4C, 5A, 5B
(See appendix B for details.)

OBJECTIVES

Students will

* demonstrate a variety of locomotor and animal movements,
* practice moving to music, and
* explain why fruits and vegetables are good for their bodies.

EQUIPMENT

* CD player and continuous music (music CD track 13)
* TV, DVD player, and DVD 1 (Instructional Routines)
* 8 to 10 cones
* 2 each of the following colored beanbags: red, yellow, blue, purple, and orange
* 6 green beanbags

RESOURCES

 General

At-a-Glance PE Lesson Plan card

 Wellness Week 1 → K-2 Resources

Animal Antics activity cards
Week 1 signs file with the following signs:

* Be active your way every day!
* Eat the rainbow way: every color, every day!

CHANTS

Leader: "How many fruits and veggies today?"

Students: "Five to nine, every day!"

DELIVERING THE LESSON

1. Instant Activity: Move and Freeze

> ⭐ **teacher tip** • • •
> You may not get through the whole lesson the first time
> through. Decide which part of the lesson is most important for
> your students to experience.

Introduction

"I have some exciting news! Next week is Wellness Week, and we will be participating in the **Fitness for Life: Elementary School** program. **Fitness for Life** will help you learn about the importance of fitness, physical activity, and healthy eating. More importantly, the **Fitness for Life** program has cool video routines that we will do in PE and in your classroom, as well as fun physical activities for our PE classes. So let's get started. When I say 'go,' I want you to skip inside the activity area in your own space. . . . Go!"

Activity

Students come into the activity space using a teacher-designated locomotor skill, such as skipping, galloping, or sliding in open space, staying inside the designated activity area. On your stop signal, have them freeze in an athletic position (knees bent, shoulder width apart, hands on their knees) with their eyes on you. All students should freeze within five seconds with their bodies under control and eyes on you. Repeat this activity several times using various locomotor activities, getting bodies warmed up and students ready to listen. When students are moving and freezing in control, move on to the fitness activity.

Extensions

* Change the locomotor movement (e.g., walk, grapevine, jog).
* Change the quality of the movement (e.g., quietly, low, high).
* Change the pathway (e.g., zigzags, curves, squares).
* Move in unison to music (e.g., alone, with a partner, with a group).

 observation • • •
Look around the room to see if students are moving safely. Encourage safe and controlled movements in open space. Do not allow running until you see safe and controlled movement, especially with kindergarteners.

2. Fitness Activity: Animal Antics

Introduction

"Animals move in so many ways. Animals move every day! Humans are animals that need regular activity. Let's get some activity by moving as if we were animals."

Activity

Place 8 to 10 Animal Antics activity cards on cones around your activity space. Have students begin at any cone, look at the animal, perform that animal movement en route to another animal activity card, and then perform that animal movement to another cone. Encourage students to explore all of the animal movements. Promote the use of a language other than English by pointing out the Spanish translation of the animal movements on the activity cards.

(?) comprehension check • • •
• "Which animal movements made your arms stronger?"
• "Which animal movements stretched your muscles?"
• "Could someone show me an example of another animal movement?"

Animal movements are fun and contribute to many parts of fitness.

Extensions

✳ Create more Animal Antics cards. Consider different themes (swamp animals, jungle animals, arctic animals).

✳ Have students create their own Animal Antics cards at home or with their classroom teacher.

3. Lesson Focus: Video Routine Practice

Introduction

"Next week is Wellness Week 1. During Wellness Week 1, we will be learning about physical activity, fitness, and healthy nutrition. Today we are going to practice the video routine you will be performing in your classroom during Wellness Week 1. This video routine is fun and will challenge you to move to music."

Activity

Introduce and practice the grade-specific video routine using the following steps.

1. Insert DVD 1 and play the instructional routine that is appropriate for your class:
   - Kindergarten: Exercise on the Farm
   - First grade: Some More
   - Second grade: Get Fit
2. Have the students follow along with the routine. Observe students performing the routine and take note of the movements that give them trouble.
3. Before going through the routine again, provide a demonstration and help students with any movements that are giving them trouble. Provide tips that will help them succeed.
4. Play the routine again and compliment students on any improvements.
5. Remind students that next week is Wellness Week 1, and they will perform this routine every day in their classrooms next week.

Refinements

Observe the students' movements and listen to the reciting of the words. Provide feedback to help students stay with the music and move together.

4. Culminating Activity: Fruits and Veggies Tag

Introduction

"Fruits and vegetables give you energy, help you grow, and can keep you healthy and well. Fruits and vegetables are full of energy and vitamins that help your body fight off illnesses like colds and flu—that's one reason to eat at least 5 servings of fruits and vegetables every day. Let's play a game that uses fruits and veggies to keep us healthy and moving."

Activity

Choose six players to have the green beanbags. These are your infectious germs—they are It. They begin in the middle of the gym. Distribute the fruits and vegetables (other colored beanbags) and have the students assign fruit and vegetable names to the various colors (e.g., red is tomato or strawberry, purple is grape or eggplant). Not all students will have a beanbag. On your signal (e.g., music), those who are It try to infect as many nonfruit and nonvegetable players as possible by tagging them softly. When infected (tagged), these players freeze in their best sick and tired position (or a position designated by you) until a fruit or vegetable player comes to save them by handing them the fruit or vegetable (beanbag) and saying the first part of the chant, "How many fruits and vegetables today?" The infected player responds, "Five to nine, every day!" That player now becomes the fruit or vegetable and must save another infected person. Play for 40 seconds or so and then change infectious germs (students who are It).

Grade Variations

* Kindergarten: Skip, gallop, or slide for safety.
* First and second grades: If moving safely, students may begin to run.

Extensions

* If you teach in a bilingual or multilingual setting, incorporate languages other than English when naming the fruits and veggies. The students can help and will feel like experts!
* Encourage students to assign new fruit and vegetable names to the beanbags.
* Talk about healthy fruit and vegetable choices served in the cafeteria.

CLOSURE ROUTINE

Compliments

Identify specific behaviors that students performed well (e.g., "Thank you for playing so hard and getting your body moving. We had a great day! Movement is fun!").

Reflection and Review

* "What is the name of the video routine we learned today?"
* "What do fruits and veggies have in them that help your body grow, move, and stay healthy?"
* "Can you describe how your body felt during one of the activities?"
* "Share your favorite fruit and favorite veggie with your neighbor."

Take It Home

"Try one new animal movement and one new fruit or vegetable before next class."

ASSESSMENT

* **Performance check:** Observe students successfully executing the locomotor, animal, and video routine movements.
* **Comprehension check:** Responses to selected Comprehension Check questions and the Reflection and Review questions can serve as a check for student understanding.

1 WELLNESS WEEK

1.1 Lesson Plan

OVERVIEW

In this lesson, students will practice the video routine and have an opportunity to create and add new movements to the routine. The Lesson Focus activity is Exercise on the Farm for kindergarten students, Some More for first-grade students, and Get Fit for second-grade students.

NASPE STANDARDS

1A, 3A, 3B, 4A, 4C, 5A, 5B
(See appendix B for details.)

OBJECTIVES

Students will

* demonstrate a variety of locomotor and animal movements, including moving to music;
* explain why fruits and veggies are good for their bodies; and
* demonstrate an ability to work well with others in a cooperative activity.

EQUIPMENT

* CD player and continuous music (music CD track 12)
* TV, DVD player, and DVD 2 (Activity Routines)
* 8 to 10 cones
* 2 each of the following colored beanbags: red, yellow, blue, purple, and orange
* 6 green beanbags

RESOURCES

 General

At-a-Glance PE Lesson Plan card
G3: Physical Activity Pyramid for Kids

 **Wellness Week 1 →
K-2 Resources**

Animal Antics activity cards
Week 1 signs file with the following signs:

* Be active your way every day!
* Eat the rainbow way: every color, every day!

CHANTS

Leader: "How many fruits and veggies today?"

Students: "Five to nine, every day!"

> ⭐ **teacher tip** • • •
> You may not get through the whole lesson the first time through. Decide which part of the lesson is most important for your students to experience.

DELIVERING THE LESSON

1. Instant Activity: Move and Freeze

Introduction

"Welcome to Wellness Week! Let's get prepared to participate in some fun **Fitness for Life** activities. When I say 'go,' I want you to gallop inside the activity area in your own space. . . . Go!"

Activity

Students come into the activity space using a teacher-designated locomotor skill such as skipping, galloping, or sliding in open space, staying inside the designated activity area. On your stop signal, have them freeze in an athletic position (knees bent, shoulder width apart, hands on their knees) with their eyes on you. All students should freeze within five seconds with their bodies under control and eyes on you. Repeat this activity several times using various locomotor activities, getting bodies warmed up and students ready to listen. When students are moving and freezing in control, move on to the fitness activity.

> ↺ **review** • • •
> Review the important points of the freeze or athletic position with the students. Ask them to show you or tell you what the important points are (eyes on teacher, knees bent, shoulder width apart, hands on their knees).

Extensions

* ✳ Change the locomotor movement (e.g., walk, grapevine, jog).
* ✳ Change the quality of the movement (e.g., quietly, low, high).
* ✳ Change the pathway (e.g., zigzags, curves, squares).
* ✳ Move in unison to music (e.g., alone, with a partner, with a group).

2. Fitness Activity: Animal Antics

Introduction

"Animals move in so many ways. Animals move every day! Humans are animals that need regular activity. Let's get some activity by moving as if we were animals."

Activity

Place 8 to 10 Animal Antics activity cards on cones around your activity space. Have students begin at any cone, look at the animal, perform that animal movement en route to another animal activity card, and then perform that animal movement to another cone.

Encourage children to come up with new ideas for animal movements.

Encourage students to explore all of the animal movements. Promote the use of a language other than English by pointing out the Spanish translation of the animal movements on the activity cards.

Print and post the Physical Activity Pyramid for Kids sign. Stop the students periodically and briefly describe each step of the pyramid. Emphasize the importance of moderate activity such as walking to school, being active on the playground, or moving from place to place as if they were a certain type of animal.

Extensions

✳ Create more Animal Antics cards. Consider different themes (swamp animals, jungle animals, arctic animals).

✳ Have students create their own Animal Antics cards at home or with their classroom teacher.

 comprehension check • • •
- "Which animal movements made your legs stronger?"
- "Which animal movements stretched your muscles?"
- "Can someone make a noise like one of the animals?"

3. Lesson Focus: Video Routine Variations

Introduction

"Last time we practiced the video routine you are performing in your classroom. Today we are going to use our creativity and make up some new moves for the routine."

Activity

Practice the grade-specific video routine using the following steps.

1. Insert DVD 2 and play the video routine that is appropriate for your class:

    • Kindergarten: Exercise on the Farm

    • First grade: Some More

    • Second grade: Get Fit

2. Have the students follow along with the routine. Observe students performing the routine and take note of the movements that give them trouble.

? comprehension check •••
Ask students to explain what the video messages are trying to tell them. Reinforce the message by using some of your own examples or having students share examples.

👁 observation •••
Observe student groups to see if they are working well with others in a cooperative activity.

3. Before going through the routine again, provide a demonstration and help students with any movements that are giving them trouble. Provide tips that will help them succeed.

4. Break the students into 16 pairs, 8 groups, or 4 groups using a grouping strategy of your choice (see page 25). These group sizes allow you to pair groups together to make an even number of fewer (and larger) groups as the activity progresses.

5. Tell the students that you will play the video routine, and their job is to make up new movements for the routine that are in time with the music.

6. Play the video routine for your class, and visit the student groups to see their movements.

7. At the end of the routine, highlight a few moves that students came up with.

8. Have each group get with another group (e.g., 16 pairs become 8 groups) and play the music again. Have the two groups share their moves with each other.

9. Allow some time for the groups to combine their moves, and play the video routine so they can practice. Visit the new groups to see how they are combining their movements.

10. Repeat steps 8 and 9 until you have two large groups or the whole class working together with new movements.

⭐ teacher tip •••
Explain the importance of working with others. Identify the important elements of working with others, such as listening; sharing thoughts, feelings, and equipment; providing encouragement; and making sure everyone feels included. Provide examples of how this might sound or look in class.

11. Encourage students to share their new moves with their classroom teachers.

4. Culminating Activity: Fruits and Veggies Tag

Introduction

"Fruits and vegetables give you energy, help you grow, and can keep you healthy and well. Fruits and vegetables are full of energy and vitamins that help your body fight off illnesses like colds and flu—that's one reason to eat at least 5 servings of fruits and vegetables every day. Let's play a game that uses fruits and veggies to keep us healthy and moving."

Activity

Choose six players to have the green beanbags. These are your infectious germs—they are It. They begin in the middle of the gym. Distribute the fruits and vegetables (other colored beanbags) and have the students assign fruit and vegetable names to the various colors (e.g., red is tomato or strawberry, purple is grape or eggplant). Not all students will have a beanbag. On your signal (e.g., music), those who are It try to infect as many nonfruit and nonvegetable players as possible by tagging them softly. When infected (tagged), these players freeze in their best sick and tired position (or a position designated by you) until a fruit or vegetable player comes to save them by handing them the fruit or vegetable (beanbag) and saying the first part of the chant, "How many fruits and vegetables today?" The infected player responds, "Five to nine, every day!" That player now becomes the fruit or vegetable and must save another infected person. Play for 40 seconds or so and then change infectious germs (students who are It).

Grade Variations

* Kindergarten: Skip, gallop, or slide for safety.
* First and second grades: If moving safely, students may begin to run.

Extensions

* If you teach in a bilingual or multilingual setting, incorporate languages other than English when naming the fruits and veggies. The students can help and will feel like experts!
* Encourage students to assign new fruit and vegetable names to the beanbags.
* Talk about healthy fruit and vegetable snacks that students can eat.

CLOSURE ROUTINE

Compliments

Identify specific behaviors that students performed well (e.g., "Thank you for playing so hard and getting your body moving. We had a great day! Movement is fun!").

Reflection and Review

* "Who can give an example of a moderate activity from step 1 of the Physical Activity Pyramid for Kids?"
* "What was the message in the video, and why is it important?"
* "What are some good ways to work with other students in the class?"
* "What do fruits and veggies have in them that help your body grow, move, and stay healthy?"
* "How many different fruits and veggies have you eaten today? Name each one."

Take It Home

"Try one new animal movement and one new fruit or vegetable before next class."

ASSESSMENT

* **Performance check:** Observe students successfully executing the locomotor, animal, and video routine movements, as well as working together cooperatively.
* **Comprehension check:** Responses to selected Comprehension Check questions and Reflection and Review questions can serve as a check for student understanding.

OVERVIEW

This is a great lesson for students to explore a variety of locomotor movements, animal movements, and jumping skills.

NASPE STANDARDS

1A, 2C, 2D, 3A, 3B, 4A, 4C, 5A, 5B
(See appendix B for details.)

OBJECTIVES

Students will

* demonstrate a variety of jumping skills, including rope jumping;
* explain what happens to their heartbeat when they perform jumping skills; and
* encourage others by giving compliments.

EQUIPMENT

* CD player and continuous music (music CD track 9)
* 8 to 10 cones
* Short jump ropes for every student
* 2 each of the following colored beanbags: red, yellow, blue, purple, and orange
* 6 green beanbags

RESOURCES

 General

At-a-Glance PE Lesson Plan card
G3: Physical Activity Pyramid for Kids

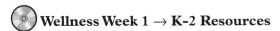 **Wellness Week 1 → K-2 Resources**

Animal Antics activity cards
Jumping for Joy task cards
Week 1 signs file with the following signs:

* Keep on trying. The more you try, the better you get!
* A healthy heart is a happy heart!

CHANTS

Leader: "Trying hard makes you sweat."

Students: "The more you try, the better you get!"

> ⭐ **teacher tip** • • •
> You may not get through the whole lesson the first time through. Decide which part of the lesson is most important for your students to experience.

DELIVERING THE LESSON

1. Instant Activity: Move and Freeze

Introduction

"Let's get prepared for some jumping activities with a quick warm-up. When I say 'go,' I want you to jog inside the activity area and in your own space. . . . Go!"

Activity

Students come into the activity space using a teacher-designated locomotor skill, such as skipping, galloping, or sliding in open space, staying inside the designated activity area. On your stop signal, have them freeze in an athletic position (knees bent, shoulder width apart, hands on their knees) with their eyes on you. All students should freeze within five seconds with their bodies under control and eyes on you. Repeat this activity several times using various locomotor activities, getting bodies warmed up and students ready to listen. When students are moving and freezing in control, move on to the fitness activity.

Extensions

* Change the locomotor movement (e.g., walk, grapevine, jog).
* Change the quality of the movement (e.g., quietly, low, high).
* Change the pathway (e.g., zigzags, curves, squares).
* Move in unison to music (e.g., alone, with a partner, with a group).

2. Fitness Activity: Animal Antics

Introduction

"Animals move in so many ways. Animals move every day! Humans are animals that need regular activity. Let's get some activity by moving as if we were animals."

Activity

Place 8 to 10 Animal Antics activity cards on cones around your activity space. Have students begin at any cone, look at the animal, perform that animal movement en route to another animal activity card, and then perform that animal movement to another cone. Encourage students to explore all of the animal movements. Promote the use of a language other than English by pointing out the Spanish translation of the animal movements on the activity cards.

3. Lesson Focus: Jumping for Joy

Introduction

"One of the best activities to move and strengthen your leg muscles and your bones is jumping. Today we are going to practice a variety of jumping skills and patterns. Jumping skills take time to learn, so we have to practice. Practice is more fun when we are encouraged by others. We can encourage others by giving compliments like, 'You're making some nice jumps, Jenny,' or 'I really like how you land softly on your jumps, Juan.' Let me hear you give compliments to others during our jumping activities today."

Activity

Have your students place their jump ropes on the floor in their own self-space, making a heart shape. Have students explore how many ways and directions they can jump, hop, or leap in, out, and over their hearts. Remember to review or teach the differences between jumping, hopping, and leaping. Teach or reinforce different jump patterns on your Jumping for Joy task cards, including the following:

> **↻ review • • •**
> Review each step of the Physical Activity Pyramid for Kids using the posted sign. Emphasize the importance of moderate activity such as walking to school or being active on the playground. Ask the following questions:
>
> - "Who can share a fun step 1 activity (moderate activity)?"
> - "What step of the pyramid has your favorite activities?"
> - "Today we are going to try some jumping activities. On what step of the pyramid would you put rope jumping?"

* Bell jump: quick, feet together, jumping forward and backward over the rope
* Straddle jump: feet apart and then together
* Scissor jump: feet splitting forward, backward, and then together
* X jump (advanced skill): straddle jump, crossing feet in the middle, and back to straddle

 observation • • •
Watch students interacting positively, and listen for encouragement between students. Model this behavior by giving positive feedback to students.

Refinements

* Observe students performing the jumping activities and provide feedback to help them improve (e.g., "Stay on your toes," "Bend your knees to land softly").
* Have students focus on the accuracy of their jumps by landing on the same spot (use lines as a guide).

Extensions

* Have students make different shapes, letters, and numbers with their jump ropes and explore jumping, hopping, and leaping over them.
* Have students travel around the room exploring other students' shapes by jumping, hopping, or leaping over them.
* Have students jump, hop, or leap in time to the music.

 comprehension check • • •
* Have students feel their hearts beating. Ask them to describe the feeling.
* "Is your heart beating faster than it was before? Why do you think that happened? Let's jump for 30 seconds and check it again."

Second Time Through

If you are teaching this lesson a second time, you may want to introduce the following activities.

Introduction

"Last time we worked on jumping movements around our jump ropes. Let's review some of those jumps and then begin to learn how to jump rope." (Have students perform some of the jumping skills from the Lesson Focus.)

"Jumping rope can be a hard activity to learn, but with lots of practice you will learn how to jump rope like me." (Demonstrate some fancy footwork and speed work.)

Activity (Kindergarten)

"Do you know who Tigger is from the *Winnie the Pooh* stories? Do you remember what Tigger likes to do best? That's right, he likes to bounce. Can you bounce (jump with feet together) like a Tigger? Can you turn a pretend jump rope, using your wrists to turn the rope while doing little, soft Tigger bounces? That's right! Now pick up your jump rope and hold it in one hand. Can you continue to do Tigger bounces and swing the jump rope in a circle, trying to bounce just as the jump rope brushes the floor? Switch hands. Nice job.

"Now hold the jump rope in both hands with the loop of the jump rope touching your heels behind you. Stretch your arms out in front of you and swing the jump rope over your head using your big shoulder muscles, keeping a very large loop and touching your toes. No bouncing yet! Can you swing it back? Let's do 10 more. Swing over, swing back, swing over, swing back.

"This time as the jump rope swings over your head, try to bounce over it like this . . . that's the way. Swing and bounce. See if you can do more than one in a row. Remember, the secret is to swing and then bounce over." (Have students keep practicing while reinforcing the swing and then the bounce.)

Activity (First and Second Grades)

Some of your students may be real beginners, some may have beginning skills, and others may be ready to move on. Students will naturally be able to do what they can. Try the following sequence.

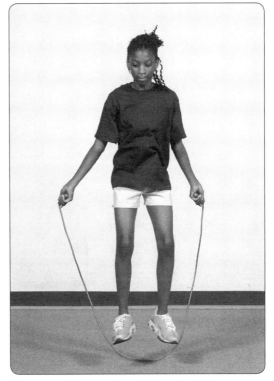

Use extensions and grade-level variations to adapt Jumping for Joy activities to meet student needs.

1. Start with students showing you their best jump-rope skills so you can get an idea of their skill level. If they can perform the basic jump (two feet together, continuous jumping, for 10 consecutive jumps), they are ready to go backward and to learn tricks.

2. Tricks to incorporate include the jump patterns you reinforced or taught the first time through the lesson. For instance, have the students practice the bell jump without the rope and then try it with the rope.

3. Reinforce critical elements, including small, soft jumps; arms to the side; watching for the rope; and swinging then jumping.

4. Challenge students to hop and do the same tricks while turning the jump rope backward.

4. Culminating Activity: Fruits and Veggies Tag

Introduction

"Fruits and vegetables give you energy, help you grow, and can keep you healthy and well. Fruits and vegetables are full of energy and vitamins that help your body fight off illnesses like colds and flu—that's one reason to eat at least 5 servings of fruits and vegetables every day. Let's play a game that uses fruits and veggies to keep us healthy and moving."

Activity

Choose six players to have the green beanbags. These are your infectious germs— they are It. They begin in the middle of the gym. Distribute the fruits and vegetables (other colored beanbags) and have the students assign fruit and vegetable names to the various colors (e.g., red is tomato or strawberry, purple is grape or eggplant). Not all students will have a beanbag. On your signal (e.g., music), those who are It

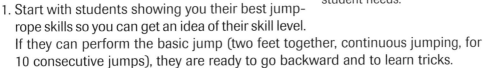

try to infect as many nonfruit and nonvegetable players as possible by tagging them softly. When infected (tagged), these players freeze in their best sick and tired position (or a position designated by you) until a fruit or vegetable player comes to save them by handing them the fruit or vegetable (beanbag) and saying the first part of the chant, "How many fruits and vegetables today?" The infected player responds, "Five to nine, every day!" That player now becomes the fruit or vegetable and must save another infected person. Play for 40 seconds or so and then change infectious germs (students who are It).

Grade Variations

* Kindergarten: Skip, gallop, or slide for safety.

* First and second grades: If moving safely, students may begin to run.

Extensions

* If you teach in a bilingual or multilingual setting, incorporate languages other than English when naming the fruits and veggies. The students can help and will feel like experts!

* Encourage students to assign new fruit and vegetable names to the beanbags.

* Have students feel their heartbeats before the game starts and during the breaks. Have them comment on the changes they feel in their heartbeats and why they think this is happening.

CLOSURE ROUTINE

Compliments

Ask students to share a compliment for the class or a class member.

Reflection and Review

* "Who can tell me a jumping pattern we learned today?"

* "Turn to your neighbor and tell what happens to your heart when you jump hard or exercise."

* "What step of the Physical Activity Pyramid for Kids would you place these jumping activities on?"

* "What activities require jumping?"

* "What animals spend a lot of time jumping?"

* "What did you learn today that will help you jump rope successfully?"

* "How did jumping rope make you feel?"

Take It Home

"Practice your jump rope skills at home. Try to get your family jumping at home. Tell them why jumping is good for the body. Remember, the more you try, the better you'll get!"

ASSESSMENT

* **Performance check:** Observe students successfully executing the locomotor, animal, and jumping movements. Listen for students giving each other compliments and encouragement.

* **Comprehension check:** Responses to selected Comprehension Check questions and Reflection and Review questions can serve as a check for student understanding.

OVERVIEW

In this lesson, students will explore a variety of tossing and catching activities.

NASPE STANDARDS

1A, 2D, 3A, 3B, 4A, 4C, 5A, 5B
(See appendix B for details.)

OBJECTIVES

Students will

* demonstrate successful tossing and catching alone and with a partner,
* demonstrate successful tossing and catching in place and on the move, and
* encourage others by giving compliments.

EQUIPMENT

* CD player and continuous music (music CD track 10)
* 8 to 10 cones
* Enough fleece balls or beanbags for everyone
* 2 each of the following colored beanbags: red, yellow, blue, purple, and orange
* 6 green beanbags

RESOURCES

 General

At-a-Glance PE Lesson Plan card

G3: Physical Activity Pyramid for Kids

 Wellness Week 1 → K-2 Resources

Animal Antics activity cards

Toss and Catch task cards

Week 1 signs file with the following sign:

* Keep on trying. The more you try, the better you get!

CHANTS

Leader: "Trying hard makes you sweat."

Students: "The more you try, the better you get!"

> ⭐ **teacher tip** • • •
> You may not get through the whole lesson the first time through. Decide which part of the lesson is most important for your students to experience.

DELIVERING THE LESSON

1. Instant Activity: Move and Freeze

Introduction

"Today we are going to work on some fun tossing and catching activities, but first we need to warm up our bodies. When I say 'go,' I want you to skip inside the activity area in your own space. . . . Go!"

Activity

Students come into the activity space using a teacher-designated locomotor skill, such as skipping, galloping, or sliding in open space, staying inside the designated activity area. On your stop signal, have them freeze in an athletic position (knees bent, shoulder width apart, hands on their knees) with their eyes on you. All students should freeze within five seconds with their bodies under control and eyes on you. Repeat this activity several times using various locomotor activities, getting bodies warmed up and students ready to listen. When students are moving and freezing in control, move on to the fitness activity.

Extensions

* Change the locomotor movement (e.g., walk, grapevine, jog).
* Change the quality of the movement (e.g., quietly, low, high).
* Change the pathway (e.g., zigzags, curves, squares).
* Move in unison to music (e.g., alone, with a partner, with a group).

2. Fitness Activity: Animal Antics

Introduction

"Animals move in so many ways. Animals move every day! Humans are animals that need regular activity. Let's get some activity by moving as if we were animals."

Activity

Place 8 to 10 Animal Antics activity cards on cones around your activity space. Have students

begin at any cone, look at the animal, perform that animal movement en route to another animal activity card, and then perform that animal movement to another cone. Encourage students to explore all of the animal

observation • • •

Look around the room to see if students are moving safely. Encourage safe and controlled movements in open space. Do not allow running until you see safe and controlled movement, especially with kindergarteners.

movements. Promote the use of a language other than English by pointing out the Spanish translation of the animal movements on the activity cards.

Extensions

✳ Perform your favorite animal movement and move toward animals like you.

✳ Perform a different animal movement and move toward animals like you.

✳ Create a new animal movement and move toward animals that move like you.

3. Lesson Focus: Tossing and Catching Skills

Introduction

"Two of the most important skills are throwing and catching. Many games require you to be able to toss and catch. Can you think of any playground games or sports that use throwing and catching? That's right—baseball, football, and basketball. Today we are going to learn how to toss and catch in our own self-space. When I say 'Beanbag,' everyone get a beanbag and begin tossing and catching it in your own space."

Activity

"Can you toss the beanbag up in the air and catch it with both hands? Toss it so that it only goes as high as you can reach. Stay in your own space. Don't move around."

Guide students through basic and advanced activities using the Toss and Catch task cards.

Second Time Through

If you are teaching this lesson a second time, you may want to introduce the following tossing and catching activities.

review • • •

Review the practice of encouraging each other through compliments. Provide a couple of examples from Lesson Plan 1.2 (see page 43). Encourage students to give each other compliments throughout the lesson.

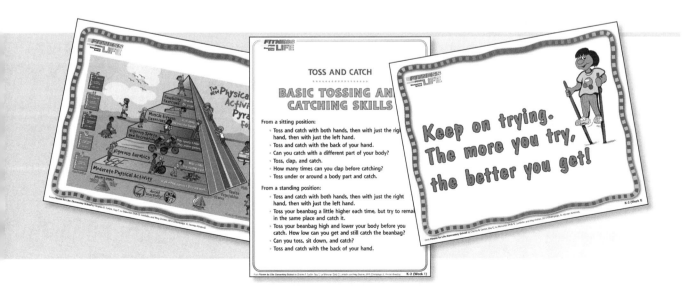

K-2 • WEEK 1
LESSON PLAN 1.3

comprehension check • • •

- "What did you have to do to make sure that you would catch the beanbag?"
- "What are some things you need to do with your hands?"
- "Did it take some practice? Did you get better?"

Introduction

"Let's review some of the tossing and catching activities from last class." (Take a few minutes to try them again.) "Today we are going to start moving while we are tossing and catching and begin working with a partner."

Individual Activities

✳ "Can you toss and catch while walking, skipping, sliding, galloping, jumping, or hopping?"

✳ "Can you toss and catch as you from move from side to side?"

✳ "Can you toss the beanbag to another place, move, and catch it?"

✳ "Can you toss the beanbag behind you, turn, move, and catch it?"

Partner Activities

"Point at the closest person. Get toe to toe. This is your partner. Decide which beanbag you will use and put the extra beanbag away. When working with a partner, you need to make careful tosses. Don't throw the beanbag too hard or too soft—always pay attention. Don't toss the beanbag if your partner is not looking at you.

"Face your partner and take three giant steps back. Practice tossing the beanbag back and forth. Don't make your partner move to catch it—toss it right to each other.

✳ "How many times can you and your partner toss it back and forth without dropping it? Make a personal record."

✳ "Each time you catch the beanbag, take a giant step backward. If you miss, you must stay there until you catch it."

Extensions

✳ If you find that the partner activities are too hard for some students, have them return to working by themselves. Start alone and stationary, and work toward moving with partners.

✳ Have successful students try fancy tosses and catches with their partners.

✳ Have students work on a solo or partner toss-and-catch routine.

 observation • • •
Watch students interacting positively and listen for encouragement between students. Model this behavior by giving positive feedback to students.

4. Culminating Activity: Fruits and Veggies Tag

Introduction

"Fruits and vegetables give you energy, help you grow, and can keep you healthy and well. Fruits and vegetables are full of energy and vitamins that help your body fight off illnesses like colds and flu—that's one reason to eat at least 5 servings of fruits and vegetables every day. Let's play a game that uses fruits and veggies to keep us healthy and moving."

Activity

Choose six players to have the green beanbags. These are your infectious germs—they are It. They begin in the middle of the gym. Distribute the fruits and vegetables (other colored beanbags) and have the students assign fruit and vegetable names to the various colors (e.g., red is tomato or strawberry, purple is grape or eggplant). Not all students will have a beanbag. On your signal (e.g., music), those who are It try to infect as many nonfruit and nonvegetable players as possible by tagging them softly. When infected (tagged), these players freeze in their best sick and tired position (or a position designated by you) until a fruit or vegetable player comes to save them by handing them the fruit or vegetable (beanbag) and saying the first part of the chant, "How many fruits and vegetables today?" The infected player responds, "Five to nine, every day!" That player now becomes the fruit or vegetable and must save another infected person. Play for 40 seconds or so and then change infectious germs (students who are It).

Grade Variations

* ✶ Kindergarten: Skip, gallop, or slide for safety.
* ✶ First and second grades: If moving safely, students may begin to run.

Extensions

* ✶ Change the locomotor movements frequently (e.g., galloping, sliding, walking).
* ✶ If you teach in a bilingual or multilingual setting, incorporate languages other than English when naming the fruits and veggies. The students can help and will feel like experts!
* ✶ Have students feel their heartbeats before the game starts and during the breaks. Have them comment on the changes they feel in their heartbeats and why they think this is happening.

Consider all the senses that this child is using to balance while tossing and catching.

CLOSURE ROUTINE

Compliments

Ask students to share a compliment for the class or a class member.

Reflection and Review

* "What things do you need to remember to catch the beanbag successfully?"
* "What happens when you take your eyes off the beanbag?"
* "What step of the Physical Activity Pyramid for Kids would you put tossing and catching activities on?"
* "What game or activity can you do at home or at school to practice tossing and catching?"
* "What are some good tips for tossing and catching with a partner?"
* "Can you give me an example of how practicing helped you get better?"

Take It Home

* "Practice tossing or catching at home with a friend or family member."
* "Find out how many games your family members know that include tossing and catching. Play one with them."

ASSESSMENT

* **Performance check:** Observe students successfully executing tossing and catching skills. Listen for students giving each other compliments and encouragement.
* **Comprehension check:** Responses to selected Comprehension Check questions and the Reflection and Review questions can serve as a check for student understanding.

EXTRA ACTIVITIES AND RESOURCES

If your school has physical education more than three times per week, consider delivering some of the lesson plans a second time or using some of the extra activities and resources in appendix A of this book (see page 245). You can also use some of the additional activities described in appendix A of the classroom guides. Ask your wellness coordinator for access to these guides.

WELLNESS WEEK 2

Fitness for Life Elementary School

These lesson plans provide students with a variety of experiences, including posing in athletic positions, moving to music, and pacing themselves while running and exploring a variety of movement skills. In Wellness Week 2, the activity theme is "vigorous physical activity (vigorous aerobics, sports, and recreation)," and the nutrition theme is "grains and foods with fat." Take time to look through the lesson plans for Wellness Week 2 and determine which objectives are most important and which activities you will use to meet those objectives. Table 2.2 summarizes the Wellness Week 2 activities for the physical education lesson plans.

For Wellness Week 2, the lesson plans include the following:

- A warm-up lesson plan to be used during the week before Wellness Week 2. The same basic warm-up lesson plan is used for kindergarten through grade 2, but the Lesson Focus (practicing the video routine) is different for each grade.
- Three lesson plans (2.1, 2.2, and 2.3) to be used during Wellness Week 2. The same basic lesson plan is used for kindergarten through grade 2, with grade-specific variations, refinements, and extensions for some of the activities.
- Extra activity ideas for schools that have physical education class more than three days a week are provided in appendix A.

Table 2.2 Summary of Wellness Week 2 Activities

Lesson Plan	Instant Activity	Fitness Activity	Lesson Focus	Culminating Activity
Warm-Up 2 (week before Wellness Week 2)	Athletes in Motion	Grab Bag	Video Routine Practice: K: Frank and Franny Fitness 1: I Can 2: La Raspa	Cardio Caper
2.1	Athletes in Motion	Grab Bag	Video Routine Variations: K: Frank and Franny Fitness 1: I Can 2: La Raspa	Cardio Caper
2.2	Athletes in Motion	Grab Bag	Ready, Set, Run	Cardio Caper
2.3	Athletes in Motion	Grab Bag	Sport Centers	Cardio Caper

Eat Well Wednesday

Each Wednesday, known as Eat Well Wednesday, all teachers and staff are encouraged to emphasize nutrition. The wellness coordinator might plan special schoolwide events. During Wellness Week 2, the nutrition event is a healthy breakfast program. If you have a physical education lesson on Eat Well Wednesday, place an emphasis on nutrition signs and messages.

Get Fit Friday

Each Friday, known as Get Fit Friday, a school-wide event focusing on physical activity will be planned. (If your school participates in this event, your wellness coordinator will provide you with more details.) The Get Fit Friday activities are called TEAM Time activities (TEAM stands for Together Everyone Achieves More). During Wellness Week 2, this activity is called Big Kids Lead. Your wellness coordinator will lead the activity at the beginning of the school day with the help of students in grades 5 and 6. All students in the school will congregate in the gym, in the multipurpose room, or outside so that they can participate together. The TEAM Time activity includes a warm-up, a special routine called Colors, and a cool-down. If time allows, you can teach these activities in advance to make it easier for students to perform them during TEAM Time. A video and script are provided on the DVD that accompanies the *Guide for Wellness Coordinators*.

Newsletter

The CD-ROM contains a newsletter for use during Wellness Week 2. It is recommended that your school's wellness coordinator edit and

Vigorous physical activity (steps 2 and 3 of the Physical Activity Pyramid for Kids) is the activity theme for Wellness Week 2.

distribute the newsletter. Alternatively, you (or the classroom teachers) can do it. Just open the appropriate file, follow the instructions to edit and customize the newsletter, and send printed copies home with students or send them electronically via e-mail. Remind students to talk to their families about Wellness Week and the information in the newsletter.

 **Wellness Week 2 → Newsletter**

Warm-Up Lesson Plan 2

OVERVIEW

In this lesson, conducted during the week before Wellness Week 2, students will learn the grade-specific video routine that they will perform in their classroom during Wellness Week 2. You can aid the classroom teachers by teaching these routines in advance to make it easier for both students and teachers and to increase the chances that the classroom teachers will do the video routines in their classrooms.

NASPE STANDARDS

1A, 2C, 3A, 3B, 4A, 4B, 4C, 5A, 5B
(See appendix B for details.)

OBJECTIVES

Students will

* explore a variety of athletic movements,
* practice moving to music, and
* explain changes that occur in their bodies when they are active.

EQUIPMENT

* CD player, 30/10 interval music (music CD track 2), and 45/15 interval music (music CD track 6)
* TV, DVD player, and DVD 1 (Instructional Routines)
* 8 red beanbags or fleece balls
* 6 to 8 cones
* Grab bag (e.g., small bag, old hat)

RESOURCES

 General

At-a-Glance PE Lesson Plan card
G3: Physical Activity Pyramid for Kids

 Wellness Week 2 → K-2 Resources

Grab Bag activity cards
6 to 8 Cardio Caper activity cards
Week 2 signs file with the following signs:

   • Choose activity from the pyramid. Do vigorous activity from steps 2 and 3!
   • A healthy heart is a happy heart!

CHANTS

Leader: "Being active is a great start . . ."

Students: ". . . being active is good for my heart!"

> ⭐ **teacher tip • • •**
> You may not get through the whole lesson the first time through. Decide which part of the lesson is most important for your students to experience.

DELIVERING THE LESSON

1. Instant Activity: Athletes in Motion

Introduction

"There is an athlete inside all of us. What does it mean to be an athlete? That's right, someone who participates in sports or physical activity, like someone who plays soccer. Let's see if you can show me some athletes in motion."

Activity

Students perform a locomotor movement in the designated area. On your signal, they freeze in open space and create a statue of an athlete in motion. You can guess what activity the athlete is performing; for instance, it might be kicking a soccer ball, swimming, or skating. Change the locomotor skills frequently and encourage students to be still as if they were made of cement or ice.

Grade Variations

✴ Kindergarten: Model and brainstorm activities first and teach what a statue is.

✴ First and second grades: Show a picture of an athlete in motion (or demonstrate) and have students try to copy the movement. Practice three athletes in motion and put them together into a sequence. Encourage students to have their athletes perform at different levels (high, medium, and low). Have students do an athlete show where half the students become statues while the others travel around guessing the activity of the athletes in suspension.

2. Fitness Activity: Grab Bag

Introduction

"Playing sports is fun, and it's also a great way to stay in shape. Let's perform some athletic movements to get strong and healthy."

Activity

Draw a card from the grab bag (e.g., small bag, old hat), and show the picture to the students while demonstrating and describing the exercise. Use 30/10 interval music (music CD track 2) for starting and stopping the activity. Students join in and perform the exercise while the music is playing. When the music stops, draw another card and then name and demonstrate the activity.

3. Lesson Focus: Video Routine Practice

Introduction

"Next week is Wellness Week 2. During Wellness Week 2, we will be learning about physical activity, fitness, and healthy nutrition. Today we are going to practice the video routine you will be performing in your classroom during Wellness Week. This video routine is fun and will challenge you to move to music."

Activity

Introduce and practice the grade-specific video routine using the following steps.

1. Insert DVD 1 and play the instructional routine that is appropriate for your class:

   • Kindergarten: Frank and Franny Fitness

   • First grade: I Can

   • Second grade: La Raspa

   ↻ **review** • • •
   "We performed music routines during the last Wellness Week. It is important to use our ears for listening to the music and our eyes to help us perform the correct movements."

2. Have the students follow along with the routine. Observe students performing the routine and take note of the movements that give them trouble.

3. Before going through the routine again, provide a demonstration and help students with any movements that are giving them trouble. Provide tips that will help them succeed.

4. Play the routine again and compliment students on any improvements.

5. Remind students that next week is Wellness Week 2, and they will perform this routine every day in their classrooms next week.

Refinements

Observe the students' movements and listen to the reciting of the words. Provide feedback to help students stay with the music and move together.

4. Culminating Activity: Cardio Caper

Introduction

"Does anyone know what the word *cardio* means? It means 'heart.' What does your heart do? That's right, your heart pumps blood around your body. Where does that blood go? Yes, to your working muscles. When you are playing hard, your heart has to beat faster to move blood to your working muscles. The blood provides oxygen and fuel to your muscles. What else happens when you play hard or exercise? That's right, you also begin to sweat and breathe harder. Let's see if we can get our hearts pumping, our bodies sweating, and our lungs breathing harder by playing a game called Cardio Caper."

Activity

Place the Cardio Caper signs on cones scattered around the perimeter of the area. Use 45/15 interval music (music CD track 6) for starting and stopping the activity. Choose eight students to be taggers and have each one get a red beanbag or fleece ball. When the music starts, everyone performs the designated locomotor movement, moving safely in open space. Students who are tagged hustle over to the closest Cardio Caper card, perform the activity on the card 10 times, and then return to the game. When the music stops, two things happen.

1. First, students stop and check their heart rate by placing a hand over their heart, noticing how fast it is beating. Then they check their sweat factor by touching their forehead. Ask the following questions: "Is your forehead sweaty? Do you feel warm? Are you breathing harder now than when you started?"

2. On your signal, taggers quickly hand their beanbags to new taggers, who are standing with a hand raised. When the music starts, the game resumes.

Grade Variations

✳ Kindergarten: Skip, gallop, or slide for safety.

✳ First and second grades: If moving safely, students may begin to run. Encourage all students to keep moving and working hard. Don't quit!

↻ **review** • • •
Revisit the Physical Activity Pyramid for Kids and emphasize the second and third steps of the pyramid (vigorous aerobics and vigorous sports and recreation). Explain that activities at steps 2 and 3 of the pyramid are good for the heart.

Refinements

* Provide feedback to students to help them perform the locomotor movements correctly.
* Provide feedback to students to help them perform the Cardio Caper activities correctly.

Extensions

* Have students try to increase their heart rate as the caper progresses.
* Have the first- and second-grade students come up with some Cardio Caper activities.
* Have students count to 10 in a language other than English when they do the Cardio Caper activities.

CLOSURE ROUTINE

Compliments

"Thank you for working so hard! Compliment your neighbors on something they did well today."

Cardio Caper activities help students learn about vigorous physical activity (steps 2 and 3 of the pyramid).

Reflection and Review

* "How could you tell if you worked hard in today's lesson?"
* "Why is it important for your heart to beat faster when you play or exercise?"
* "Why do we start to breathe harder and sweat when we play hard?"
* "What kinds of activities do you do at home that get your heart pumping?"
* "At what steps of the Physical Activity Pyramid for Kids did you work during the Cardio Caper game?"

Take It Home

"Get your family moving! Challenge them to play or exercise with you and get their hearts pumping. Check to see how hard everyone is working by feeling each other's heartbeats, chests breathing, or warm foreheads."

ASSESSMENT

* **Performance check:** Observe students successfully executing the Grab Bag activities and moving to music during the video routines.
* **Comprehension check:** Responses to Reflection and Review questions can serve as a check for student understanding.

K-2 · WEEK 2
WARM-UP 2

2.1 Lesson Plan

OVERVIEW

In this lesson, students will practice the video routine and have an opportunity to create and add new movements to the routine.

NASPE STANDARDS

1A, 2C, 3A, 3B, 4A, 4B, 4C, 5A, 5B
(See appendix B for details.)

OBJECTIVES

Students will

* explore a variety of movements, including moving to music;
* explain changes that occur in their bodies when they are active; and
* demonstrate an ability to work well with others in a cooperative activity.

EQUIPMENT

* CD player and 30/10 (music CD track 2) and 45/15 interval music (music CD track 6)
* TV, DVD player, and DVD 2 (Activity Routines)
* 8 red beanbags or fleece balls
* 6 to 8 cones
* Grab bag (e.g., small bag, old hat)

RESOURCES

 General

At-a-Glance PE
  Lesson Plan card
G3: Physical Activity
  Pyramid for Kids

Wellness Week 2 → K-2 Resources

Grab Bag activity cards

6 to 8 Cardio Caper activity cards

Week 2 signs file with the following signs:

- Choose activity from the pyramid. Do vigorous activity from steps 2 and 3!
- A healthy heart is a happy heart!

CHANTS

Leader: "Being active is a great start . . ."

Students: ". . . being active is good for my heart!"

> ⭐ **teacher tip • • •**
> You may not get through the whole lesson the first time through. Decide which part of the lesson is most important for your students to experience.

DELIVERING THE LESSON

1. Instant Activity: Athletes in Motion

Introduction

"There is an athlete inside all of us. What does it mean to be an athlete? That's right, someone who participates in sports or physical activity, like someone who plays soccer. Let's see if you can show me some athletes in motion."

Activity

Students perform a locomotor movement in the designated area. On your signal, they freeze in open space and create a statue of an athlete in motion. You can guess what activity the athlete is performing; for instance, it might be kicking a soccer ball, swimming, or skating. Change the locomotor skills frequently and encourage students to be still as if they were made of cement or ice.

K-2 • WEEK 2
LESSON PLAN 2.1

Grade Variations

✳ Kindergarten: Model and brainstorm activities first and teach what a statue is.

✳ First and second grades: Show a picture of an athlete in motion (or demonstrate) and have students try to copy the movement. Practice three athletes in motion and put them together into a sequence. Encourage students to have their athletes perform at different levels (high, medium, and low). Have students do an athlete show where half the students become statues while the others travel around guessing the activity of the athletes in suspension.

2. Fitness Activity: Grab Bag

Introduction

"Playing sports is fun, and it's also a great way to stay in shape. Let's perform some athletic movements to get strong and healthy."

Activity

Draw a card from the grab bag (e.g., small bag, old hat), and show the picture to the students while demonstrating and describing the exercise. Use 30/10 interval music (music CD track 2) for starting and stopping the activity. Students join in and perform the exercise while the music is playing. When the music stops, draw another card and then name and demonstrate the activity.

 comprehension check • • •

"How can you tell if you are playing or exercising hard enough to build a strong heart? Think about the signals your body gives you when you are playing hard. You feel your heart beating fast, your temperature rising, your lungs breathing fast, or the sweat on your face."

Extensions

✳ Have students contribute new movements to the Grab Bag.

✳ Add a choice card and have students who choose the same activity move toward each other.

3. Lesson Focus: Video Routine Variations

Introduction

"Last class we practiced the video routine you are performing in your classroom. Today we are going to use our creativity and make up some new moves for the routine."

Activity

Practice the grade-specific video routine using the following steps.

1. Insert DVD 2 and play the video routine that is appropriate for your class:
   • Kindergarten: Frank and Franny Fitness
   • First grade: I Can
   • Second grade: La Raspa

2. Have the students follow along with the routine. Observe students performing the routine and take note of the movements that give them trouble.

> **comprehension check** • • •
> Ask students to explain what the video messages are trying to tell them. Help reinforce the message by using some of your own examples or having students share examples.

3. Before going through the routine again, provide a demonstration and help students with any movements that are giving them trouble. Provide tips that will help them succeed.

4. Break the students into 16 pairs, 8 groups, or 4 groups using a grouping strategy of your choice (see page 25). These group sizes allow you to pair groups together to make an even number of fewer (and larger) groups as the activity progresses.

5. Instruct the students that you will play the video routine, and their job is to make up new movements for the routine that are in time with the music.

6. Play the video routine for your class, and visit the student groups to see their movements.

7. At the end of the routine, highlight a few moves that students came up with.

8. Have each group get with another group (e.g., 16 pairs become 8 groups) and play the music again. Have the two groups share their moves with each other.

> **observation** • • •
> Observe student groups to see if they are working well with others in a cooperative activity.

9. Allow some time for the groups to combine their moves, and play the video routine so they can practice. Visit the new groups to see how they are combining their movements.

10. Repeat steps 8 and 9 until you have two large groups or the whole class working together with new movements.

11. Encourage students to share their new moves with their classroom teachers.

> **review** • • •
> Review the important elements of working with others, such as listening; sharing thoughts, feelings, and equipment; providing encouragement; and making sure everyone feels included. Ask the students to share examples of what this might sound or look like in the class.

4. Culminating Activity: Cardio Caper

Introduction

"Does anyone know what the word *cardio* means? It means 'heart.' What does your heart do? That's right, your heart pumps blood around your body. Where does that blood go? Yes, to your working muscles. When you are playing hard, your heart has to beat faster to move blood to your working muscles. The blood provides oxygen and fuel to your muscles. What else happens when you play hard or exercise? That's right, you also begin to sweat and breathe harder. Let's see if we can get our hearts pumping, our bodies sweating, and our lungs breathing harder by playing a game called Cardio Caper."

K-2 • WEEK 2
LESSON PLAN 2.1

> **↺ review** • • •
> Revisit the Physical Activity Pyramid for Kids and emphasize the second and third steps of the pyramid (vigorous aerobics and vigorous sports and recreation). Explain that activities at steps 2 and 3 of the pyramid are good for the heart.

Activity

Place the Cardio Caper signs on cones scattered around the perimeter of the area. Use 45/15 interval music (music CD track 6) for starting and stopping the activity. Choose eight students to be taggers and have each one get a red beanbag or fleece ball. When the music starts, everyone performs the designated locomotor movement, moving safely in open space. Students who are tagged hustle over to the closest Cardio Caper card, perform the activity on the card 10 times, and then return to the game. When the music stops, two things happen.

1. First, students stop and check their heart rate by placing a hand over their heart, noticing how fast it is beating. Then they check their sweat factor by touching their forehead. Ask the following questions: "Is your forehead sweaty? Do you feel warm? Are you breathing harder now than when you started?"
2. On your signal, taggers quickly hand their beanbags to new taggers, who are standing with a hand raised. When the music starts, the game resumes.

Grade Variations

* Kindergarten: Skip, gallop, or slide for safety.
* First and second grades: If moving safely, students may begin to run. Encourage all students to keep moving and working hard. Don't quit!

Refinements

* Provide feedback to students to help them perform the locomotor movements correctly.
* Provide feedback to students to help them perform the Cardio Caper activities correctly.

Extensions

* Have students try to increase their heart rate as the caper progresses.
* Have first- and second-grade students come up with some Cardio Caper activities.
* Have students count to 10 in a language other than English when they do the Cardio Caper activities.

CLOSURE ROUTINE

Compliments

"Thank you for working so hard! Compliment your neighbors on something they did well today."

Reflection and Review

* "What step of the Physical Activity Pyramid for Kids has activities that are especially good for the heart?"

* "How would you know if you worked at steps 2 and 3 (vigorous activity) of the pyramid today? Think about the changes that happen in your body when you play or exercise hard."

* "Share one activity with your neighbor that you improved at today."

* "Can anyone remember what the video message was and what it was trying to tell us? Did anyone play or exercise with your family and get your heart pumping?"

Take It Home

"Get your family members moving! Challenge them to play or exercise with you. Check to see if they are working hard by feeling their hearts beating, seeing their chests breathing fast, or feeling the warmth on their forehead."

Soccer is considered a vigorous sport (step 3 of the Physical Activity Pyramid for Kids).

ASSESSMENT

* **Performance check:** Observe students successfully executing the Grab Bag activities, moving to music during the video routines, and performing the Cardio Caper exercises.

* **Comprehension check:** Responses to selected Comprehension Check questions and the Reflection and Review questions can serve as a check for student understanding.

2.2 Lesson Plan •••••••••••••••••••••••••••••••••

OVERVIEW

This lesson focuses on cardiorespiratory fitness and gives students an opportunity to practice pacing themselves using the Fitnessgram PACER (Progressive Aerobic Cardiovascular Endurance Run) test.

NASPE STANDARDS

1A, 3A, 3B, 4A, 4C, 5A, 5B
(See appendix B for details.)

OBJECTIVES

Students will

* explore a variety of athletic movements,

* practice pacing to the Fitnessgram PACER signals, and

* explain why exercise makes their hearts beat faster and their bodies heat up.

EQUIPMENT

* CD player, 30/10 interval music (music CD track 2), 45/15 interval music (music CD track 6), and PACER music (music CD track 14)

* 8 red beanbags or fleece balls

* 6 to 8 cones

* Grab bag (e.g., small bag, old hat)

* Watch the PACER test at the Fitnessgram page of the **FFL: Elementary** Web site at www.fitnessforlife.org.

RESOURCES

 General

At-a-Glance PE Lesson Plan card

G3: Physical Activity Pyramid for Kids

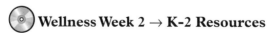 **Wellness Week 2 → K-2 Resources**

Grab Bag activity cards

6 to 8 Cardio Caper activity cards

Week 2 signs file with the following signs:

- Choose activity from the pyramid. Do vigorous activity from steps 2 and 3!
- A healthy heart is a happy heart!
- Keep on going to get fit. Never give up! Never quit!

CHANTS

Leader: "Being active is a great start . . ."

Students: ". . . being active is good for my heart!"

> **teacher tip** • • •
> You may not get through the whole lesson the first time through. Decide which part of the lesson is most important for your students to experience.

DELIVERING THE LESSON

1. Instant Activity: Athletes in Motion

Introduction

"There is an athlete inside all of us. What does it mean to be an athlete? That's right, someone who participates in sports or physical activity, like someone who plays soccer. Let's see if you can show me some athletes in motion."

Activity

Students perform a locomotor movement in the designated area. On your signal, they freeze in open space and create a statue of an athlete in motion. You can guess what activity the athlete is performing; for instance, it might be kicking a soccer ball, swimming, or skating. Change the locomotor skills frequently and encourage students to be still as if they were made of cement or ice.

Grade Variations

✳ Kindergarten: Model and brainstorm activities first and teach what a statue is.

✳ First and second grades: Show a picture of an athlete in motion (or demonstrate) and have students try to copy the movement. Practice three athletes in motion and put them together into a sequence. Encourage students to have their athletes perform at different levels (high, medium, and low). Have students do an athlete show where half the students become statues while the others travel around guessing the activity of the athletes in suspension.

2. Fitness Activity: Grab Bag

Introduction

"We have been exploring various athletic movements with the Grab Bag. Let's try to come up with some new activities and encourage each other to perform the movements for the whole time the music is playing."

For the Athletes in Motion activity, students copy the movements shown in pictures such as this photo of a pitcher.

Activity

Draw a card from the grab bag (e.g., small bag, old hat), and show the picture to the students while demonstrating and describing the exercise. Use 30/10 interval music (music CD track 2) for starting and stopping the activity. Students join in and perform the exercise while the music is playing. When the music stops, draw another card and then name and demonstrate the activity.

Extensions

✳ Have students contribute new movements to the Grab Bag.

✳ Add a choice card and have students who choose the same activity move toward each other.

✳ Have students identify the movements using a language other than English.

✳ Create new cards with a theme for the movements (e.g., warm-weather activities, cold-weather sports, water sports, snow sports).

3. Lesson Focus: Ready, Set, Run

Introduction

"To keep our bodies healthy, we need to move them at least 60 minutes a day. One of the best ways to move is to run. Running also helps us to build a strong heart muscle and something called *cardiorespiratory fitness.* Good cardiorespiratory fitness allows you to keep moving for long periods of time without stopping. Let's practice a fun running test that measures your cardiorespiratory fitness. It's called the PACER. The PACER is a test that starts out slow and easy and then gets faster and harder. So, we all have to pace ourselves. Pacing means to match our speed with another person, a rhythm, or a signal. We have to pace ourselves when we run the PACER test, so start slow!"

Activity

As a lead-up to the Fitnessgram PACER test, measure and mark two lines 20 meters apart. Have students line up along one of the lines. Explain to your students that they are going to do a fun run called the PACER. When the voice on the music (music CD track 14) says "Start," students jog to the other line and wait. When they hear the beep, they jog back to the other line.

Have students continue doing this for 10 to 15 lengths. Once students begin jogging, remind them to change directions on the beep. Encourage students to time their running so that they make it to the other line on or before the beep. Don't worry if they don't. Students don't get eliminated; they just turn and run when they hear the beep.

(?) comprehension check

"On what steps of the Physical Activity Pyramid for Kids would you place the PACER?"

Second Time Through

If you are teaching this lesson a second time, you may want to introduce the following activities.

Introduction

"Last time we practiced the fun running test called the PACER. Who can tell me what this test measures? That's right, cardiorespiratory fitness. Today we are going to try the test again and use our pacing skills that we learned by practicing the PACER last class."

Refinements

Have the students concentrate on running together in a single line (i.e., side by side) across the distance.

Extensions

* Have the students try various locomotor movements for the first few laps (e.g., walk, skip, or gallop).
* Challenge them to see how many laps they can stay together as a straight line.

4. Culminating Activity: Cardio Caper

Introduction

"Does anyone know what the word *cardio* means? It means 'heart.' What does your heart do? That's right, your heart pumps blood around your body. Where does that blood go? Yes, to your working muscles. When you are playing hard, your heart has to beat faster to move blood to your working muscles. The blood provides oxygen and fuel to your muscles. What else happens when you play hard or exercise? That's right, you also begin to sweat and breathe harder. Let's see if we can get our hearts pumping, our bodies sweating, and our lungs breathing harder by playing a game called Cardio Caper."

> **review** • • •
> Revisit the Physical Activity Pyramid for Kids and emphasize the second and third steps of the pyramid (vigorous aerobics and vigorous sports and recreation). Explain that activities at steps 2 and 3 of the pyramid are good for the heart.

Activity

Place the Cardio Caper signs on cones scattered around the perimeter of the area. Use 45/15 interval music (music CD track 6) for starting and stopping the activity. Choose eight students to be taggers and have each one get a red beanbag or fleece ball. When the music starts, everyone performs the designated locomotor movement, moving safely in open space. Students who are tagged hustle over to the closest Cardio Caper card, perform the activity on the card 10 times, and then return to the game. When the music stops, two things happen.

1. First, students stop and check their heart rate by placing a hand over their heart, noticing how fast it is beating. Then they check their sweat factor by touching their forehead. Ask the following questions: "Is your forehead sweaty? Do you feel warm? Are you breathing harder now than when you started?"

2. On your signal, taggers quickly hand their beanbags to new taggers, who are standing with a hand raised. When the music starts, the game resumes.

Grade Variations
* Kindergarten: Skip, gallop, or slide for safety.
* First and second grades: If moving safely, students may begin to run. Encourage all students to keep moving and working hard. Don't quit!

Refinements
* Provide feedback to students to help them perform the locomotor movements correctly.
* Provide feedback to students to help them perform the Cardio Caper activities correctly.

Extensions
* When the music stops, have the students freeze, close their eyes, and tune in to the sensations in their bodies. What feelings, sounds, or smells can they describe?
* Have first- and second-grade students come up with some Cardio Caper activities.
* Have students count to 10 in a language other than English when they do the Cardio Caper activities.

CLOSURE ROUTINE

Compliments

"Thanks for a great class. Remember to exercise your heart! Moving your body gets your heart thump, thump, thumping."

> **interdisciplinary** • • •
> If you have a picture of heart or a heart model, this would be a great time to show your students what the heart looks like. Identify one or two key structures of the heart (e.g., atria, ventricles, aorta, valves). Discuss how the heart is a muscle and needs exercise to stay strong and fit. What happens if it stops beating? How do you keep it healthy?

Reflection and Review

* "What parts of your body did you notice when you stopped the PACER?"

* "What are you feeling in those body parts?"

* "What do we all need to do to run together?" (Use our eyes.)

* "What activity made your heart beat hardest today?"

Take It Home

* "Invite your family members to do some running with you. Pace yourselves so you can run together for a few minutes."

* "Get your family members outside and get their hearts beating hard. Feel their hearts to check that they are beating hard."

ASSESSMENT

* **Performance check:** Observe students successfully executing the Grab Bag activities and pacing themselves during the PACER test.

* **Comprehension check:** Responses to selected Comprehension Check questions and the Reflection and Review questions can serve as a check for student understanding.

2.3 Lesson Plan ··

OVERVIEW

In this lesson, students will explore a variety of sport activities using a station approach.

NASPE STANDARDS

1A, 3A, 3B, 4A, 4C, 5A, 5B
(See appendix B for details.)

OBJECTIVES

Students will

* explore a variety of sport movements,
* explain changes that occur in the body when they are active, and
* display consideration of others while participating in the station activities.

EQUIPMENT

* CD player, 30/10 interval music (music CD track 2), 45/15 interval music (music CD track 6), and continuous music (music CD track 12)
* 8 red beanbags or fleece balls
* 6 to 8 cones
* Grab bag (e.g., small bag, old hat)
* Various physical education equipment (depends on sport centers chosen)

RESOURCES

 General

At-a-Glance PE Lesson Plan card

 Wellness Week 2 → K-2 Resources

Grab Bag activity cards

6 to 8 Cardio Caper activity cards

Sport Centers activity cards

Week 2 signs file with the following signs:

* Choose activity from the pyramid. Do vigorous activity from steps 2 and 3!
* A healthy heart is a happy heart!
* Keep on trying. The more you try, the better you get!

CHANTS

Leader: "Keep on going to get fit."

Students: "Never give up! Never quit!"

Leader: "Being active is a great start . . ."

Students: ". . . being active is good for my heart!"

> **teacher tip** • • •
> You may not get through the whole lesson the first time through. Decide which part of the lesson is most important for your students to experience.

DELIVERING THE LESSON

1. Instant Activity: Athletes in Motion

Introduction

"There is an athlete inside all of us. What does it mean to be an athlete? That's right, someone who participates in sports or physical activity, like someone who plays soccer. Let's see if you can show me some athletes in motion."

Activity

Students perform a locomotor movement in the designated area. On your signal, they freeze in open space and create a statue of an athlete in motion. You can guess what activity the athlete is performing; for instance, it might be kicking a soccer ball, swimming, or skating. Change the locomotor skills frequently and encourage students to be still as if they were made of cement or ice.

Grade Variations

✳ Kindergarten: Model and brainstorm activities first and teach what a statue is.

✳ First and second grades: Show a picture of an athlete in motion (or demonstrate) and have students try to copy the movement. Practice three athletes in motion and put them together into a sequence. Encourage students to have their athletes perform at different levels (high, medium, and low). Have students do an athlete show where half the students become statues while the others travel around guessing the activity of the athletes in suspension.

2. Fitness Activity: Grab Bag

Introduction

"We have been exploring various athletic movements with the Grab Bag. Let's try to come up with some new activities and encourage each other to perform the movements for the whole time the music is playing."

Activity

Draw a card from the grab bag (e.g., small bag, old hat), and show the picture to the students while demonstrating and describing the exercise. Use 30/10 interval music (music CD track 2) for starting and stopping the activity. Students join in and perform the exercise while the music is playing. When the music stops, draw another card and then name and demonstrate the activity.

Extensions

✳ Have students identify the movements using a language other than English.

✳ Create some new cards with a theme for the movements (e.g., warm-weather activities, cold-weather activities, water sports, snow sports).

3. Lesson Focus: Sport Centers

Introduction

"There are many activities that you can do to be active. Today you are going to explore many types of skills and activities. Some activities will be hard in the beginning, so you will need to practice to get better. If you don't get it the first time, keep trying. Keep trying, and never, ever give up! One last thing—you will be working at these stations with others, so I would like to see you give each other space, share equipment, and communicate with each other."

Activity

Design several centers with the equipment you have. The Sport Centers activity cards present some sample centers, but you can also design centers for tossing and catching with beanbags and scoops, scarf juggling or throwing and catching, balance-beam walking, and so on.

 comprehension check • • •

In the break between stations, ask the following:

• "What changes can you feel in your body after performing that last sport center?"

• "At what step of the Physical Activity Pyramid for Kids would you place the Sport Centers activities?"

Explain and demonstrate the centers to your students. Because students at this age might not read well, keep everything simple. Divide the students into equal groups and make sure you have enough equipment at each center so that all students will have their own piece of equipment to practice with. Have students practice at their center for two to three minutes. When the music stops or on another signal, they clean up their center and point at the next one. When you say "Rotate," they advance to the next clockwise center and begin working there.

Second Time Through

If you are teaching this lesson a second time, you may want to integrate some of the following ideas.

Introduction

"Last time we practiced our sport skills at different learning centers. Did anyone come up with an idea for a new center? Let's practice at these centers again to improve our sport skills."

Refinements

* Observe students performing the various skills. Provide feedback to help students succeed at the skill.

* Have students encourage each other at the stations. Model this behavior by providing positive feedback to students.

 **observation** • • •
Observe student groups to see if they are considering each other while working at the stations (i.e., giving each other space, sharing equipment, communicating).

Extensions

* Include student ideas at the centers.

* Challenge students to perform the skills consecutively, at different speeds, using different body parts, or with a partner.

At a jump-rope center, students can count the number of times they can jump forward and backward without a miss.

4. Culminating Activity: Cardio Caper

Introduction

"Does anyone know what the word *cardio* means? It means 'heart.' What does your heart do? That's right, your heart pumps blood around your body. Where does that blood go? Yes, to your working muscles. When you are playing hard, your heart has to beat faster to move blood to your working muscles. The blood provides oxygen and fuel to your muscles. What else happens when you play hard or exercise? That's right, you also begin to sweat and breathe harder. Let's see if we can get our hearts pumping, our bodies sweating, and our lungs breathing harder by playing a game called Cardio Caper."

> ↺ **review** • • •
> Revisit the Physical Activity Pyramid for Kids and emphasize the second and third steps of the pyramid (vigorous aerobics and vigorous sports and recreation). Explain that activities at steps 2 and 3 of the pyramid are good for the heart.

Activity

Place the Cardio Caper signs on cones scattered around the perimeter of the area. Use 45/15 interval music (music CD track 6) for starting and stopping the activity. Choose eight students to be taggers and have each one get a red beanbag or fleece ball. When the music starts, everyone performs the designated locomotor movement, moving safely in open space. Students who are tagged hustle over to the closest Cardio Caper card, perform the activity on the card 10 times, and then return to the game. When the music stops, two things happen.

1. First, students stop and check their heart rate by placing a hand over their heart, noticing how fast it is beating. Then they check their sweat factor by touching their forehead. Ask the following questions: "Is your forehead sweaty? Do you feel warm? Are you breathing harder now than when you started?"
2. On your signal, taggers quickly hand their beanbags to new taggers, who are standing with a hand raised. When the music starts, the game resumes.

Grade Variations

✳ Kindergarten: Skip, gallop, or slide for safety.
✳ First and second grades: If moving safely, students may begin to run. Encourage all students to keep moving and working hard. Don't quit!

Refinements

✳ Provide feedback to students to help them perform the locomotor movements correctly.
✳ Provide feedback to students to help them perform the Cardio Caper activities correctly.

Extensions

✳ Have first- and second-grade students come up with some Cardio Caper activities.
✳ Have students count to 10 in a language other than English when they do the Cardio Caper activities.

CLOSURE ROUTINE

Compliments

Have some students share a compliment about a class member or the whole class.

> **interdisciplinary** • • •
>
> If you have a picture of heart or a heart model, this would be a great time to show your students what the heart looks like. Identify one or two key structures of the heart (e.g., atria, ventricles, aorta, valves). Discuss how the heart is a muscle and needs exercise to stay strong and fit. What happens if it stops beating? How do you keep it healthy?

Reflection and Review

* "What senses did you use at the sport centers?"
* "What was your favorite sport center? Why?"
* "What did you improve at today? How did you get better?"
* "Share something that you learned from another student."

Take It Home

"Create and practice a sport center with a family member."

ASSESSMENT

* **Performance check:** Observe students successfully executing the skills at the sport centers, performing Cardio Caper activities, and considering others at the sport centers.
* **Comprehension check:** Responses to selected Comprehension Check questions and the Reflection and Review questions can serve as a check for student understanding.

EXTRA ACTIVITIES AND RESOURCES

If your school has physical education more than three times per week, consider delivering some of the lesson plans a second time or using some of the extra activities and resources in appendix A of this book (see page 245). You can also use some of the additional activities described in appendix A of the classroom guides. Ask your wellness coordinator for access to these guides.

WELLNESS WEEK 3

Fitness for Life Elementary School

These lesson plans provide students with a variety of experiences, including conducting a warm-up and a cool-down, engaging in flexibility exercises, exploring muscle fitness stunts and challenges, and moving to music. In Wellness Week 3, the activity theme is "muscle fitness and flexibility exercises," and the nutrition theme is "food for strong bones and muscles." The lesson plans emphasize these themes and reinforce the changes that take place in our bodies when we engage in activity. Take time to look through the lesson plans for Wellness Week 3 and determine which objectives are most important and which activities you will use to meet those objectives. Table 2.3 summarizes the Wellness Week 3 activities for the physical education lesson plans.

For Wellness Week 3, the lesson plans include the following:

- A warm-up lesson plan to be used during the week before Wellness Week 3. The same basic warm-up lesson plan is used for kindergarten through grade 2.
- Three lesson plans (3.1, 3.2, and 3.3) to be used during Wellness Week 3. The same basic lesson plan is used for kindergarten through grade 2.
- Extra activity ideas for schools that have physical education class more than three days a week are provided in appendix A.

Table 2.3 Summary of Wellness Week 3 Activities

Lesson Plan	Instant Activity	Fitness Activity	Lesson Focus	Culminating Activity
Warm-Up 3 (week before Wellness Week 3)	Warm It Up	Move Your Body	Video Routine Practice: K: We Get Fit 1: CYIM Fit 2: Wave It	Cool It Down
3.1	Warm It Up	Move Your Body	Video Routine Variations: K: We Get Fit 1: CYIM Fit 2: Wave It	Cool It Down
3.2	Active Every Day	Move Your Body	Bend It, Stretch It	Flexibility Tag
3.3	Active Every Day	Move Your Body	Muscle Stunts and Challenges	Muscle-Builder Tag

Eat Well Wednesday

Each Wednesday, known as Eat Well Wednesday, all teachers and staff are encouraged to emphasize nutrition. The wellness coordinator might plan special schoolwide events. During Wellness Week 3, the nutrition event is a yogurt bar in the cafeteria. If you have a physical education lesson on Eat Well Wednesday, place an emphasis on nutrition signs and messages.

Get Fit Friday

Each Friday, known as Get Fit Friday, a schoolwide event focusing on physical activity will be planned. (If your school participates in this event, your wellness coordinator will provide you with more details.) The Get Fit Friday activities are called TEAM Time activities (TEAM stands for Together Everyone Achieves More). During Wellness Week 3, this activity is called Little Kids Lead. Your wellness coordinator and students from kindergarten, first grade, and second grade will lead all students in three activities. First, kindergarten students will lead an activity called We Get Fit, then first-grade students will lead an activity called CYIM Fit, and finally second-grade students will lead an activity called Wave It. These activities will have been learned in physical education or in the classroom earlier in the week.

Newsletter

The CD-ROM contains a newsletter for use during Wellness Week 3. It is recommended that your school's wellness coordinator edit and distribute the newsletter. Alternatively, you (or the classroom teachers) can do it. Just open the appropriate file, follow the instructions to edit and customize the newsletter, and send printed copies home with students or send them electronically via e-mail. Remind students to talk to their families about Wellness Week and the information in the newsletter.

 Wellness Week 3 → Newsletter

The activity theme for Wellness Week 3 is muscle fitness and flexibility exercises (steps 4 and 5 of the Physical Activity Pyramid for Kids).

K-2 · WEEK 3 INTRODUCTION

Warm-Up Lesson Plan **3**

OVERVIEW

In this lesson, conducted during the week before Wellness Week 3, students will learn the video routine that they will perform in their classroom during Wellness Week 3. You can aid the classroom teachers by teaching these routines in advance to make it easier for both students and teachers and to increase the chances that the classroom teachers will do the video routines in their classrooms. In addition, students will learn about the importance of the warm-up and cool-down.

NASPE STANDARDS

1A, 2C, 3A, 3B, 4A, 4B, 4C, 5A, 5B
(See appendix B for details.)

OBJECTIVES

Students will

* demonstrate an ability to move to the beat of the music,
* explain why a warm-up and a cool-down are important for physical activity, and
* identify the changes that take place in the body after a warm-up and cool-down.

EQUIPMENT

* CD player, 30/30 interval music (music CD track 4), and slow cool-down music (music CD track 3)
* TV, DVD player, and DVD 1 (Instructional Routines)
* 6 cones

RESOURCES

 General

At-a-Glance PE Lesson Plan card
G3: Physical Activity Pyramid for Kids

 Wellness Week 3 → K-2 Resources

Move Your Body activity cards
Week 3 signs file with the following signs:

* Choose activity from the pyramid. Do muscle fitness exercises (step 4) and flexibility exercises (step 5)!
* Before you hustle, warm up your muscles!

CHANTS

Leader: "One body is all you get."

Students: "I'm going to make it fit!"

> ⭐ **teacher tip** • • •
> You may not get through the whole lesson the first time through. Decide which part of the lesson is most important for your students to experience.

DELIVERING THE LESSON

1. Instant Activity: Warm It Up

Introduction

"What does it mean to warm up your body? How do you know when you are warmed up? During this game you will find the answers to these questions. Pay attention to your body. How do you feel right this moment? Check your heart rate. Is your heart beating slow or fast? Check your forehead. Are you sweaty or not? How's your breathing—slow or fast, hard or light?"

Activity

This is a tag game where everyone is It. Specify the locomotor movement and the body reward (i.e., the exercise students have to do when they get tagged). For example, you could say, "When I say 'Go,' we're going to play a game of walking tag. Everybody is It and must watch out for everybody else. If you get tagged, you must perform a body reward of 10 jumping jacks. Go!" Play for approximately 30 seconds. Freeze! Change the locomotor movements (e.g., skip, gallop, slide) and the body rewards (e.g., 10 ski jumps, 10 hops).

> ❓ **comprehension check** • • •
> "Check your heart. What has happened? Check your forehead. Are you sweaty? Check your breathing. What do you hear? Yes, that's right, you have warmed up your body. Your body has heated up, you are breathing faster, and your heart is beating faster. Now you're ready to play!"

Refinements

Provide students with feedback so they can perform the body rewards with proper technique.

Extensions

* Allow students to select the locomotor movement.
* Ask students to provide some ideas for body rewards.

2. Fitness Activity: Move Your Body

Introduction

"Now that our muscles are warm, we're going to be performing all sorts of movements with our bodies. Are you ready? Let's go!"

Activity

Place six Move Your Body activity cards on cones around the activity area. Divide students evenly among the centers using a grouping strategy of your choice (see page 25). At each station, there is an activity at the top and the bottom. Students perform the top activity when the music starts (music CD track 4), and they perform the bottom activity to get to the next station. Encourage students to begin exercising immediately.

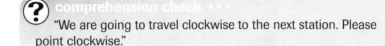

? comprehension check •••
"We are going to travel clockwise to the next station. Please point clockwise."

Refinements

Provide feedback so students can perform the Move Your Body activities correctly.

Extensions

* Use student-created Move Your Body activity cards.
* Have students follow a partner's movements.
* Have students create Move Your Body activity cards and use languages other than English to identify the activities.

3. Lesson Focus: Video Routine Practice

Introduction

"Next week is Wellness Week 3. During Wellness Week 3, we will be learning about physical activity, fitness, and healthy nutrition. Today we are going to practice the video routine you will be performing in your classroom during Wellness Week 3. This video routine is fun and will challenge you to move to music."

Activity

Introduce and practice the grade-specific video routine using the following steps.

1. Insert DVD 1 and play the instructional routine that is appropriate for your class:
   - Kindergarten: We Get Fit
   - First grade: CYIM Fit
   - Second grade: Wave It
2. Have the students follow along with the routine. Observe students performing the routine and take note of the movements that give them trouble.
3. Before going through the routine again, provide a demonstration and help students with any movements that are giving them trouble. Provide tips that will help them succeed.
4. Play the routine again and compliment students on any improvements.
5. Remind students that next week is Wellness Week 3, and they will perform this routine every day in their classrooms next week.

Refinements

Observe the students' movements and listen to the reciting of the words. Provide feedback to help students stay with the music and move together.

4. Culminating Activity: Cool It Down

Introduction

"Now that we have been playing hard all class, it is time for us to do a cool-down. What is a cool-down? A cool-down involves us moving slower, walking at an easy pace, breathing deep, and ending with some stretching. Not only does it slow our hearts down gradually, but stretching helps our muscles to become long and flexible."

Activity

Have students walk in open space, stop, and lead them through a variety of slow-moving exercises and a variety of upper- and lower-body stretches. Slow cool-down music is good here (music CD track 3).

> **review • • •**
> Revisit the Physical Activity Pyramid for Kids and point out that the students are working on flexibility exercises from step 5.

Extensions

* Have students hold the stretches for 10 to 15 seconds. Count in another language.
* Have students provide ideas for cool-down stretches.
* Have students bring some cool-down music.

CLOSURE ROUTINE

Compliments

Have some students share compliments about their classmates.

Reflection and Review

* "What is the name of the video routine we learned today?"

* "Why is a warm-up important? What did you feel when you warmed up?"

* "How do you know if your muscles are ready to exercise?"

* "Why is a cool-down important? What did you feel when you cooled down?"

* "When we stretch our muscles, on what step of the Physical Activity Pyramid for Kids are we exercising?"

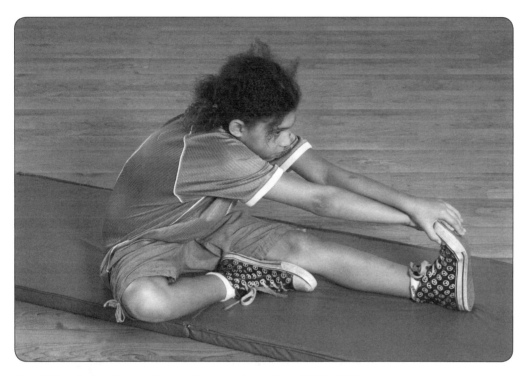

Stretching during the cool-down is a great way to build flexibility.

Take It Home

* "Engage in an activity with a family member. Sandwich that activity between a warm-up and a cool-down."

* "Create a Move Your Body activity card at home or in class."

ASSESSMENT

* **Performance check:** Observe students moving to music during the video routines and performing the Move Your Body activities correctly.

* **Comprehension check:** Responses to selected Comprehension Check questions and the Reflection and Review questions can serve as a check for student understanding.

3 WELLNESS WEEK

3.1 Lesson Plan

OVERVIEW

In this lesson, students will practice the video routine and have an opportunity to create and add new movements to a routine.

NASPE STANDARDS

1A, 2C, 3A, 3B, 4A, 4B, 4C, 5A, 5B
(See appendix B for details.)

OBJECTIVES

Students will

* demonstrate an ability to move to the beat of the music,
* identify parts of the body involved in various activities, and
* demonstrate an ability to work well with others in a cooperative activity.

EQUIPMENT

* CD player with 30/30 interval music (music CD track 4) and slow cool-down music (music CD track 3)
* TV, DVD player, and DVD 2 (Activity Routines)
* 6 cones

RESOURCES

 General

At-a-Glance PE Lesson Plan card

G3: Physical Activity Pyramid for Kids

Wellness Week 3 → K-2 Resources

Move Your Body activity cards

Week 3 signs file with the following signs:

- Choose activity from the pyramid. Do muscle fitness exercises (step 4) and flexibility exercises (step 5)!
- Before you hustle, warm up your muscles!

CHANTS

Leader: "One body is all you get."

Students: "I'm going to make it fit!"

> ⭐ **teacher tip • • •**
> You may not get through the whole lesson the first time through. Decide which part of the lesson is most important for your students to experience.

DELIVERING THE LESSON

1. Instant Activity: Warm It Up

Introduction

"What does it mean to warm up your body? How do you know when you are warmed up? During this game you will find the answers to these questions. Pay attention to your body. How do you feel right this moment? Check your heart rate. Is your heart beating slow or fast? Check your forehead. Are you sweaty or not? How's your breathing—slow or fast, hard or light?"

Activity

This is a tag game where everyone is It. Specify the locomotor movement and the body reward (i.e., the exercise students have to do when they get tagged). For example, you could say, "When I say 'Go,' we're going to play a game of walking tag. Everybody is It and must watch out for everybody else. If you get tagged, you must perform a body reward of 10 jumping jacks. Go!" Play for approximately 30 seconds. Freeze! Change the locomotor movements (e.g., skip, gallop, slide) and the body rewards (e.g., 10 ski jumps, 10 hops).

K-2 • WEEK 3
LESSON PLAN 3.1

(?) comprehension check • • •

"Check your heart. What has happened? Check your forehead. Are you sweaty? Check your breathing. What do you hear? Yes, that's right, you have warmed up your body. Your body has heated up, you are breathing faster, and your heart is beating faster. Now you're ready to play!"

Refinements

Provide students with feedback so they can perform the body rewards with proper technique.

Extensions

✳ Allow students to select the locomotor movement.

✳ Ask students to provide some ideas for body rewards.

2. Fitness Activity: Move Your Body

Introduction

"Now that our muscles are warm, we're going to be performing all sorts of movements with our bodies. Are you ready? Let's go!"

Activity

Place six Move Your Body activity cards on cones around the activity area. Divide students evenly among the centers using a grouping strategy of your choice (see page 25). At each station, there is an activity at the top and the bottom. Students perform the top activity when the music starts (music CD track 4), and they perform the bottom activity to get to the next station. Encourage students to begin exercising immediately.

Refinements

Provide feedback so students can perform the Move Your Body activities correctly.

Move your body to have fun.

(?) comprehension check • • •

"What parts of your body are involved in the Move Your Body activities?" (Identify specific activities when you ask the students.)

Extensions

✳ Use student-created Move Your Body activity cards.

✳ Have students follow a partner's movements.

✳ Have students create Move Your Body activity cards and use languages other than English to identify the activities.

3. Lesson Focus: Video Routine Variations

Introduction

"Last class we practiced the video routine you are performing in your classroom. Today we are going to use our creativity and make up some new moves for the routine."

Activity

Practice the grade-specific video routine using the following steps.

1. Insert DVD 2 and play the video routine that is appropriate for your class:
   - Kindergarten: We Get Fit
   - First grade: CYIM Fit
   - Second grade: Wave It

2. Have the students follow along with the routine. Observe students performing the routine and take note of the movements that give them trouble.

> **❓ comprehension check ···**
> Ask students to explain what the video messages are trying to tell them. Reinforce the message by using some of your own examples or having students share examples.

3. Before going through the routine again, provide a demonstration and help students with any movements that are giving them trouble. Provide tips that will help them succeed.

4. Break the students into 16 pairs, 8 groups, or 4 groups using a grouping strategy of your choice (see page 25). These group sizes allow you to pair groups together to make an even number of fewer (and larger) groups as the activity progresses.

5. Instruct the students that you will play the video routine, and their job is to make up new movements for the routine that are in time with the music.

6. Play the video routine for your class, and visit the student groups to see their movements.

7. At the end of the routine, highlight a few moves that students came up with.

8. Have each group get with another group (e.g., 16 pairs become 8 groups) and play the music again. Have the two groups share their moves with each other.

9. Allow some time for the groups to combine their moves, and play the video routine so they can practice. Visit the new groups to see how they are combining their movements.

> **👁 observation ···**
> Observe student groups to see if they are working well with others in a cooperative activity.

10. Repeat steps 8 and 9 until you have two large groups or the whole class is working together with new movements.

11. Encourage students to share their new moves with their classroom teachers.

> **↻ review ···**
> Review the important elements of working with others, such as listening; sharing thoughts, feelings, and equipment; providing encouragement; and making sure everyone feels included. Ask the students to share examples of what this might sound or look like in the class.

K-2 · WEEK 3
LESSON PLAN 3.1

4. Culminating Activity: Cool It Down

Introduction

"Now that we have been playing hard all class, it is time for us to do a cool-down. What is a cool-down? A cool-down involves us moving slower, walking at an easy pace, breathing deep, and ending with some stretching. Not only does it slow our hearts down gradually, but stretching helps our muscles to become long and flexible."

Activity

Have students walk in open space, stop, and lead them through a variety of slow-moving exercises and a variety of upper- and lower-body stretches. Slow cool-down music is good here (music CD track 3).

Extensions

* Have students hold the stretches for 10 to 15 seconds. Count in another language.
* Have students provide ideas for cool-down stretches.
* Have students bring some cool-down music.

CLOSURE ROUTINE

Compliments

Have some students share compliments about their classmates.

> **(?) comprehension check • • •**
> Ask the children what parts of the body are being stretched throughout the cool-down.

Reflection and Review

* "What was the message in the video routine today?"
* "What was the message trying to tell us?"
* "How do you know if your muscles are ready to exercise?"
* "What senses help you know that you are warmed up?"
* "What parts of the body did you feel a stretch in today?"

Take It Home

* "Engage in an activity with a family member. Sandwich that activity between a warm-up and a cool-down."
* "Create a Move Your Body activity card at home or in class."

ASSESSMENT

* **Performance check:** Observe students moving to music during the video routines, performing the Move Your Body activities correctly, and working cooperatively in groups.
* **Comprehension check:** Responses to selected Comprehension Check questions and the Reflection and Review questions can serve as a check for student understanding.

Lesson Plan 3.2

OVERVIEW

In this lesson, students will have the opportunity to try a variety of movements that focus on flexibility.

NASPE STANDARDS

1A, 2C, 3A, 3B, 4A, 4B, 4C, 5A, 5B
(See appendix B for details.)

OBJECTIVES

Students will

* engage in a variety of stretches following a warm-up,
* demonstrate proper technique for a variety of stretches, and
* explain how a warm-up affects flexibility.

EQUIPMENT

* CD player with 30/30 interval music (music CD track 4) and yoga interval music (music CD track 3)
* 6 cones
* Stretchy putty
* 6 to 8 green beanbags, fleece balls, scarves, or rubber animals for tag

RESOURCES

 General

At-a-Glance PE Lesson Plan card

G3: Physical Activity Pyramid for Kids

 Wellness Week 3 → K-2 Resources

Move Your Body activity cards

Bend It, Stretch It task cards

Week 3 signs file with the following signs:

- Choose activity from the pyramid. Do muscle fitness exercises (step 4) and flexibility exercises (step 5)!
- Before you hustle, warm up your muscles!
- Be active your way every day!

CHANTS

Leader: "One body is all you get."

Students: "I'm going to make it fit!"

> ⭐ **teacher tip** • • •
>
> You may not get through the whole lesson the first time through. Decide which part of the lesson is most important for your students to experience.

DELIVERING THE LESSON

1. Instant Activity: Active Every Day

Introduction

In this game, the teacher's call is followed by the students' action. This activity focuses on getting children active every day.

Activity

When you call "Be active!" the students respond "Every day!" Then you state an action using the phrase, "I can be active by . . .

* "walking to school" (students walk around the area),
* "surfing" (students pretend to balance on a surfboard and ride the wave),

* "walking the dog" (students pretend to walk a dog),

* "jumping rope" (students pretend to jump rope, showing fancy footwork), or

* anything creative that you or your students come up with.

> **(?) comprehension check • • •**
>
> "As you can see, pretending is a great way to get active at school or at home. What has happened to your body? Can you feel any changes? Yes, it has become sweaty and warm. That's what warming up is all about—raising your body temperature so you are safe to exercise and play hard!"

Extensions

* Have students provide some actions.

* Create a theme (e.g., firefighter movements, sailor movements, carpenter movements).

2. Fitness Activity: Move Your Body

Introduction

"Now that our muscles are warm, we're going to be performing all sorts of movements with our bodies. Are you ready? Let's go!"

Activity

Place six Move Your Body activity cards on cones around the activity area. Divide students evenly among the centers using a grouping strategy of your choice (see page 25). At each station, there is an activity at the top and the bottom. Students perform the top activity when the music starts (music CD track 4), and they perform the bottom activity to get to the next station. Encourage students to begin exercising immediately.

> **(?) comprehension check • • •**
>
> "We are going to travel counterclockwise to the next station. Please point counterclockwise."

Refinements

Provide feedback so students can perform the Move Your Body activities correctly.

Extensions

* Use student-created Move Your Body activity cards.

* Have students follow a partner's movements.

* Have students create Move Your Body activity cards and use languages other than English to identify the activities.

3. Lesson Focus: Bend It, Stretch It

Introduction

"We have been learning about physical fitness concepts. We have already learned about cardiorespiratory fitness. Today we are going to learn about flexibility. Do you know what flexibility means? It's the ability of body parts to move in many ways. To be flexible, you also need warm muscles that can stretch. Stretching your muscles helps you to become more flexible."

> **(↻) review • • •**
>
> Revisit the Physical Activity Pyramid for Kids and point out that they are working on flexibility exercises from step 5. Ask students to identify some activities that require muscle fitness.

K-2 • WEEK 3
LESSON PLAN 3.2

"When do you think you are more flexible, in the morning or at night before you go to bed? The answer is at night, after you have had all day to move your muscles. It is important to warm up your body before you stretch it. Do any of you know what this is?" (Hold up stretchy putty.) "Today I am going to use the putty to show how your muscles respond to warming up."

* "What if I pulled really hard on this putty right now? What do you think would happen? Let's see." (Pull hard and the putty breaks in half.)
* "What if I warm it up in my hands by squeezing it?" (Start warming it up.) "What do you think will happen now? Let's see." (This time the putty stretches long and thin.)

"Why do you think I was able to stretch the putty this time but it broke the first time? That's right, the second time it was warmed up. Just like the putty, your muscles are easier to stretch when they are warmed up. Have we warmed up our muscles today in class? That's right, I think we did. Are you warm and sweaty? That is an indicator that you are warmed up and it's safe to stretch out your muscles."

Activity

Lead the students through a variety of upper- and lower-body static stretches using the Bend It, Stretch It task cards. Don't forget to tell them the name of each stretch and the body part it stretches.

Safety reminder: Hold the stretch for 10 "flexibilities" or any other appropriate five-syllable word. No bouncing or jerking, and use relaxed joints, not locked.

> **observation** • • •
> Observe students performing the flexibility exercises. Provide feedback that helps them perform the movements correctly.

Extensions

Begin connecting a muscle name or muscle group with each stretch you perform. For instance, when doing the modified hurdler stretch, ask students which muscle they feel stretching. Tell them the name of the muscle (hamstrings).

Second Time Through

If you are teaching this lesson a second time, you may want to introduce the following activities.

Introduction

"In our last class, we learned that we need to warm up our muscles before we stretch, just like the putty. Today we are going to do a combination of bending and stretching activities to review the stretches that we know and to move and bend our bodies in different ways."

Activity

When the music begins, lead the students in a stretch, and when the music stops, give the students a movement or bending challenge (music CD track 3). A few examples follow. More ideas are on the Bend It, Stretch It task cards.

* **Stretch:** Stretch to the sky, up on your tippy toes, and hold.
* **Move:** Fly like a bird, gracefully moving your wings up and down.

4. Culminating Activity: Flexibility Tag

Introduction

"We have been learning about the importance of flexibility and learning many new stretches to keep our muscles flexible and long. Can you show me an upper-body stretch that you remember? Can you show me a lower-body stretch? Show me your favorite stretch."

> **⊗ interdisciplinary • • •**
> Introduce the practice of yoga to students. Talk about where it originated (India; geography), why people participated (body and mind; health) and selected terminology (Sanskrit terms: *Namaste* = "The light in me honors the light in you"; *asanas* = seat or poses). Use the Internet to learn more.

Activity

Choose six to eight players to be taggers. Everyone else is scattered within the activity area. On your signal, the taggers begin to move using the designated locomotor skill, softly tagging those who are not It. If students are tagged or step out-of-bounds, they must perform the designated stretch and hold it for a count of 10 flexibilities. Review stretches that you taught within the lesson focus. Change taggers often.

Refinements

Observe students performing stretches. Provide feedback to ensure proper technique.

Extensions

* Once students get the idea, have them choose their own stretches or designate an upper- or lower-body stretch, or even get very specific (for instance, "Perform a stretch that stretches your hamstrings").
* Have students perform a different stretch every time they are tagged.
* Have students count their stretching holds using a language other than English (e.g., *uno flexibilidad*).

CLOSURE ROUTINE

Compliments

Have students share compliments about their classmates.

Flexibility Tag promotes stretching for flexibility.

Reflection and Review

 * "What feelings do you get when you stretch?"
 * "What does it mean to be flexible?"
 * "How long should you hold a stretch?"
 * "Should you bounce or jerk?"
 * "What do you need to do to a muscle before your stretch it? How do you do that?"
 * "Show me a stretch you learned today."
 * "What activities require good flexibility?"
 * "Why do we need to warm up our muscles before we stretch?"
 * "Tell your neighbor your favorite stretch."

Take It Home

 * "Have a family member warm-up and stretch with you. Maybe you will learn a new stretch."
 * "Teach a family member a new stretch that you learned."

ASSESSMENT

 * **Performance check:** Observe students successfully executing the stretches and the Move Your Body activities.
 * **Comprehension check:** Responses to selected Comprehension Check questions and the Reflection and Review questions can serve as a check for student understanding.

Lesson Plan 3.3

OVERVIEW

In this lesson, students will explore a variety of muscle fitness stunts and challenges.

NASPE STANDARDS

1A, 2C, 3A, 3B, 4A, 4B, 4C, 5A, 5B
(See appendix B for details.)

OBJECTIVES

Students will

* participate in a variety of muscle fitness activities following a warm-up,
* demonstrate proper technique for a variety of muscle challenges, and
* explain why it is important to have strong muscles.

EQUIPMENT

* CD player with 30/30 interval music (music CD track 4) and 45/15 interval music (music CD track 5)
* 6 cones
* 6 to 8 green beanbags, fleece balls, scarves, or rubber animals for tag

RESOURCES

 General

At-a-Glance PE Lesson Plan card
G3: Physical Activity Pyramid for Kids

 Wellness Week 3 → K-2 Resources

Move Your Body activity cards
Muscle Stunts and Challenges task cards
Week 3 signs file with the following signs:

* Choose activity from the pyramid. Do muscle fitness exercises (step 4) and flexibility exercises (step 5)!
* Before you hustle, warm up your muscles!
* Be active your way every day!

CHANTS

Leader: "One body is all you get."

Students: "I'm going to make it fit!"

> ⭐ **teacher tip • • •**
> You may not get through the whole lesson the first time through. Decide which part of the lesson is most important for your students to experience.

DELIVERING THE LESSON

1. Instant Activity: Active Every Day

Introduction

In this game, the teacher's call is followed by the students' action. This activity focuses on getting children active every day.

Activity

When you call "Be active!" the students respond "Every day!" Then you state an action using the phrase, "I can be active by . . .

* "walking to school" (students walk around the area),
* "surfing" (students pretend to balance on a surfboard and ride the wave),

* "walking the dog" (students pretend to walk a dog),

* "jumping rope" (students pretend to jump rope, showing fancy footwork), or

* anything creative that you or your students come up with.

 comprehension check • • •
"What activities challenged your leg (arm, stomach) muscles?"

Extensions

* Have students provide some actions.

* Create a theme (e.g., firefighter movements, sailor movements, carpenter movements).

2. Fitness Activity: Move Your Body

Introduction

"Now that our muscles are warm, we're going to be performing all sorts of movements with our bodies. Are you ready? Let's go!"

Activity

Place six Move Your Body activity cards on cones around the activity area. Divide students evenly among the centers using a grouping strategy of your choice (see page 25). At each station, there is an activity at the top and the bottom. Students perform the top activity when the music starts (music CD track 4), and they perform the bottom activity to get to the next station. Encourage students to begin exercising immediately.

 comprehension check • • •
Ask students to identify which parts of the body are exercised by selected Move Your Body activities.

Refinements

Provide feedback so students can perform the Move Your Body activities correctly.

Extensions

* Use student-created Move Your Body activity cards.

* Have students follow a partner's movements.

* Have students create Move Your Body activity cards and use languages other than English to identify the activities.

3. Lesson Focus: Muscle Stunts and Challenges

Introduction

"Today we are going to learn about muscle fitness. If you have muscle fitness, you are strong and can play or work for a long amount of time. Today we are going to experience a variety of stunts and challenges that exercise your muscles."

⟳ **review** • • •
Revisit the Physical Activity Pyramid for Kids and point out muscle fitness activities. Ask students to identify a few activities that require muscle fitness.

Activity

Demonstrate the activity and students follow. Activities are on the Muscle Stunts and Challenges task cards. These exercises are challenging for kindergarteners, but they love to try.

Extensions

✳ Intersperse the muscle fitness activities with locomotor movements to give students a chance to rest between stunts.

✳ Music is a good motivator (use music CD track 5).

Second Time Through

If you are teaching this lesson a second time, you may want to introduce the following activities.

Introduction

"Today we are going to practice the muscle fitness activities that we learned last class. Let's see if we can hold our poses longer. Maybe we can even make up some new ones!"

Activity

Lead the students randomly through the Muscle Stunts and Challenges task cards.

> **observation** • • •
> Observe students performing the muscle stunts and challenges. Provide feedback that helps them perform the movements correctly.

Extensions

✳ Challenge your students to come up with some new stunts and challenges.

✳ Have your students come up with names for stunts in languages other than English.

> **interdisciplinary** • • •
> If you have access to a poster or model that displays human muscles, share the names and locations of some major muscles (e.g., biceps, rectus abdominis, gluteus maximus) or muscle groups (e.g., hamstrings, abdominal muscles, quadriceps, calf muscles).

4. Culminating Activity: Muscle-Builder Tag

Introduction

"We have been learning about the importance of muscular fitness and learning many new challenges to keep our muscles strong."

> **review** • • •
> "Can you show me a challenge that makes your arms stronger? Can you show me a challenge that makes your abdominal muscles stronger? Show me your favorite 'get strong' challenge that you learned today."

Muscle-Builder Tag challenges several muscle groups.

Activity

Choose six to eight players to be taggers. Everyone else is scattered within the activity area. On your signal, the taggers begin to move using the designated locomotor skill, softly tagging those who are not It. If students are tagged or step out-of-bounds, they must perform a designated Muscle-Builder challenge and hold it for a count of 10 "muscle builders" (i.e., 1 muscle builder, 2 muscle builders). Change taggers often.

Extensions

* Students can choose their favorite Muscle-Builder challenge when tagged.
* Have students perform a different Muscle-Builder challenge each time they are tagged.
* Have students count their Muscle Builders in another language (e.g., the Spanish translation of "muscle builder" is *constructor del músculo*).

CLOSURE ROUTINE

Compliments

Have some students share compliments about their classmates.

Reflection and Review

* "Why is it important to have strong muscles?"
* "What was the hardest muscle stunt? Why? What muscle did it target?"
* "What muscles are your favorites to challenge? Why?"
* "Share with your neighbor the most important muscles for your favorite sport."
* "How can we know if we have improved our muscle fitness?"

K-2 · WEEK 3
LESSON PLAN 3.3

Take It Home

＊ "Challenge a family member to a muscle stunt. See who can hold it the longest."

＊ "Create a new muscle stunt with a family member and give it a cool name."

＊ "While watching TV, perform a muscle stunt every time you see a commercial. Challenge your family members to do the same."

ASSESSMENT

＊ **Performance check:** Observe students successfully executing the muscle fitness challenges.

＊ **Comprehension check:** Responses to selected Comprehension Check questions and the Reflection and Review questions can serve as a check for student understanding.

EXTRA ACTIVITIES AND RESOURCES

If your school has physical education more than three times per week, consider delivering some of the lesson plans a second time or using some of the extra activities and resources in appendix A of this book (see page 245). You can also use some of the additional activities described in appendix A of the classroom guides. Ask your wellness coordinator for access to these guides.

WELLNESS WEEK

4

Fitness for Life Elementary School

These lesson plans provide students with a variety of experiences, including performing an Olympic circuit targeting health-related fitness, moving to music, engaging in balancing activities, and practicing soccer skills. In Wellness Week 4, the activity theme is "integration (energy balance)," and the nutrition theme is "healthy foods help us move." Take time to look through the lesson plans for Wellness Week 4 and determine which objectives are most important and which activities you will use to meet those objectives. Table 2.4 summarizes the Wellness Week 4 activities for the physical education lesson plans.

For Wellness Week 4, the lesson plans include the following:

- A warm-up lesson plan to be used during the week before Wellness Week 4. The same basic warm-up lesson plan is used for kindergarten through grade 2, but the Lesson Focus (practicing the video routine) is different for each grade.

- Three lesson plans (4.1, 4.2, and 4.3) to be used during Wellness Week 4. The same basic lesson plan is used for kindergarten through grade 2, with grade-specific variations for some of the activities.

- Extra activity ideas for schools that have physical education class more than three days a week are provided in appendix A.

Table 2.4 Summary of Wellness Week 4 Activities

Lesson Plan	Instant Activity	Fitness Activity	Lesson Focus	Culminating Activity
Warm-Up 4 (week before Wellness Week 4)	Healthy Body Tag	Olympic Athlete Workout	Video Routine Practice: K: Shake It 1: Stomp and Balance 2: It's the One	Veggie Medley
4.1	Healthy Body Tag	Olympic Athlete Workout	Video Routine Variations: K: Shake It 1: Stomp and Balance 2: It's the One	Veggie Medley
4.2	Healthy Body Tag	Olympic Athlete Workout	Are You Balanced?	Healthy Food Medley
4.3	Healthy Body Tag	Olympic Athlete Workout	Kick It!	Fruit Salad

Eat Well Wednesday

Each Wednesday, known as Eat Well Wednesday, all teachers and staff are encouraged to emphasize nutrition. The wellness coordinator might plan special schoolwide events. During Wellness Week 4, the nutrition event is a fruit and vegetable bar with bottled water in the cafeteria. If you have a physical education lesson on Eat Well Wednesday, place an emphasis on nutrition signs and messages.

Get Fit Friday

Each Friday, known as Get Fit Friday, a schoolwide event focusing on physical activity will be planned. (If your school participates in this event, your wellness coordinator will provide you with more details.) The Get Fit Friday activities are called TEAM Time activities (TEAM stands for Together Everyone Achieves More). During Wellness Week 4, this activity is called Mid Kids Lead. Your wellness coordinator will teach several third- and fourth-grade students

The activity theme for Wellness Week 4 is integration (energy balance).

how to do the routine ahead of time so that they can help lead. Then the wellness coordinator and the selected students will lead the TEAM Time activity at the beginning of the school day. All students in the school will congregate in the gym, multipurpose room, or outside so that they all can participate together. The activity includes a warm-up, a Hawaiian Surfing routine, and a cool-down. If time allows, you can teach these activities in advance to make it easier for students to perform them during TEAM Time. A video and script are provided on the DVD that accompanies the *Guide for Wellness Coordinators*.

ACES Day

In 1984, Len Saunders created a program called Project ACES (All Children Exercising Simultaneously). May is National Physical Fitness Month, and the first week in May is National Physical Education Week. Each year in the first week of May, children throughout the world participate in Project ACES by doing exercise at the same time on the same day. The children in your school can participate by performing the TEAM Time activity on ACES Day at the designated time. More information is available at http://lensaunders.com/aces/aces.html.

Newsletter

The CD-ROM contains a newsletter for use during Wellness Week 4. It is recommended that your school's wellness coordinator edit and distribute the newsletter. Alternatively, you (or the classroom teachers) can do it. Just open the appropriate file, follow the instructions to edit and customize the newsletter, and send printed copies home with students or send them electronically via e-mail. Remind students to talk to their families about Wellness Week and the information in the newsletter.

Wellness Week 4 → Newsletter

Warm-Up Lesson Plan 4

OVERVIEW

In this lesson, conducted during the week before Wellness Week 4, students will learn the video routine that they will perform in their classroom during Wellness Week 4. You can aid the classroom teachers by teaching these routines in advance to make it easier for both students and teachers and to increase the chances that the classroom teachers will do the video routines in their classrooms.

NASPE STANDARDS

1A, 2C, 3A, 3B, 4A, 4B, 4C, 5A, 5B
(See appendix B for details.)

OBJECTIVES

Students will

* practice combining a sequence of movements to music;
* perform movements targeted at cardiorespiratory fitness, muscle fitness, and flexibility; and
* be able to connect exercises with components of health-related fitness.

EQUIPMENT

* CD player and 30/30 interval music (music CD track 4)
* TV, DVD player, and DVD 1 (Instructional Routines)
* 4 red beanbags, 4 blue beanbags, and 4 green beanbags
* 12 cones

RESOURCES

 General

At-a-Glance PE Lesson Plan card
G3: Physical Activity Pyramid for Kids
G4: MyPyramid for Kids

 Wellness Week 4 → K-2 Resources

Olympic Athlete Workout activity cards
Week 4 signs file with the following signs:
   • Get off your seat and move your feet!
   • Healthy foods help us move! Choose your foods wisely!

CHANTS

Leader: "Get off your seat . . ."

Students: ". . . and move my feet!"

★ **teacher tip • • •**
You may not get through the whole lesson the first time through. Decide which part of the lesson is most important for your students to experience.

DELIVERING THE LESSON

1. Instant Activity: Healthy Body Tag

Introduction

"We have now learned about cardiorespiratory (heart) fitness, muscle fitness, and flexibility. We also have learned that we need to warm up our bodies before we stretch or play games. Today we are going to put all of our knowledge together."

Activity

In this tag game, students tagged by colored beanbags must perform a specific body reward. Specify the locomotor movement and the activity area. Have students move on your signal. On the first time through, use one or two colors and specify the body rewards. Connect the body rewards to the fitness concept. Add new colors in subsequent lessons.

* Students tagged by red taggers (cardiorespiratory fitness) must perform a healthy heart activity (e.g., jumping jacks, straddle jumps) 10 times (see lesson 1.2 for jump patterns).

* Students tagged by blue taggers (muscle fitness) must perform a muscle fitness challenge (e.g., curl-ups, crab cross-lateral dance), either holding it for 10 counts or doing 10 repetitions of the exercise (see lesson 3.3 for stunts and challenges).

* Students tagged by green taggers (flexibility) must perform a stretch and hold it for at least 10 counts (see lesson 3.2 for stretches).

Kindergarten Variations

* Begin with just one colored beanbag and fitness concept and then add on.

* Tell students which body reward they will be performing so they know what to do.

* Connect the body reward and the color back to the physical fitness concept it represents (e.g., red for heart or cardio).

(?) comprehension check • • •
Demonstrate a body reward and ask students to identify which parts of fitness it builds. Ask them which parts of the body it benefits. Ask them which muscles it targets.

Refinements

* Provide feedback to students to help them perform the specified locomotor movements correctly.

* Provide feedback to students to help them perform the body rewards correctly.

Extensions

* Allow students to choose the appropriate body reward when tagged.

* Encourage students to create new body rewards.

2. Fitness Activity: Olympic Athlete Workout

Introduction

"All athletes must work out to get strong and fit. What kind of exercises do they need to do to get fit? That's right, something to get them strong, such as muscle fitness activities. Can you name some? Flexibility is important, too. How do we develop flexibility? Stretching, that's right. Can you show me a stretch for your upper body or lower body? Can you think of anything else athletes need? That's right, cardiorespiratory fitness. Today we are going to do the Olympic Athlete Workout to get our bodies active, strong, and flexible. Can you figure out what each center does for your body and which part of physical fitness it helps?"

Activity

Place the Olympic Athlete Workout signs on cones around the perimeter of the teaching area. Make a racetrack with cones inside the teaching area. Students begin exercising at a designated center when the music starts (use music CD track 4). When the music stops, they move to the racetrack and run or walk for the next 30 seconds of music. When the music stops again, they move to the closest center and begin exercising. This pattern continues until they have visited all circuit centers (i.e., center, racetrack, center, racetrack, center).

> ↻ **review** • • •
> Review the Physical Activity Pyramid for Kids and ask students to identify on what steps the Olympic Athlete Workout activities would be.

Refinements

Encourage students to pace themselves so they can move the whole time the music is playing.

Extensions

Change the locomotor movements (e.g., gallop, hop, slide).

3. Lesson Focus: Video Routine Practice

Introduction

"Next week is Wellness Week 4. During Wellness Week 4, we will be learning about physical activity, fitness, and healthy nutrition. Today we are going to practice the video routine you will be performing in your classroom during Wellness Week. This video routine is fun and will challenge you to move to music."

Activity

Introduce and practice the grade-specific video routine using the following steps.

1. Insert DVD 1 and play the instructional routine that is appropriate for your class:
   - Kindergarten: Shake It
   - First grade: Stomp and Balance
   - Second grade: It's the One
2. Have the students follow along with the routine. Observe students performing the routine and take note of the movements that give them trouble.
3. Before going through the routine again, provide a demonstration and help students with any movements that are giving them trouble. Provide tips that will help them succeed.
4. Play the routine again and compliment students on any improvements.
5. Remind students that next week is Wellness Week 4, and they will perform this routine every day in their classrooms next week.

Refinements

Observe the students' movements and listen to the reciting of the words. Provide feedback to help students stay with the music and move together.

4. Culminating Activity: Veggie Medley

Introduction

"You need to eat a variety of foods to maintain a healthy body. Vegetables are especially wonderful because they give you energy, nutrients, and vitamins. Can you name any vegetables? What vegetables are your favorites? Tell your neighbor a vegetable you have eaten recently."

Activity

Three players are It and stand in the center of the activity area between two safety lines established on either end of the playing area. All other students (runners) stand behind one of the safety lines. You or the students select three vegetables (e.g., broccoli, carrots, and squash). Each runner then selects a vegetable from among the three but keeps it a secret. You (or one tagger) call out one of the designated vegetables. All runners who chose that vegetable attempt to cross to the other line without getting tagged. If a runner is tagged, that student becomes a tagger. If "Mixed vegetables" is called, all runners must cross to the opposite sideline.

> **X interdisciplinary • • •**
>
> Print, post, and share MyPyramid with the class. Talk about the rainbow of food choices (grains, vegetables, fruits, milk, and meats and beans). Ask students to share their favorite food and connect it to the appropriate food group.

Make sure students understand the following rules:

* Stay inside the boundaries.
* Use safe, soft tags.
* Stay on your feet; don't run into the walls.
* Be honest; if you are tagged, join the taggers in the middle.

Refinements

Emphasize moving under control using the specified locomotor movement (e.g., gallop, walk, skip).

Extensions

* Have student vegetables start in different positions (e.g., plank, crabwalk, balanced on one foot).
* Use Spanish vegetable names (e.g., instead of vegetable medley, use *mezcla vegetal*).
* Use fruits instead of vegetables and the signal "Fruit salad" instead of "Mixed vegetables."

CLOSURE ROUTINE

Compliments

Have some students share compliments about their classmates.

Reflection and Review

* "Can you name three parts of physical fitness?"
* "Give me an example of a cardiorespiratory fitness (or muscle fitness or flexibility) exercise."

✳ "Why is it important for you to 'get off your seat and move your feet'?"

✳ "How many servings of fruits and vegetables should you have each day?"

✳ "Share your favorite vegetable with your neighbor."

✳ "Share your favorite fruit with your neighbor."

Take It Home

✳ "Have a family member take you to a farmer's market and pick out one new fruit or vegetable that you have never tried before. Report back to the class."

✳ "My challenge to you today is to match your seat time with activity time. If you play a video game or watch TV for an hour, you need to be active for an hour. Get off your seat and move your feet!"

ASSESSMENT

✳ **Performance check:** Observe students correctly executing muscle fitness, cardiorespiratory fitness, and flexibility activities.

✳ **Comprehension check:** Responses to selected Comprehension Check questions and the Reflection and Review questions can serve as a check for student understanding.

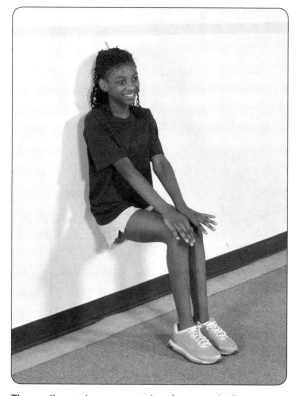

The wall seat is an example of a muscle fitness exercise.

Lesson Plan 4.1

OVERVIEW

In this lesson, students will practice the video routine and have an opportunity to create and add new movements to the routine. In addition, students will explore a variety of muscle fitness and flexibility exercises.

NASPE STANDARDS

1A, 2C, 3A, 3B, 4A, 4B, 4C, 5A, 5B
(See appendix B for details.)

OBJECTIVES

Students will

* practice combining a sequence of movements to music;
* perform movements targeted at cardiorespiratory fitness, muscle fitness, and flexibility; and
* demonstrate an ability to work well with others in a cooperative activity.

EQUIPMENT

* CD player and 30/30 interval music (music CD track 4)
* TV, DVD player, and DVD 2 (Activity Routines)
* 4 red beanbags, 4 blue beanbags, and 4 green beanbags
* 12 cones

RESOURCES

 General

At-a-Glance PE Lesson Plan card
G3: Physical Activity Pyramid for Kids
G4: MyPyramid for Kids

 Wellness Week 4 → K-2 Resources

Olympic Athlete Workout activity cards
Week 4 signs file with the following signs:

• Get off your seat and move your feet!
• Healthy foods help us move! Choose your foods wisely!

CHANTS

Leader: "Get off your seat . . ."

Students: ". . . and move my feet!"

> ⭐ **teacher tip** • • •
> You may not get through the whole lesson the first time through. Decide which part of the lesson is most important for your students to experience.

DELIVERING THE LESSON

1. Instant Activity: Healthy Body Tag

Introduction

"We have now learned about cardiorespiratory (heart) fitness, muscle fitness, and flexibility. We also have learned that we need to warm up our bodies before we stretch or play games. Today we are going to put all of our knowledge together."

Activity

In this tag game, students tagged by colored beanbags must perform a specific body reward. Specify the locomotor movement and the activity area. Have students move on your signal. On the first time through, use one or two colors and specify the body rewards. Connect the body rewards to the fitness concept. Add new colors in subsequent lessons.

* Students tagged by red taggers (cardiorespiratory fitness) must perform a healthy heart activity (e.g., jumping jacks, straddle jumps) 10 times (see lesson 1.2 for jump patterns).

* Students tagged by blue taggers (muscle fitness) must perform a muscle fitness challenge (e.g., curl-ups, crab cross-lateral dance) either holding it for 10 counts or doing 10 repetitions of the exercise (see lesson 3.3 for stunts and challenges).

* Students tagged by green taggers (flexibility) must perform a stretch and hold it for at least 10 counts (see lesson 3.2 for stretches).

Kindergarten Variations

* Begin with just one colored beanbag and fitness concept and then add on.

* Tell students which body reward they will be performing so they know what to do.

* Connect the body reward and the color back to the physical fitness concept it represents (e.g., red for heart or cardio).

Refinements

✳ Provide feedback to students to help them perform the specified locomotor movements correctly.

✳ Provide feedback to students to help them perform the body rewards correctly.

(?) comprehension check • • •
Have a student perform a body reward and ask students to identify which parts of fitness it builds. Ask them which parts of the body it benefits. Ask them which muscles it targets.

Extensions

✳ Allow students to choose the appropriate body reward when tagged.

✳ Encourage students to create new body rewards.

✳ Have students identify their body reward in Spanish or another language (e.g., push-up = *levante,* jump = *saltar*).

2. Fitness Activity: Olympic Athlete Workout

Introduction

"All athletes must work out to get strong and fit. What kind of exercises do they need to do to get fit? That's right, something to get them strong, such as muscle fitness activities. Can you name some? Flexibility is important, too. How do we develop flexibility? Stretching, that's right. Can you show me a stretch for your upper body or lower body? Can you think of anything else athletes need? That's right, cardiorespiratory fitness. Today we are going to do the Olympic Athlete Workout to get our bodies active, strong, and flexible. Can you figure out what each center does for your body and which part of physical fitness it helps?"

Activity

Place the Olympic Athlete Workout signs on cones around the perimeter of the teaching area. Make a racetrack with cones inside the teaching area. Students begin exercising at a designated center when the music starts (use music CD track 4). When the music stops, they move to the racetrack and run or walk for the next 30 seconds of music. When the music stops again, they move to the closest center and begin exercising. This pattern continues until they have visited all circuit centers (i.e., center, racetrack, center, racetrack, center).

⟳ **review** • • •
Review the Physical Activity Pyramid for Kids and ask students to identify on what steps the Olympic Athlete Workout activities would be.

Refinements

Encourage students to pace themselves so they can move the whole time the music is playing.

Extensions

* Change the locomotor movements (e.g., gallop, hop, slide).
* Increase the time spent at each station using tracks 5, 6, 7, or 8 on the music CD.

⊗ **interdisciplinary** • • •
Talk with classroom teachers and encourage them to have students create Olympic Athlete Workout activity cards in art class. Students could also write on the cards (language arts), describing the kind of fitness the activity builds and which sports require that kind of fitness. Finally, students could identify the countries that excel at that sport (geography) and find them on the map. Students could also learn the names of sports in other languages.

The Olympic Athlete Workout helps students learn about flexibility.

3. Lesson Focus: Video Routine Variations

Introduction

"Last class we practiced the video routine you are performing in your classroom. Today we are going to use our creativity and make up some new moves for the routine."

Activity

Practice the grade-specific video routine using the following steps.

1. Insert DVD 2 and play the video routine that is appropriate for your class:
   - Kindergarten: Shake It
   - First grade: Stomp and Balance
   - Second grade: It's the One

2. Have the students follow along with the routine. Observe students performing the routine and take note of the movements that give them trouble.

3. Before going through the routine again, provide a demonstration and help students with any movements that are giving them trouble. Provide tips that will help them succeed.

   > **↻ review • • •**
   > Review the important elements of working with others, such as listening; sharing thoughts, feelings, and equipment; providing encouragement; and making sure everyone feels included. Ask the students to share examples of what this might sound or look like in the class.

4. Break the students into 16 pairs, 8 groups, or 4 groups using a grouping strategy of your choice (see page 25). These group sizes allow you to pair groups together to make an even number of fewer (and larger) groups as the activity progresses.

5. Instruct the students that you will play the video routine, and their job is to make up new movements for the routine that are in time with the music.

6. Play the video routine for your class, and visit the student groups to see the movements they are trying.

7. At the end of the routine, highlight a few moves that students came up with.

8. Have each group get with another group (e.g., 16 pairs become 8 groups) and play the music again. Have the two groups share their moves with each other.

9. Allow some time for the groups to combine their moves, and play the video routine so they can practice. Visit the new groups to see how they are combining their movements.

10. Repeat steps 8 and 9 until you have two large groups or the whole class is working together with new movements.

11. Encourage students to share their new moves with their classroom teachers.

   > **👁 observation • • •**
   > Observe student groups to see if they are working well with others in a cooperative activity.

4. Culminating Activity: Veggie Medley

Introduction

"You need to eat a variety of foods to maintain a healthy body. Vegetables are especially wonderful because they give you energy, nutrients, and vitamins. Can you name any vegetables? What vegetables are your favorites? Tell your neighbor a vegetable you have eaten recently."

> ↻ review • • •
> Review the food groups from MyPyramid. Ask students to provide examples of foods that they have eaten and what group they belong to.

Activity

Three players are It and stand in the center of the activity area between two safety lines established on either end of the playing area. All other students (runners) stand behind one of the safety lines. You or the students select three vegetables (e.g., broccoli, carrots, and squash). Each runner then selects a vegetable from among the three but keeps it a secret. You (or one tagger) call out one of the designated vegetables. All runners who chose that vegetable attempt to cross to the other line without getting tagged. If a runner is tagged, that student becomes a tagger. If "Mixed vegetables" is called, all runners must cross to the opposite sideline.

Make sure students understand the following rules:

* Stay inside the boundaries.
* Use safe, soft tags.
* Stay on your feet; don't run into the walls.
* Be honest; if you are tagged, join the taggers in the middle.

Refinements

Emphasize moving under control using the specified locomotor movement (e.g., gallop, walk, skip).

Extensions

* Have student vegetables start in different positions (e.g., plank, crabwalk, balanced on one foot).
* Use Spanish vegetable names (e.g., vegetable medley = *mezcla vegetal*).
* Use fruits instead of vegetables and the signal "Fruit salad" instead of "Mixed vegetables."

CLOSURE ROUTINE

Compliments

Have some students share compliments about their classmates.

Reflection and Review

✳ "Can you name one of the food groups from MyPyramid? How does food help us play and be active?"

✳ "Share your favorite food with your neighbor and identify what food group it belongs to."

✳ "On what step of the Physical Activity Pyramid for Kids did you exercise today?"

Take It Home

✳ "Have a family member take you to a farmer's market and pick out one new fruit or vegetable that you have never tried before. Report back to the class."

✳ "My challenge to you today is to match your seat time with activity time. If you play a video game or watch TV for an hour, you need to be active for an hour. Get off your seat and move your feet!"

ASSESSMENT

✳ **Performance check:** Observe students correctly executing muscle fitness, cardiorespiratory fitness, and flexibility activities; moving to music; and working cooperatively with others while trying new movements to music.

✳ **Comprehension check:** Responses to selected Comprehension Check questions and the Reflection and Review questions can serve as a check for student understanding.

4.2 Lesson Plan

OVERVIEW

In this lesson, students will explore a variety of balancing activities.

NASPE STANDARDS

1A, 2C, 3A, 3B, 4A, 4B, 4C, 5A, 5B
(See appendix B for details.)

OBJECTIVES

Students will

* be able to connect exercises with components of health-related fitness,
* demonstrate a variety of balanced poses, and
* identify healthy foods.

EQUIPMENT

* CD player and 30/30 interval music (music CD track 4)
* 4 red beanbags, 4 blue beanbags, and 4 green beanbags
* 12 cones

RESOURCES

 General

At-a-Glance PE Lesson Plan card

G3: Physical Activity Pyramid for Kids

G4: MyPyramid for Kids

 Wellness Week 4 → K-2 Resources

Olympic Athlete Workout activity cards

Are You Balanced? task cards

Week 4 signs file with the following sign:

* Get off your seat and move your feet!

CHANTS

Leader: "Get off your seat . . ."

Students: ". . . and move my feet!"

⭐ **teacher tip** • • •
You may not get through the whole lesson the first time
through. Decide which part of the lesson is most important for
your students to experience.

DELIVERING THE LESSON

1. Instant Activity: Healthy Body Tag

Introduction

"We have now learned about cardiorespiratory (heart) fitness, muscle fitness, and
flexibility. We also have learned that we need to warm up our bodies before we stretch
or play games. Today we are going to put all of our knowledge together."

Activity

In this tag game, students tagged by colored beanbags must perform a specific
body reward. Specify the locomotor movement and the activity area. Have students
move on your signal. On the first time through, use one or two colors and specify the
body rewards. Connect the body rewards to the fitness concept. Add new colors in
subsequent lessons.

✱ Students tagged by red taggers (cardiorespiratory fitness) must perform a
   healthy heart activity (e.g., jumping jacks, straddle jumps) 10 times (see lesson
   1.2 for jump patterns).

✱ Students tagged by blue taggers (muscle fitness) must perform a muscle fitness
   challenge (e.g., curl-ups, crab cross-lateral dance) either holding it for 10 counts
   or doing 10 repetitions of the exercise (see lesson 3.3 for stunts and challenges).

✱ Students tagged by green taggers (flexibility) must perform a stretch and hold
   it for at least 10 counts (see lesson 3.2 for stretches).

Kindergarten Variations

* Begin with just one colored beanbag and fitness concept and then add on.

* Tell students which body reward they will be performing so they know what to do.

* Connect the body reward and the color back to the physical fitness concept it represents (e.g., red for heart or cardio).

(?) **comprehension check** • • •
Have a student perform a body reward and ask students to identify which parts of fitness it builds. Ask them which parts of the body it benefits. Ask them which muscles it targets.

Refinements

* Provide feedback to students to help them perform the specified locomotor movements correctly.

* Provide feedback to students to help them perform the body rewards correctly.

Extensions

* Allow students to choose the appropriate body reward when tagged.

* Encourage students to create new body rewards.

* Have students identify their body reward in Spanish or another language (e.g., push-up = *levante,* jump = *saltar*).

2. Fitness Activity: Olympic Athlete Workout

Introduction

"All athletes must work out to get strong and fit. What kind of exercises do they need to do to get fit? That's right, something to get them strong, such as muscle fitness activities. Can you name some? Flexibility is important, too. How do we develop flexibility? Stretching, that's right. Can you show me a stretch for your upper body or lower body? Can you think of anything else athletes need? That's right, cardiorespiratory fitness. Today we are going to do the Olympic Athlete Workout to get our bodies active, strong, and flexible. Can you figure out what each center does for your body and which part of physical fitness it helps?"

Activity

Place the Olympic Athlete Workout signs on cones around the perimeter of the teaching area. Make a racetrack with cones inside the teaching area. Students begin exercising at a designated center when the music starts (use music CD track 4). When the music stops, they move to the racetrack and run or walk for the next 30 seconds of music. When the music stops again, they move to the closest center and begin exercising. This pattern continues until they have visited all circuit centers (i.e., center, racetrack, center, racetrack, center).

(↻) **review** • • •
Review the Physical Activity Pyramid for Kids and ask students to identify on what steps the Olympic Athlete Workout activities would be.

Refinements

Encourage students to pace themselves so they can move the whole time the music is playing.

Extensions

* Change the locomotor movements (e.g., gallop, hop, slide).

interdisciplinary • • •

Talk with classroom teachers and encourage them to have students create Olympic Athlete Workout activity cards in art class. Students could also write on the cards (language arts), describing the kind of fitness the activity builds and which sports require that kind of fitness. Finally, students could identify the countries that excel at that sport (geography) and find them on the map. Students could also learn the names of sports in other languages.

* Increase the time spent at each station using tracks 5, 6, 7, or 8 on the music CD.

* Incorporate student-created Olympic Athlete Workout activity cards.

3. Lesson Focus: Are You Balanced?

Introduction

"Being in balance means you are able to keep your body still. To be in balance, you must use your muscles to hold your body in place. You will also need to use your senses of sight and feeling to remain balanced. Today we will learn some new balancing activities and practice some old stunts and balances. Remember to focus your eyes on a spot, keeping your head very still. Strong muscles!"

Activity

Have students scatter throughout the space. Choose a balance activity from the Are You Balanced? task cards, introduce and model it, and then have your students do it. Encourage them to hold the balance for five seconds or more. Some students will have a difficult time with a basic one-legged balance. If you perform a balancing exercise on one leg (e.g., left), always perform the same activity on the other leg.

Refinements

* Remind students that focusing their eyes on a target (object) will help them balance.
* Observe students holding strong and stable poses. Provide feedback to help them improve.
* Encourage students to hold the poses for the full count.

Extensions

Encourage students to be creative.

* "Can you balance on four body parts? Show me another way."
* "Can you balance on three body parts? Show me another way."
* "Can you balance on five body parts? Show me another way."

Are You Balanced? activities require the integration of several senses.

* "Can you make your balance wide or narrow? Show me another way."
* "Can you balance low or high?"
* Have students work with a partner and match their partner's balance poses.
* Have students name their poses in a language other than English.
* Have students create a balance routine that flows smoothly.

4. Culminating Activity: Healthy Food Medley

Introduction

"You need to eat a variety of foods to maintain a healthy body. Can you name a healthy food from each of the five food groups? I need a fruit, a vegetable, a grain, a dairy food, and a meat or bean."

Activity

Three players are It and stand in the center of the activity area between two safety lines established on either end of the playing area. All other students (runners) stand behind one of the safety lines. You or the students select three healthy foods (e.g., banana, nonfat yogurt, and chicken). Each runner then selects a food from among the three but keeps it a secret. You (or one tagger) call out one of the designated foods. All runners who chose that food attempt to cross to the other line without getting tagged. If a runner is tagged, that student becomes a tagger. If "Health food junkie" is called, all runners must cross to the opposite sideline.

Refinements

* Provide feedback to students to help them perform the specified locomotor movements correctly.
* Remind students to move under control using the specified locomotor movements (e.g., gallop, walk, skip).

Extensions

* Have student healthy foods start in different positions (e.g., plank, crabwalk, balanced on one foot).
* Use Spanish food names (e.g., chicken = *pollo*).

CLOSURE ROUTINE

Compliments

Have some students share compliments about their classmates.

Reflection and Review

* "What sports or activities require balance? On what step of the Physical Activity Pyramid for Kids are those sports?"
* "What are some senses that help you perform balancing acts?"
* "Can anyone tell me what it means to have a balanced diet?"
* "What food group does yogurt (broccoli, pineapple, bread) belong to?"
* "Share your favorite balancing act with your neighbor."

Take It Home

✳ "Can you balance for a full commercial break? Practice balance activities during commercials at home. Include your family members."

✳ "Practice a flowing balance routine with a family member or a friend. Pick some fun music to balance to."

ASSESSMENT

✳ **Performance check:** Observe students successfully executing the body rewards and balancing positions.

✳ **Comprehension check:** Responses to selected Comprehension Check questions and the Reflection and Review questions can serve as a check for student understanding.

4.3 Lesson Plan

OVERVIEW

In this lesson, students will explore a variety of striking and manipulative skills with their feet.

NASPE STANDARDS

1A, 2C, 3A, 3B, 4A, 4B, 4C, 5A, 5B
(See appendix B for details.)

OBJECTIVES

Students will

* demonstrate a variety of striking and manipulative skills with their feet, and
* explain why physical activities are good for the brain.

EQUIPMENT

* CD player, 30/30 interval music (music CD track 4), and continuous music (music CD track 11 or 12)
* 4 red beanbags, 4 blue beanbags, and 4 green beanbags
* 12 cones
* One 8-inch (20 cm) soft ball or small soccer ball for each student

RESOURCES

 General

At-a-Glance PE Lesson Plan card
G3: Physical Activity Pyramid for Kids
G4: MyPyramid for Kids

 Wellness Week 4 → K-2 Resources

Olympic Athlete Workout activity cards
Soccer Centers activity cards
Week 4 signs file with the following signs:
* Get off your seat and move your feet!
* Play every day, sun or rain. Playing is good for your brain!

CHANTS

Leader: "Get off your seat…"

Students: ". . . and move my feet!"

1. Instant Activity: Healthy Body Tag

Introduction

"We have now learned about cardiorespiratory (heart) fitness, muscle fitness, and flexibility. We also have learned that we need to warm up our bodies before we stretch or play games. Today we are going to put all of our knowledge together."

Activity

In this tag game, students tagged by colored beanbags must perform a specific body reward. Specify the locomotor movement and the activity area. Have students move on your signal. On the first time through, use one or two colors and specify the body rewards. Connect the body rewards to the fitness concept. Add new colors in subsequent lessons.

* Students tagged by red taggers (cardiorespiratory fitness) must perform a healthy heart activity (e.g., jumping jacks, straddle jumps) 10 times (see lesson 1.2 for jump patterns).

* Students tagged by blue taggers (muscle fitness) must perform a muscle fitness challenge (e.g., curl-ups, crab cross-lateral dance) either holding it for 10 counts or doing 10 repetitions of the exercise (see lesson 3.3 for stunts and challenges).

* Students tagged by green taggers (flexibility) must perform a stretch and hold it for at least 10 counts (see lesson 3.2 for stretches).

Kindergarten Variations

* Begin with just one colored beanbag and fitness concept and then add on.

* Tell students which body reward they will be performing so they know what to do.

* Connect the body reward and the color back to the physical fitness concept it represents (e.g., red for heart or cardio).

comprehension check • • •

• "Show me an exercise that improves your cardiorespiratory fitness (muscle fitness, flexibility)."

• "Why is cardiorespiratory fitness (muscle fitness, flexibility) important?"

Refinements

* Provide feedback to students to help them perform the specified locomotor movements correctly.

* Provide feedback to students to help them perform the body rewards correctly.

Extensions

* Allow students to choose the appropriate body reward when tagged.

* Encourage students to create new body rewards.

* Have students identify their body reward in Spanish or another language (e.g., push-up = *levante,* jump = *saltar*).

2. Fitness Activity: Olympic Athlete Workout

Introduction

"All athletes must work out to get strong and fit. What kind of exercises do they need to do to get fit? That's right, something to get them strong, such as muscle fitness activities. Can you name some? Flexibility is important, too. How do we develop flexibility? Stretching, that's right. Can you show me a stretch for your upper body or lower body? Can you think of anything else athletes need? That's right, cardiorespiratory fitness. Today we are going to do the Olympic Athlete Workout to get our bodies active, strong, and flexible. Can you figure out what each center does for your body and which part of physical fitness it helps?"

Activity

Place the Olympic Athlete Workout signs on cones around the perimeter of the teaching area. Make a racetrack with cones inside the teaching area. Students begin exercising at a designated center when the music starts (use music CD track 4). When the music stops, they move to the racetrack and run or walk for the next 30 seconds of music. When the music stops again, they move to the closest center and begin exercising. This pattern continues until they have visited all circuit centers (i.e., center, racetrack, center, racetrack, center).

Refinements

Encourage students to pace themselves so they can move the whole time the music is playing.

 review • • •

"How can we check if we are working hard enough to build a strong heart?" (Heart rate, warm body and sweating, breathing rate)

Extensions

✳ Change the locomotor movements (e.g., gallop, hop, slide).

✳ Increase the time spent at each station using tracks 5, 6, 7, or 8 on the music CD.

✳ Incorporate student-created Olympic Athlete Workout activity cards.

3. Lesson Focus: Kick It!

Introduction

"Soccer is the most popular sport in the world. It is played in nearly every country. In the United States it is called *soccer,* but what does the rest of the world call it? Yes, football. When you play soccer, you must control the ball with your feet and body but not your hands, unless you play what position? Yes, that's right, the goalie! Today we are going to review and practice many of the skills we use in soccer, using our feet to control or kick a ball. When you play soccer, you need to use a lot of senses such as touch, sight, and hearing. When you participate in physical activities, you challenge your brain to use many senses at once. This is why physical activity is good for the brain."

⊗ **interdisciplinary** • • •

Talk with classroom teachers and encourage them to have students create Olympic Athlete Workout activity cards in art class. Students could also write on the cards (language arts), describing the kind of fitness the activity builds and which sports require that kind of fitness. Finally, students could identify the countries that excel at that sport (geography) and find them on the map. Students could also learn the names of sports in other languages.

Activity

Demonstrate the activities at the various soccer centers (use Soccer Centers activity cards). Break the students into five groups using a grouping strategy of your choice (see page 25). Students will be at each soccer center for two to three minutes while the music is playing (use music CD track 11 or 12). When the music stops, they will clean up their center, and when you say "Rotate," they rotate to the next center.

 comprehension check • • •

• "On what step of the Physical Activity Pyramid for Kids would you place soccer?"

• "What parts of fitness are important for soccer?"

Refinements

✳ Observe students at each station. Provide feedback to help them improve their skills at each station.

✳ Encourage students to kick it for the whole duration of the station.

Extensions

✳ Challenge students to increase the number of successful repetitions of a soccer skill.

✳ Challenge students to keep the ball under control for the whole time at a station.

✳ Introduce skills in a language other than English (e.g., in Spanish, pass = *paso,* kick = *patada*).

4. Culminating Activity: Fruit Salad

Introduction

"You need to eat a variety of foods to maintain a healthy body. Fruits are especially wonderful because they give you energy, nutrients, and vitamins. Can you name any fruits? What fruits are your favorites? Tell your neighbor a fruit you have eaten recently."

Activity

Three players are It and stand in the center of the activity area between two safety lines established on either end of the playing area. All other students (runners) stand behind one of the safety lines. You or the students select three fruits (e.g., banana, apple, and orange). Each runner then selects a fruit from among the three but keeps it a secret. You (or one tagger) call out one of the designated fruits. All runners who chose that fruit attempt to cross to the other line without getting tagged. If a runner is tagged, that student becomes a tagger. If "Fruit salad" is called, all runners must cross to the opposite sideline.

> ⟳ **review** • • •
>
> "What are the names of all the food groups? If I were a tomato (peach, piece of cheese, noodle), what food group would I be in?"

Refinements

* Provide feedback to students to help them perform the specified locomotor movements correctly.
* Remind students to move under control using the specified locomotor movements (e.g., gallop, walk, skip).

Extensions

* Have student fruits start in different positions (e.g., plank, crabwalk, balanced on one foot).
* Use Spanish fruit names (e.g., fruit salad = *ensalada de frutas*).

CLOSURE ROUTINE

Compliments

Have some students share compliments about their classmates.

Reflection and Review

* "What is soccer called in other countries?"
* "What senses do we use to play soccer?"
* "Why are physical activities good for our brains?"
* "What are some Spanish terms for soccer skills?"
* "What senses do we use when we eat?"

Soccer can be used to teach about other cultures.

Take It Home

✳ "Include your family members in a game of soccer or just practice your skills with a friend. Remember, playing is good for the brain."

✳ "Practice some soccer skills with a family member. Teach that person the Spanish names for some skills. Remember, playing is good for the brain."

ASSESSMENT

✳ **Performance check:** Observe students successfully executing the striking and manipulative skills with their feet.

✳ **Comprehension check:** Responses to selected Comprehension Check questions and the Reflection and Review questions can serve as a check for student understanding.

EXTRA ACTIVITIES AND RESOURCES

If your school has physical education more than three times per week, consider delivering some of the lesson plans a second time or using some of the extra activities and resources in appendix A of this book (see page 245). You can also use some of the additional activities described in appendix A of the classroom guides. Ask your wellness coordinator for access to these guides.

PART
III

LESSON PLANS FOR GRADES 3-6

Part III contains the **Fitness for Life: Elementary School** physical education lesson plans for third, fourth, fifth, and sixth grades, organized by Wellness Week. Before you start using the lesson plans, be sure to read part I of this book (especially "Using the Lesson Plans" on page 15) and familiarize yourself with the DVDs, resources CD-ROM, and music CD bound into the back of the book.

WELLNESS WEEK

1

Fitness for Life Elementary School

These lesson plans provide students with a variety of experiences, including locomotor and animal movements, moving to music, jumping movements, rope jumping, and tossing and catching skills. In Wellness Week 1, the activity theme is "moderate physical activity," the nutrition theme for grades 3-5 is "fruits and vegetables (eat 5 a day)," and the nutrition theme for grade 6 is "fruits and vegetables (you are what you eat)." These themes are reinforced through activities, signs, and chants. Take time to look through the lesson plans for Wellness Week 1 and determine which objectives are most important and which activities you will use to meet those objectives. Table 3.1 summarizes the Wellness Week 1 activities for the physical education lesson plans.

For Wellness Week 1, the lesson plans include the following:

- A warm-up lesson plan to be used during the week before Wellness Week 1. The same basic warm-up lesson plan is used for grades 3 through 6, but the Lesson Focus (practicing the video routine) is different for each grade.

- Three lesson plans (1.1, 1.2, and 1.3) to be used during Wellness Week 1. The same basic lesson plan is used for grades 3 through 6, with grade-specific variations, refinements, and extensions for some of the activities.

- Extra activity ideas for schools that have physical education class more than three days a week are provided in appendix A.

Table 3.1   Summary of Wellness Week 1 Activities

Lesson Plan	Instant Activity	Fitness Activity	Lesson Focus	Culminating Activity
Warm-Up 1 (week before Wellness Week 1)	Move and Freeze	Physical Activity Pyramid for Kids Circuit	Video Routine Practice: 3: It's Our Plan 4: Robot 5: Hip Hop 5 6: Hip Hop 6	Fruits and Veggies Tag
1.1	Move and Freeze	Physical Activity Pyramid for Kids Circuit	Video Routine Variations: 3: It's Our Plan 4: Robot 5: Hip Hop 5 6: Hip Hop 6	Fruits and Veggies Tag
1.2	Move and Freeze	Physical Activity Pyramid for Kids Circuit	Jump Squad	Safety Scramble
1.3	Move and Freeze	Physical Activity Pyramid for Kids Circuit	What's the Catch?	Safety Scramble

Eat Well Wednesday

Each Wednesday, known as Eat Well Wednesday, all teachers and staff are encouraged to emphasize nutrition. The wellness coordinator might plan special schoolwide events. During Wellness Week 1, the nutrition event is a fruit and vegetable bar in the cafeteria. If you have a physical education lesson on Eat Well Wednesday, place an emphasis on nutrition signs and messages.

Get Fit Friday

Each Friday, known as Get Fit Friday, a schoolwide event focusing on physical activity will be planned. (If your school participates in this event, your wellness coordinator will provide you with more details.) The Get Fit Friday activities are called TEAM Time activities (TEAM stands for Together Everyone Achieves More). During Wellness Week 1, this activity will be the School Walk. All students gather in the gym, in the multipurpose room, or outside before beginning the School Walk. Your wellness coordinator will set up and lead the activity.

Moderate physical activity (step 1 of the Physical Activity Pyramid for Kids) is the activity theme for Wellness Week 1.

Newsletter

The CD-ROM contains a newsletter for use during Wellness Week 1. It is recommended that your school's wellness coordinator edit and distribute the newsletter. Alternatively, you (or the classroom teachers) can do it. Just open the appropriate file, follow the instructions to edit and customize the newsletter, and send printed copies home with students or send them electronically via e-mail. Remind students to talk to their families about Wellness Week and the information in the newsletter.

 **Wellness Week 1 → Newsletter**

Warm-Up Lesson Plan 1

OVERVIEW

In this lesson, conducted during the week before Wellness Week 1, students will learn the grade-specific video routine that they will perform in their classroom during Wellness Week 1. You can aid the classroom teachers by teaching these routines in advance to make it easier for both students and teachers and to increase the chances that the classroom teachers will do the video routines in their classrooms.

NASPE STANDARDS

* **Grades 3-5:** 1A, 1B, 4A, 4I, 5F, 5G, 6H
* **Grade 6:** 1D, 1E, 1F, 5F, 5G

(See appendix B for details.)

OBJECTIVES

Students will

* demonstrate a variety of locomotor and manipulative skills,
* demonstrate basic dance steps to music, and
* explain why fruits and vegetables are good for their bodies.

EQUIPMENT

* CD player and 45/15 interval music (music CD track 6)
* TV, DVD player, and DVD 1 (Instructional Routines)
* 6 cones
* Circuit equipment (depends on activity cards chosen)
* 2 each of the following colored beanbags: red, yellow, blue, purple, and orange
* 6 green beanbags

RESOURCES

 General

At-a-Glance PE Lesson Plan card

G3: Physical Activity Pyramid for Kids

G4: MyPyramid for Kids

Wellness Week 1 → 3-6 Resources

Physical Activity Pyramid for Kids activity cards

Week 1 signs file with the following signs:

- Whatever you love to play, get 60 minutes every day!
- Eat the rainbow way: every color, every day!

CHANTS

Leader: "How many minutes do you need today?"

Students: "We need 60 every day!"

⭐ **teacher tip • • •**
You may not get through the whole lesson the first time through. Decide which part of the lesson is most important for your students to experience.

DELIVERING THE LESSON

1. Instant Activity: Move and Freeze

Introduction

"I have some exciting news! Next week is Wellness Week, and we will be participating in the **Fitness for Life: Elementary School** program. **Fitness for Life** will help you learn about the importance of fitness, physical activity, and healthy eating. More importantly, the **Fitness for Life** program has cool video routines that we will do in PE and in your classroom, as well as fun physical activities for our PE classes. So let's get started. When I say 'go,' I want you to skip inside the activity area in your own space. . . . Go!"

Activity

Students come into the activity space using a teacher-designated locomotor skill, such as skipping, galloping, or sliding in open space, staying inside the designated activity area. On your stop signal, have them freeze in an athletic position (knees bent, shoulder width apart, hands on their knees) with their eyes on you. All students should freeze within five seconds with their bodies under control and eyes on you. Repeat this activity several times using various locomotor activities, getting bodies warmed up and students ready to listen. When students are moving and freezing in control, move on to the fitness activity.

Extensions

* Change the locomotor movement (e.g., walk, grapevine, jog).
* Change the quality of the movement (e.g., quietly, low, high).
* Change the pathway (e.g., zigzags, curves, squares).
* Move in unison to music (e.g., alone, with a partner, with a group).

2. Fitness Activity: Physical Activity Pyramid for Kids Circuit

Introduction

"Today we will be working on activities from the Physical Activity Pyramid for Kids." (Show students the pyramid poster.) "The pyramid has five steps that each represent a type of activity.

* "At the bottom of the pyramid, or step 1, are moderate physical activities. These are activities that don't make you sweat or breathe hard, but they involve moving around. Can you give me some examples?"
* "At step 2 are vigorous aerobic activities. Aerobic activities at step 2 build cardiorespiratory fitness."
* "At step 3 are vigorous sports and recreation. These are vigorous activities that build cardiorespiratory fitness and require you to breathe hard and sweat."
* "At step 4 are muscle fitness exercises, and at step 5 are flexibility exercises."
* "Activities at steps 4 and 5 can help you build muscular endurance, strength, and flexibility. Can you think of activities that require strength or flexibility?"
* "Sedentary (resting) activities such as watching TV and playing video games are not part of the pyramid, but are shown below the pyramid. Too much TV watching and video gaming keep you from being active and are not good for your health."

"Like any pyramid, the Physical Activity Pyramid for Kids has a wide base and narrows to a point at the top. This week we are emphasizing moderate activity at the bottom. Moderate activity is activity that most people can do on a regular basis, and that is why it is at the bottom of the pyramid."

Activity

Choose one Physical Activity Pyramid for Kids activity card from each category and attach it to a cone at that station. The first activity in each category is the easiest to set up and administer. Consider the equipment demands and setup between classes.

Get students into groups of four to six using a grouping strategy of your choice (see page 25). Have each group go to a station and look at the activity card for instructions. When the music starts, students begin the activity at their station. Students move to the next station when the music stops, and they begin the activity at that station when the music starts again.

 comprehension check • • •

- "What station has activities that are at the first step of the pyramid (moderate physical activity)? Second? Third? Fourth?"
- "Using your fingers, which step of the pyramid has your favorite activity?"
- "Which movements challenged your upper body? Lower body?"

3. Lesson Focus: Video Routine Practice

Introduction

"Next week is Wellness Week 1. During Wellness Week 1, we will be learning about physical activity, fitness, and healthy nutrition. Today we are going to practice the video routine you will be performing in your classroom during Wellness Week 1. This video routine is fun and will challenge you to move to music."

Activity

Introduce and practice the grade-specific video routine using the following steps.

1. Insert DVD 1 and play the instructional routine that is appropriate for your class:
   - Third grade: It's Our Plan
   - Fourth grade: Robot
   - Fifth grade: Hip Hop 5
   - Sixth grade: Hip Hop 6
2. Have the students follow along with the routine. Observe students performing the routine and take note of the movements that give them trouble.
3. Before going through the routine again, provide a demonstration and help students with any movements that are giving them trouble. Provide tips that will help them succeed.
4. Play the routine again and compliment students on any improvements.
5. Remind students that next week is Wellness Week 1, and they will perform this routine every day in their classrooms next week.

Refinements

Observe the students' movements and listen to the reciting of the words. Have students focus on staying with the music and moving together.

4. Culminating Activity: Fruits and Veggies Tag

Introduction

"Fruits and vegetables give you energy, help you grow, and can keep you healthy and well. Fruits and vegetables are full of energy and vitamins that help your body fight off illnesses like colds and flu—that's one reason to eat at least 5 servings of fruits and vegetables every day. Let's play a game that uses fruits and veggies to keep us healthy and moving."

Activity

Choose six players to have the green beanbags. These are your infectious germs— they are It. They begin in the middle of the gym. Distribute the fruits and vegetables (other colored beanbags) and have the students assign fruit and vegetable names to the various colors (e.g., red is tomato or strawberry, purple is grape or eggplant). Not all students will have a beanbag. On your signal (e.g., music), those who are It try to infect as many nonfruit and nonvegetable players as possible by tagging them softly. When infected (tagged), these players freeze in their best sick and tired position (or a position designated by you) until a fruit or vegetable player comes to save them by handing the infected player the fruit or vegetable (beanbag) and saying, "Fruits and vegetables keep you well." The player now becomes the fruit or vegetable and must save another infected person. Play for 40 seconds or so and then change infectious germs (students who are It).

Grade Variations

* Third grade: Skip, gallop, or slide for safety. If moving safely, students may begin to run.
* Fourth through sixth grades: Allow students to run if they can control their bodies.
* Sixth grade: Have the students who are It move differently from the other students. If students are working safely, allow fruits to make short tosses to infected students.

Refinements

Have students focus on moving using the teacher-designated locomotor movements, even when being chased.

Extensions

* Have students use their imaginations to come up with new fruits and vegetables that match the color of the beanbags.
* If you teach in a bilingual or multilingual setting, incorporate these languages when naming the fruits and vegetables.
* If students are working safely, allow fruits and vegetables to make short tosses to infected students.
* Talk about healthy fruit and vegetable choices served in the cafeteria.

Volleying around a beach ball with friends is a moderate physical activity (step 1 of the Physical Activity Pyramid).

CLOSURE ROUTINE

Compliments

Identify specific behaviors that students performed well (e.g., "I really liked the energy and enthusiasm you showed during the video routines").

Reflection and Review

* "How many steps are there on the Physical Activity Pyramid for Kids?"
* "Turn to your neighbors and tell them your favorite step."
* "What is the name of the video routine we learned today?"
* "Why are fruits and vegetables important for good health?"
* "Turn to your neighbors and tell them your favorite vegetable or fruit."

Take It Home

* "Find out which step of the Physical Activity Pyramid for Kids includes a family member's favorite activity."
* "Find out your family members' favorite vegetables and fruits."

ASSESSMENT

* **Performance check:** Observe students successfully executing the Physical Activity Pyramid for Kids movements, moving to music during the video routines, and using the correct locomotor movements during the culminating activity.
* **Comprehension check:** Responses to the Comprehension Check questions and Reflection and Review questions serve as a check for student understanding.

Lesson Plan 1.1

OVERVIEW

In this lesson, students will practice the Wellness Week 1 video routine and have an opportunity to create and add new movements to the routine.

NASPE STANDARDS

* **Grades 3-5:** 1A, 1B, 1C, 3B, 4A, 4I, 5A, 5B, 5E, 5H, 5J, 6B, 6D, 6F
* **Grade 6:** 1D, 1F, 5F, 5L, 6I, 6J

(See appendix B for details.)

OBJECTIVES

Students will

* demonstrate a variety of locomotor and manipulative skills,
* demonstrate an ability to work well with others in a cooperative activity, and
* explain why fruits and vegetables are good for their bodies.

EQUIPMENT

* CD player and 45/15 interval music (music CD track 6)
* TV, DVD player, and DVD 2 (Activity Routines)
* 6 cones
* Circuit equipment (depends on activity cards)
* 2 each of the following colored beanbags (red, yellow, blue, purple, and orange)
* 6 green beanbags

RESOURCES

 General

At-a-Glance PE Lesson Plan card
G3: Physical Activity Pyramid for Kids
G4: MyPyramid for Kids

 Wellness Week 1 → 3-6 Resources

Physical Activity Pyramid for Kids activity cards
Week 1 signs file with the following signs:

* Whatever you love to play, get 60 minutes every day!
* Eat the rainbow way: every color, every day!

CHANTS

Leader: "How many minutes do you need today?"

Students: "We need 60 every day!"

> ⭐ **teacher tip** • • •
>
> You may not get through the whole lesson the first time through. Decide which part of the lesson is most important for your students to experience.

DELIVERING THE LESSON

1. Instant Activity: Move and Freeze

Introduction

"This week is Wellness Week 1, and we will be participating in some lessons that will help you learn about the importance of physical activity, fitness, and healthy eating. Last week we practiced the video routines that you will be doing in your classroom. Today we are going to work together to create some of our own moves to add to the video routines. So let's get started. When I say 'go,' I want you to jog inside the activity area in your own space. . . . Go!"

3–6 • WEEK 1
LESSON PLAN 1.1

Activity

Students come into the activity space using a teacher-designated locomotor skill, such as skipping, galloping, or sliding in open space, staying inside the designated activity area. On your stop signal, have them freeze in an athletic position (knees bent, shoulder width apart, hands on their knees) with their eyes on you. All students should freeze within five seconds with their bodies under control and eyes on you.

Repeat this activity several times using various locomotor activities, getting bodies warmed up and students ready to listen. When students are moving and freezing in control, move on to the fitness activity.

review • • •
Review the important points of the freeze or athletic position with the students. Ask them to show you or tell you what the important points are (eyes on teacher, knees bent, shoulder width apart, hands on their knees).

Extensions

* Change the locomotor movement (e.g., walk, grapevine, jog).
* Change the quality of the movement (e.g., quietly, low, high).
* Change the pathway (e.g., zigzags, curves, squares).
* Move in unison to music (e.g., alone, with a partner, with a group).

2. Fitness Activity: Physical Activity Pyramid for Kids Circuit

Introduction

"Today we will be working on activities from the Physical Activity Pyramid for Kids." (Revisit the steps of the pyramid and the parts of fitness that are enhanced by working at each step—for example, steps 2 and 3 improve cardiorespiratory fitness, step 4 improves muscular endurance and strength, and step 5 improves flexibility.) "Last time you might have worked really hard at the start of the station and were not able to stay active for the whole time at the station. Pace yourself at each station so you can stay active for the whole time. Can anyone tell me what it means to pace yourself?"

Activity

Choose one Physical Activity Pyramid for Kids activity card from each category and attach it to a cone at that station. The first activity in each category is the easiest to set up and administer. Consider the equipment demands and setup between classes.

Get students into groups of four to six using a grouping strategy of your choice (see page 25). Have each group go to a station and look at the pyramid activity card for instructions. When the music starts, students begin the activity at their station. Students move to the next station when the music stops, and they begin the activity at that station when the music starts again.

review • • •
Ask students to identify the steps of the pyramid, provide an example of an activity on that step, and describe what part of fitness is developed by participating in that activity.

Refinements

Observe the quality of the movements that students are performing at each station. Provide students with simple feedback to help them perform the activities correctly.

In one of the circuit stations, students try to hula hoop to the music using different body parts.

Extensions

✳ Use different Physical Activity Pyramid for Kids activity cards.

✳ Have students create an activity card for each step of the pyramid.

✳ Have students bring their own music for the circuit.

3. Lesson Focus: Video Routine Variations

Introduction

"Last class we practiced the video routine you are performing in your classroom. Today we are going to use our creativity and make up some new moves for the routine."

Activity

Practice the grade-specific video routine using the following steps.

1. Insert DVD 2 and play the video routine that is appropriate for your class:
   - Third grade: It's Our Plan
   - Fourth grade: Robot
   - Fifth grade: Hip Hop 5
   - Sixth grade: Hip Hop 6

2. Have the students follow along with the routine. Observe students performing the routine and take note of the movements that give them trouble.

3. Before going through the routine again, provide a demonstration and help students with any movements that are giving them trouble. Provide tips that will help them succeed.

(?) comprehension check • • •
Ask students to explain what the video messages are trying to tell them. Reinforce the message by using some of your own examples or having students share examples.

4. Break the students into 16 pairs, 8 groups, or 4 groups using a grouping strategy of your choice (see page 25). These group sizes allow you to pair groups together to make an even number of fewer (and larger) groups as the activity progresses.

5. Instruct the students that you will play the video routine, and their job is to make up new movements for the routine that are in time with the music.

6. Play the video routine for your class, and visit the student groups to see the movements they are trying.

7. At the end of the routine, highlight a few moves that students came up with.

8. Have each group get with another group (e.g., 16 pairs become 8 groups) and play the music again. Have the two groups share their moves with each other.

9. Allow some time for the groups to combine their moves, and play the video routine so they can practice. Visit the new groups to see how they are combining their movements.

10. Repeat steps 8 and 9 until you have two large groups or the whole class working together with new movements.

11. Encourage students to share their new moves with their classroom teachers.

> **observation • • •**
> Observe student groups to see if they are working well with others in a cooperative activity.

> **teacher tip • • •**
> Explain the importance of working with others. Identify the important elements of working with others, such as listening; sharing thoughts, feelings, and equipment; providing encouragement; and making sure everyone feels included. Provide examples of what this might sound or look like in the class.

4. Culminating Activity: Fruits and Veggies Tag

Introduction

"Fruits and vegetables give you energy, help you grow, and can keep you healthy and well. Fruits and vegetables are full of energy and vitamins that help your body fight off illnesses like colds and flu—that's one reason to eat at least 5 servings of fruits and vegetables every day. Let's play a game that uses fruits and veggies to keep us healthy and moving."

Activity

Choose six players to have the green beanbags. These are your infectious germs—they are It. They begin in the middle of the gym. Distribute the fruits and vegetables (other colored beanbags) and have the students assign fruit and vegetable names to the various colors (e.g., red is tomato or strawberry, purple is grape or eggplant). Not all students will have a beanbag. On your signal (e.g., music), those who are It try to infect as many nonfruit and nonvegetable players as possible by tagging them softly. When infected (tagged), these players freeze in their best sick and tired position (or a position designated by you) until a fruit or vegetable player comes to save them by handing the infected player the fruit or vegetable (beanbag) and saying, "Fruits and vegetables keep you well." The player now becomes the fruit or vegetable and must save another infected person. Play for 40 seconds or so and then change infectious germs (students who are It).

Grade Variations

✳ Third grade: Skip, gallop, or slide for safety. If moving safely, students may begin to run.

✳ Fourth through sixth grades: Allow students to run if they can control their bodies.

✳ Sixth grade: Have the students who are It move differently from the other students. If students are working safely, allow fruits and veggies to make short tosses to infected students.

Refinements

Have students focus on moving correctly using the teacher-designated locomotor movements, even when being chased.

Extensions

 * Have students use their imaginations to come up with new fruits and vegetables that match the color of the beanbags.

 * If you teach in a bilingual or multilingual setting, incorporate languages other than English when naming the fruit and veggies. The students can help and will feel like experts!

 * Talk about healthy fruit and vegetable snacks.

CLOSURE ROUTINE

Compliments

Have students share a compliment about the group members they worked with during the Video Routine Variations activity.

Reflection and Review

 * "How many steps are there in the Physical Activity Pyramid for Kids?"

 * "Turn to your neighbors and tell them your favorite step."

 * "What was the importance of the video message? Name a vegetable that makes a good raw snack."

Take It Home

"Bring one new raw fruit or veggie as a snack tomorrow."

ASSESSMENT

 * **Performance check:** Observe students successfully executing the Physical Activity Pyramid for Kids Circuit movements, moving to music during the video routines, and working together cooperatively.

 * **Comprehension check:** Responses to the Comprehension Check questions and Reflection and Review questions serve as a check for student understanding.

Lesson Plan 1.2

OVERVIEW

In this lesson, students will explore activities at different steps of the Physical Activity Pyramid for Kids and engage in a variety of jumping activities.

NASPE STANDARDS

* **Grades 3-5:** 1C, 2E, 4A, 4B, 4C, 4I, 5F
* **Grade 6:** 1D, 2G, 2H, 2I, 4J, 5L, 6K

(See appendix B for details.)

OBJECTIVES

Students will

* practice and demonstrate a variety of rope-jumping skills,
* encourage others during the lesson, and
* accurately identify safety equipment for a variety of physical activities.

EQUIPMENT

* CD player and 45/15 interval music (music CD track 6, 7, or 8)
* Circuit equipment (depends on activity cards chosen)
* 6 cones
* 2 each of the following colored beanbags: red, yellow, blue, purple, and orange
* 6 green beanbags
* Short jump rope for each student
* A few long ropes for advanced jumpers
* 40 to 60 scarves or beanbags (or a combination of the two)
* 4 hula hoops

RESOURCES

 General

At-a-Glance PE Lesson Plan card

G3: Physical Activity Pyramid for Kids

 Wellness Week 1 → 3-6 Resources

Physical Activity Pyramid for Kids activity cards

Jump Squad task cards

Week 1 signs file with the following signs:

- Start with safety! Finish with fun!
- Encouragement helps you and me. Positive is the way to be!

CHANTS

Leader: "How many minutes do you need today?"

Students: "We need 60 every day!"

⭐ **teacher tip** • • •
You may not get through the whole lesson the first time through. Decide which part of the lesson is most important for your students to experience.

DELIVERING THE LESSON

1. Instant Activity: Move and Freeze

Introduction

"Let's get prepared for some jumping activities with a quick warm-up. When I say 'go,' I want you to gallop inside the activity area and in your own space. . . . Go!"

Activity

Students come into the activity space using a teacher-designated locomotor skill, such as skipping, galloping, or sliding in open space, staying inside the designated activity area. On your stop signal, have them freeze in an athletic position (knees bent, shoulder width apart, hands on their knees) with their eyes on you. All students should freeze within five seconds with their bodies under control and eyes on you. Repeat this activity several times using various locomotor activities, getting bodies warmed up and students ready to listen. When students are moving and freezing in control, move on to the fitness activity.

review • • •

"Last class we talked about working with others in activity. Can you share some of the ways we can work together effectively? Encouraging others in physical activity is especially important because it can motivate us to try harder, practice a little more, and get better. Who can give me an example of how we can encourage each other?"

Refinement

Observe students using various locomotor skills. Provide students with feedback to help them perform the locomotor skills correctly.

Extensions

* Change the locomotor movement (e.g., walk, grapevine, jog).
* Change the quality of the movement (e.g., quietly, low, high).
* Change the pathway (e.g., zigzags, curves, squares).
* Move in unison to music (e.g., alone, with a partner, with a group).

2. Fitness Activity: Physical Activity Pyramid for Kids Circuit

Introduction

"Today we will be trying some new activities in the Physical Activity Pyramid for Kids circuit. Let's quickly go over the steps of the pyramid." Ask students to identify the five steps in the pyramid.

teacher tip • • •

If your school has a class set of pedometers, this would be a good week to introduce them to the class. Pedometers count steps and are good tools for monitoring the volume of physical activity. Students could see how many steps they take at each Physical Activity Pyramid for Kids station. Which step of the Physical Activity Pyramid gets students to step the most?

Activity

Choose one Physical Activity Pyramid for Kids activity card from each category and attach it to a cone at that station. The first activity in each category is the easiest to set up and administer. Consider the equipment demands and setup between classes.

Get students into groups of four to six using a grouping strategy of your choice (see page 25). Have each group go to a station and look at the activity card for instructions. When the music starts, students begin the activity at their station. Students move to the next station when the music stops, and they begin the activity at that station when the music starts again.

comprehension check • • •

"At what step of the pyramid are you being active at your station? What part of fitness are you developing by working at that station?"

Refinements

Remind students to encourage and support each other at each station. Model this behavior by providing positive feedback to students.

Extensions

* Add in new cards for some or all steps of the pyramid.
* Have students create an activity card for each step of the pyramid.
* Have students bring their own music for the circuit.

3. Lesson Focus: Jump Squad

Introduction

"Jumping is a skill that is important for many sports and recreational activities. Rope jumping is one way to practice your jumping skills and build fitness for sports. Does anyone know what kind of fitness rope jumping can build? That's right, cardiorespiratory and muscle endurance. Jumping rope is a hard skill to learn, but with lots of practice you will be able to jump rope like me." (Demonstrate some fancy footwork and speed work.) "Keep practicing and never give up, because the more you try the better you'll get. When I say 'Jump squad,' everyone get a jump rope and begin jumping rope in your own space."

> **observation** • • •
> Move around the area and observe the jumping skills of your students. This will give you an idea of the jumping tasks that you will work on.

Activity

You may have students who do not know how to jump rope and students who are very good rope jumpers. Following are instructions and activities for both groups. Use the Jump Squad task cards to guide you through the progressions.

Beginner Progression

* "Can you bounce (jump with feet together)?"
* "Can you turn a pretend jump rope, using your wrists to turn the rope while doing little, soft jumps?"
* "Pick up your jump rope, fold it in half, and hold both handles in one hand. Can you continue to jump and swing the rope in a circle, trying to bounce just as the jump rope brushes the floor? Switch hands."
* "Hold the jump rope in both hands with the loop of the jump rope touching your heels behind you. Stretch your arms out in front of you and swing the jump rope over your head using your big shoulder muscles, keeping a very large loop and touching your toes. No bouncing yet! Can you swing it back? Let's do 10 more. Swing over, swing back, swing over, swing back."
* "This time as the jump rope swings over your head, try to jump over it. Swing and bounce. See if you can do more than one in a row."

Advanced Progression

✳ Perform the basic jump (two feet together, continuous jumping, for 10 consecutive jumps).

✳ Perform 10 jumps backward.

✳ Perform hopping. Switch legs. Alternate legs. Repeat with backward jumping.

✳ Challenge students to try jumping side to side or front to back while jumping rope.

✳ Challenge students to try straddle jumps, scissor jumps, and X jumps.

✳ Introduce the double jump.

✳ Have students travel around the area while jumping rope, keeping a safe distance from others (forward and backward).

comprehension check • • •

For third through fifth grades:
- "Which jumping activities made your heart beat really fast? Why does this happen?"
- "What parts of your legs did the jumping activities challenge? Can you name the muscles? At what step of the Physical Activity Pyramid for Kids would you place rope jumping? Is it moderate physical activity (step 1) or vigorous aerobics (step 2)?"

For sixth grade:
- "What parts of fitness are challenged by rope jumping?" (cardiorespiratory and muscle endurance)
- "What specific muscles are challenged?"
- "How can we build cardiorespiratory fitness and muscular endurance?"

Grade Variations

Sixth grade: Have students identify which jumping skills (e.g., rope turning, jump timing) they are having trouble with and what activities they could practice to improve those jumping skills.

Second Time Through

If you are teaching this lesson a second time, you may want to introduce the following activities.

Introduction

"Last time you all worked hard at your jump rope skills. Today we are going try some new skills, practice skills you learned from your family at home, and work with music. The more you practice, the better you get."

Refinements

✳ Start with some basics from the Jump Squad task cards and observe students' technique. Provide feedback and tips when necessary.

✳ Focus on helping students make consistent rope turns.

Extensions

✳ Allow students time to practice skills learned at home.

✳ Have students try to jump to the rhythm of the music using existing jump skills.

✳ Have students perform jumping skills that incorporate tricks with the rope and the feet (look skills up on the Internet).

Rope jumping requires the use of several senses.

✳ Have students work with partners or in small groups to do the following:
  • Follow the Leader: Students try to match the skills of others.
  • Jump routine: Students create a jump routine with a sequence of skills.
✳ Allow students to work with the long rope if they are supporting others.

4. Culminating Activity: Safety Scramble

Introduction

"Today we are going to play a game that challenges your knowledge of safety equipment for physical activity. It will also challenge your imagination. It's called Safety Scramble."

Activity

Get students into four groups using a grouping strategy of your choice (see page 25). Groups get together at four separate hula hoops that are spread equidistant apart in the activity area. Inside each hula hoop there should be an equal number of safety items (10-15 beanbags or 10-15 scarves; these are the safety items). When the music starts, students try to collect as many safety items as possible from any of the other group's hoops. Tell the students how they can move (e.g., walk, skip, run). They can only take one safety item at a time and must place it directly into their hoop (no throwing). When the music stops, students freeze, and you yell out an activity and a number, such as "Volleyball, two." The object of the game is to be the first team to its hoop, suited up for safety, and pretending to perform the activity. Using the "Volleyball, two" example, the first team at its hoop in a volleyball position with beanbags balanced on both knees would be the winner. All team members must have the required number of safety equipment items. Therefore, if a team has not collected enough beanbags and many of its beanbags have been taken, its members will not be able to suit up.

Start with one of the activities listed here. Demonstrate the finished position for each activity for students (e.g., volleyball position with a beanbag on each knee).

✳ Biking: All team members must have a safety item (helmet) balanced on their head, with their hands on the pretend handlebars.
✳ Volleyball: All team members must be in a ready position with one safety item (knee pads) balancing on each knee.
✳ Beach day: All team members must be on all fours with two safety items (sunscreen) balanced on their backs.
✳ Skateboarding: All team members must have three safety items (wrist guards or knee guards) balanced on the backs of the hands or tops of the knees and one on their head (helmet) while balancing on one foot.

Grade Variations

✳ Third grade: Have students walk, skip, gallop, or slide for safety.
✳ Fourth through sixth grades: If moving safely, students may begin to run. Encourage these students to come up with lesser-known activities and use their imaginations.

Refinement

✳ Make a rule that students cannot touch anyone.
✳ Have students move throughout the activity using the teacher-designated locomotor movements, even when scrambling to finish.

Extensions

- ✳ Have students come up with activities that require safety equipment.
- ✳ Remove safety items (beanbags) from each team's hula hoop to make it more challenging.
- ✳ If you teach in a bilingual or multilingual setting, incorporate these languages when naming activities and safety items.

CLOSURE ROUTINE

Compliments

Share a compliment about a class member or the class as a whole.

Reflection and Review

- ✳ "Which activities require jumping skills?"
- ✳ "What kinds of athletes would use rope jumping to train their fitness?"
- ✳ "What is a good tip for someone learning to jump rope?"
- ✳ "What safety equipment is most important for your favorite activity? When do you put it on?"

Take It Home

"See if a family member or friend can show you some new jumping moves before next class."

ASSESSMENT

- ✳ **Performance check:** Observe students successfully executing the pyramid circuit movements and jumping activities.
- ✳ **Comprehension check:** Responses to the Comprehension Check questions and Reflection and Review questions serve as a check for student understanding.

1 WELLNESS WEEK

1.3 Lesson Plan

OVERVIEW

In this lesson, students will continue working on activities at various steps of the Physical Activity Pyramid for Kids, and they will engage in a variety of tossing and catching activities.

NASPE STANDARDS

* **Grades 3-5:** 1C, 2D, 2E, 3A, 4A, 4B, 4C, 4I, 5E, 5G, 5J, 6D
* **Grade 6:** 1D, 2F, 2G, 2H, 4J, 5G, 5L, 6J, 6K

(See appendix B for details.)

OBJECTIVES

Students will

* identify activities that build different parts of health-related fitness,
* practice a variety of manipulative skills, and
* support each other during practice through verbal encouragement.

EQUIPMENT

* CD player and 45/15 interval music (music CD track 6, 7, or 8)
* Circuit equipment (depends on activity cards chosen)
* 6 cones
* Variety of beanbags and balls
* 4 hula hoops
* 40 to 60 scarves or beanbags (or a combination of the two)

RESOURCES

 General

At-a-Glance PE Lesson Plan card
G3: Physical Activity Pyramid for Kids

 Wellness Week 1 → 3-6 Resources

Physical Activity Pyramid for Kids activity cards
What's the Catch? activity cards

Week 1 signs file with the following signs:

- Start with safety! Finish with fun!
- Encouragement helps you and me. Positive is the way to be!
- Keep on trying. The more you try, the better you get!

SIGNS AND CHANTS

Leader: "Who can do it and tell me why?"

Students: "We can do it if we try!"

> ⭐ **teacher tip** • • •
>
> You may not get through the whole lesson the first time through. Decide which part of the lesson is most important for your students to experience.

DELIVERING THE LESSON

1. Instant Activity: Move and Freeze

Introduction

"Today we are going to work on some fun tossing and catching activities, but first we need to warm up our bodies. When I say 'go,' I want you to skip inside the activity area in your own space. . . . Go!"

Activity

Students come into the activity space using a teacher-designated locomotor skill, such as skipping, galloping, or sliding in open space, staying inside the designated activity area. On your stop signal, have them freeze in an athletic position (knees bent, shoulder width apart, hands on their knees) with their eyes on you. All students should freeze within five seconds with their bodies under control and eyes on you.

Repeat this activity several times using various locomotor activities, getting bodies warmed up and students ready to listen. When students are moving and freezing in control, move on to the fitness activity.

> ↻ **review** • • •
>
> "Today we are going to be practicing throwing and catching skills. We need to support each other during practice through encouragement. I want to hear you all encouraging each other throughout today's lesson."

Extensions

- ✳ Change the locomotor movement (e.g., walk, grapevine, jog).
- ✳ Change the quality of the movement (e.g., quietly, low, high).
- ✳ Change the pathway (e.g., zigzags, curves, squares).
- ✳ Move in unison to music (e.g., alone, with a partner, with a group).

2. Fitness Activity: Physical Activity Pyramid for Kids Circuit

Introduction

"You have been working hard at different pyramid stations all week. I have introduced some new stations today (and some created by members of the class). Please pace yourself so you can be active for all the stations."

Activity

Choose one Physical Activity Pyramid for Kids activity card from each category and attach it to a cone at that station. The first activity in each category is the easiest to set up and administer. Consider the equipment demands and setup between classes.

Get students into groups of four to six using a grouping strategy of your choice (see page 25). Have each group go to a station and look at the activity card for instructions. When the music starts, students begin the activity at their station. Students move to the next station when the music stops, and they begin the activity at that station when the music starts again.

> ↻ review • • •
> Have students identify what parts of fitness are developed with activities at different steps of the pyramid.

Refinements

Remind students to encourage and support each other at each station. Model this behavior by providing positive feedback to students.

Extensions

* Allow students to choose the stations they want to work at.
* Have students create an activity card for each step of the pyramid.
* Have students bring some of their own music for the circuit.

3. Lesson Focus: What's the Catch?

Introduction

"Today we are going to explore different ways of throwing and catching. Can someone give us some tips for successful throwing? Can someone give us some tips for successful catching? What activities require throwing and catching? Throwing and catching are skills that require practice. We can all throw and catch, but can you match the catches at these stations?"

Activity

Replace the Physical Activity Pyramid for Kids activity cards with six What's the Catch? activity cards. Split the class into six groups using a grouping strategy of your choice (see page 25), and send them to a station. While students read the cards, distribute the different equipment to each station. On your signal, or when the music starts (music CD track 6, 7, or 8), have students perform the tasks at each station. When the music stops, have the students place the equipment into the hula hoop at the station before moving on.

 comprehension check • • •

- "Which stations challenge you to make accurate throws?"
- "How is tossing to yourself different from tossing with a partner?"
- "What are some tips for tossing and catching with a partner while moving?"
- "What stations required good communication?"
- "What stations required good listening?"

Grade Variations

Sixth grade: Have students identify which tossing and catching skills they are having trouble with and what activities they could practice to improve those tossing and catching skills.

Refinements

* Observe students' technique more closely. Provide feedback and tips when necessary.
* Explain to students at the move-and-catch station why leading the partner with a toss is important.

Extensions

* Encourage students to work with new partners and encourage their partners.
* Encourage students to use a language other than English when counting at stations.
* Have students share a fancy toss or catch that they created or learned from someone.
* At the individual stations, have students try following the leader (i.e., match the skills of another student).

4. Culminating Activity: Safety Scramble

Introduction

"Today we are going to play a game that challenges your knowledge of safety equipment for physical activity. It will also challenge your imagination. It's called Safety Scramble."

Activity

Get students into four groups using a grouping strategy of your choice (see page 25). Groups get together at four separate hula hoops that are spread equidistant apart in the activity area. Inside each hula hoop there should be an equal number of safety items (10-15 beanbags or 10-15 scarves; these are the safety items). When the music starts, students try to collect as many safety items as possible from any of the other group's hoops. Tell the students how they can move (e.g., walk, skip, run). They can only take one safety item at a time and must place it directly into their hoop (no throwing). When the music stops, students freeze, and you yell out an activity and a number, such as "Volleyball, two." The object of the game is to be the first team to its hoop, suited up for safety, and pretending to perform the activity. Using the "Volleyball, two" example, the first team at its hoop in a volleyball position with beanbags balanced on both knees would be the winner. All team members must have the required number of safety equipment items. Therefore, if a team has not collected enough beanbags and many of its beanbags have been taken, its members will not be able to suit up.

Start with one of the activities listed here. Demonstrate the finished position for each activity for students (e.g., volleyball position with a beanbag on each knee).

* Biking: All team members must have a safety item (helmet) balanced on their head, with their hands on the pretend handlebars.
* Volleyball: All team members must be in a ready position with one safety item (knee pads) balancing on each knee.
* Beach day: All team members must be on all fours with two safety items (sunscreen) balanced on their backs.
* Skateboarding: All team members must have three safety items (wrist guards or knee guards) balanced on the backs of the hands or tops of the knees and one on their head (helmet) while balancing on one foot.

Grade Variations

* Third grade: Have students walk, skip, gallop, or slide for safety.
* Fourth through sixth grades: If moving safely, students may begin to run. Encourage these students to come up with lesser-known activities and use their imaginations.

Refinement

* Make a rule that students cannot touch anyone.
* Have students move throughout the activity using the teacher-designated locomotor movements, even when scrambling to finish.

Extensions

* Have students come up with activities that require safety equipment.
* Remove safety items (beanbags) from each team's hula hoop to make it more challenging.
* If you teach in a bilingual or multilingual setting, explore the languages by incorporating them when naming activities and safety items.

CLOSURE ROUTINE

Compliments

Have students share a compliment about a class member or the class as a whole.

Reflection and Review

* "What tossing and catching stations were at step 1 of the Physical Activity Pyramid for Kids? Were there any stations at steps 2 or 3?"

* "Who can share something that they learned from a partner?"

* "What tossing or catching skills did you improve at? Why?"

* "How does it make you feel when you are successful?"

* "What senses did you use today to help you perform the activities?"

* "Can you think of how safety equipment can affect our senses?"

* "Why does the beanbag always come back to the earth?"

Take It Home

* "Put together a fancy toss-and-catch routine with a family member."

* "With a family member, perform an activity from one or more steps of the pyramid."

ASSESSMENT

* **Performance check:** Observe students successfully executing the pyramid circuit movements and tossing and catching activities.

* **Comprehension check:** Responses to the Comprehension Check questions and Reflection and Review questions serve as a check for student understanding.

EXTRA ACTIVITIES AND RESOURCES

If your school has physical education more than three times per week, consider delivering some of the lesson plans a second time through or using some of the extra activities and resources in appendix A of this book (see page 245). You can also use some of the additional activities described in appendix A of the classroom guides. Ask your wellness coordinator for access to these guides.

Encourage students to do tossing and catching routines at home.

WELLNESS WEEK 2

Fitness for Life Elementary School

These lesson plans provide students with a variety of experiences, including exploring activities at step 2 of the Physical Activity Pyramid for Kids, moving to music, practicing the Fitnessgram PACER test, and learning about concepts such as empty calories, the FITT formula, and the overload principle. In Wellness Week 2, the activity theme is "vigorous physical activity (vigorous aerobics, sports, and recreation)," the nutrition theme for grades 3-5 is "grains and empty calories," and the nutrition theme for grade 6 is "grains and high-calorie foods." These themes are reinforced through activities, signs, and chants. Take time to look through the lesson plans for Wellness Week 2 and determine which objectives are most important and which activities you will use to meet those objectives. Table 3.2 summarizes the Wellness Week 2 activities for the physical education lesson plans.

For Wellness Week 2, the lesson plans include the following:

- A warm-up lesson plan to be used during the week before Wellness Week 2. The same basic warm-up lesson plan is used for grades 3 through 6, but the Lesson Focus (practicing the video routine) is different for each grade.

- Three lesson plans (2.1, 2.2, and 2.3) to be used during Wellness Week 2. The same basic lesson plan is used for grades 3 through 6, with grade-specific variations, refinements, and extensions for some of the activities.

- Extra activity ideas for schools that have physical education class more than three days a week are provided in appendix A.

Table 3.2 Summary of Wellness Week 2 Activities

Lesson Plan	Instant Activity	Fitness Activity	Lesson Focus	Culminating Activity
Warm-Up 2 (week before Wellness Week 2)	Athletes in Motion	Moving to Music	Video Routine Practice: 3: Go Aerobics Go 4: Latin Aerobics 5: Tinikling 6: Salsaerobics	Soda Swarm
2.1	Athletes in Motion	Moving to Music	Video Routine Variations: 3: Go Aerobics Go 4: Latin Aerobics 5: Tinikling 6: Salsaaerobics	Soda Swarm
2.2	Tempo Tag	Moving to Music	PACER Practice	Small-Sided Sports
2.3	Tempo Tag	Moving to Music	Sport Skills Circuit	Small-Sided Sports

Eat Well Wednesday

Each Wednesday, known as Eat Well Wednesday, all teachers and staff are encouraged to emphasize nutrition. The wellness coordinator might plan special schoolwide events. During Wellness Week 2, the nutrition event is a healthy breakfast program. If you have a physical education lesson on Eag Well Wednesday, place an emphasis on nutrition signs and messages.

Get Fit Friday

Each Friday, known as Get Fit Friday, a schoolwide event focusing on physical activity will be planned. (If your school participates in this event, your wellness coordinator will provide you with more details.) The Get Fit Friday activities are called TEAM Time activities (TEAM stands for Together Everyone Achieves More). During Wellness Week 2, this activity is called Big Kids Lead. The wellness coordinator will lead the activity at the beginning of the school day with the help of students in grades 5 and 6. All students in the school will congregate in the gym, multipurpose room, or outside so that they can participate together. The TEAM Time activity includes a warm-up, a special routine called Colors, and a cool-down. If time allows, you can teach these activities in advance to make it easier for students to perform them during TEAM Time. A video and script are provided on the DVD that accompanies the *Guide for Wellness Coordinators*.

Newsletter

The CD-ROM contains a newsletter for use during Wellness Week 2. It is recommended that your school's wellness coordinator edit and distribute the newsletter. Alternatively, you (or the classroom teachers) can do it. Just open the appropriate file, follow the instructions to edit and customize the newsletter, and send printed copies home with students or send them electronically via e-mail. Remind students to talk to their families about Wellness Week and the information in the newsletter.

 Wellness Week 2 → Newsletter

Vigorous physical activity (steps 2 and 3 of the Physical Activity Pyramid for Kids) is the activity theme for Wellness Week 2.

Warm-Up Lesson Plan 2

OVERVIEW

In this lesson, conducted during the week before Wellness Week 2, students will practice moving to music and will learn the grade-specific video routine that they will perform in their classroom during Wellness Week 2. You can aid the classroom teachers by teaching these routines in advance to make it easier for both students and teachers and to increase the chances that the classroom teachers will do the video routines in their classrooms.

NASPE STANDARDS

* **Grades 3-5:** 1A, 1B, 2A, 4B, 4I, 5B, 5F, 6H
* **Grade 6:** 1D, 1F, 2G, 2I, 3G, 4J

(See appendix B for details.)

OBJECTIVES

Students will

* be active for at least 50 percent of class time,
* move to the beat of the music using a variety of locomotor movements, and
* describe some empty-calorie foods and explain what *empty calorie* means.

EQUIPMENT

* CD player, 30/30 interval music (music CD track 4), and 45/15 interval music (music CD track 5)
* TV, DVD player, and DVD 1 (Instructional Routines)
* 4 hula hoops
* 40 to 60 different-colored beanbags (orange, green, red, blue, purple, yellow, brown, and black)

RESOURCES

 General

At-a-Glance PE Lesson Plan card

G3: Physical Activity Pyramid for Kids

 Wellness Week 2 → 3-6 Resources

Moving to Music task cards

Week 2 signs file with the following signs:

* To be fit, you must think FITT!
* Avoid empty calories! Calories with few nutrients are empty calories.

CHANTS

Leader: "The heart is a muscle . . ."

Students: ". . . that allows me to hustle!"

> ⭐ **teacher tip** • • •
> You may not get through the whole lesson the first time through. Decide which part of the lesson is most important for your students to experience.

DELIVERING THE LESSON

1. Instant Activity: Athletes in Motion

Introduction

"There is an athlete inside all of us. What does it mean to be an athlete? That's right, someone who participates in sports or physical activity, like someone who figure skates or rock climbs. Let's see if you can show me some athletes in motion."

Activity

Students perform a locomotor movement in the designated area. On your signal, they freeze in open space and create a statue of an athlete in motion. Guess what activity the athlete is performing; for instance, it might be kicking a soccer ball, swimming, or skating. Change the locomotor skills frequently, and encourage students to be still, as if they were made of cement or ice.

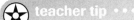 **teacher tip • • •**
Start with locomotor movements at a lower intensity (e.g., sliding and galloping), and build to more intense locomotor movements (e.g., skipping and running).

Extensions

* Have students freeze on different numbers of body parts.
* Have students freeze at different levels (low, high).
* Have older students perform the athlete's action in slow motion instead of freezing.

 **review • • •**
Point out a few student statues and ask students on what step of the Physical Activity Pyramid for Kids they would place each activity (probably 2 or 3). Also ask what kind of fitness is important for that activity.

2. Fitness Activity: Moving to Music

Introduction

"This week we will be working on activities from the second and third steps of the Physical Activity Pyramid for Kids. Can you remember what was at step 2 and step 3? That's right, step 2 is vigorous aerobics, and step 3 is vigorous sports and recreation. Activities at steps 2 and 3 are vigorous activities that make you breathe hard and sweat. What part of fitness do vigorous activities at steps 2 and 3 of the pyramid help you build? That's right, cardiorespiratory fitness. Activities at steps 2 and 3 also require specialized skills that need to be practiced, especially those at step 3. Today we are going to build our cardiorespiratory fitness while moving our bodies to music."

Activity

Students will move to music in different ways, with and without a partner. Use the ideas on the Moving to Music task cards. Have students spread out in the activity area. Play some interval music (use music CD track 4) and see if students can clap to the music, stomp to the music, or walk to the music. You may have to have them watch you first. Once they have the idea, introduce the activities on the Moving to Music task cards. When the music stops, have students stop and count their heartbeats or the number of times they breathe.

Grade Variations

Sixth grade: Have students count their heartbeats or breaths for 15 seconds and then figure out how many breaths or beats per minute that equates to.

Extensions

* Explain the FITT formula acronym to students using the "To be fit, you must think FITT!" sign and the Physical Activity Pyramid for Kids sign.

- **Frequency:** How many times per week?
- **Intensity:** How hard? (Measured using heart rate or breathing rate.)
- **Time:** How long?
- **Type:** What activity or step of the pyramid?

✴ Introduce the overload principle (i.e., in order to build fitness, you need to do more than before), and explain that you can increase the frequency, time, or intensity to overload and build cardiorespiratory fitness, muscle fitness, or flexibility.

(?) comprehension check • • •

- "What movements got your heart beating fast? Can you explain why this happens?"
- "What other changes in your body can you sense that let you know you are challenging your body?"

---

 interdisciplinary • • •

This is a good time to show a model of the heart and teach the students that the heart is a muscle with four chambers and that it increases in size when it is exercised, just like other muscles. Point out which chamber develops the most in size and why (left ventricle because it is pushing blood out to the working muscles).

---

3. Lesson Focus: Video Routine Practice

Introduction

"Next week is Wellness Week 2. During Wellness Week 2, we will be learning about physical activity, fitness, and healthy nutrition. Today we are going to practice the video routine you will be performing in your classroom during Wellness Week 2. This video routine is fun and will challenge you to move to music."

Activity

Introduce and practice the grade-specific video routine using the following steps.

1. Insert DVD 1 and play the instructional routine that is appropriate for your class:
   - Third grade: Go Aerobics Go
   - Fourth grade: Latin Aerobics
   - Fifth grade: Tinikling
   - Sixth grade: Salsaerobics

2. Have the students follow along with the routine. Observe students performing the routine and take note of the movements that give them trouble.

3. Before going through the routine again, provide a demonstration and help students with any movements that are giving them trouble. Provide tips that will help them succeed.

4. Play the routine again and compliment students on any improvements.

5. Remind students that next week is Wellness Week 2, and they will perform this routine every day in their classrooms next week.

Refinements

Observe the students' movements and listen to the reciting of the words. Have students focus on staying with the music and moving together.

4. Culminating Activity: Soda Swarm

Introduction

"Soda and sweets give us a lot of calories but few vitamins. This is why we say that soda and sweets have *empty calories.* Who can tell me what a calorie is? Right, calories are the energy in food that fuels our movement. We need calories, but we want to eat foods that have calories and vitamins. We should only eat or drink foods with empty calories once in a while. This is why we call them *treats.* In this game we are trying to get as many healthy foods as we can and few treats."

Activity

Break the class into groups of four using a grouping strategy of your choice (see page 25). Groups get together at four separate hula hoops that are spread equidistant apart in the gym or activity area. Inside each hula hoop, place 10 to 15 beanbags of various colors. When the music starts (use music CD track 5), each team tries to get as

The Moving to Music activities encourage vigorous activity (steps 2 and 3 of the Physical Activity Pyramid for Kids).

many healthy foods as possible (orange, green, red, blue, and purple beanbags) while avoiding the empty-calorie sweets (brown, black, or yellow beanbags). Specify how students move and introduce the following rules:

* Players can only carry one beanbag at a time.
* They take an empty-calorie beanbag from their hoop or anyone else's hoop and drop it off at another hoop. No one wants empty calories.
* After dropping off an empty-calorie beanbag, they can take a healthy-food beanbag back to their hoop.
* No throwing beanbags.
* Healthy beanbags are worth 1 point, and empty calories are worth –2 points.
* The first team sitting back at its hoop when the music stops gets 4 bonus points.

Grade Variations

* Third grade: Skip, gallop, or slide for safety. If moving safely, students may begin to run.
* Fourth through sixth grades: Allow students to run if they can control their bodies.

Refinements

* Ensure students move using the teacher-designated locomotor movements.
* Have teams take a minute to decide on a strategy. Share strategy ideas such as delivering empty calories to teams with lots of beanbags or dividing responsibilities (some members deliver empty calories, some collect healthy foods).

Extensions

* Have students transfer the beanbag by balancing it on the head, shoulder, or foot. If they drop the beanbag, they must go back to where they got it.
* Have students report their scores in a language other than English.
* Have students take a 15-second heart rate after each game. Start the first game with locomotor movements that are less intense (e.g., walking) and progressively increase the intensity (e.g., slide, skip, run). Reinforce the concept of intensity using this approach.

CLOSURE ROUTINE

Compliments

Have some students share compliments about their classmates.

Reflection and Review

* "What is the name of the video routine we learned today?"
* "At what steps of the pyramid were we active today?"
* "How can we tell how hard we are working during physical activity?"
* "Explain to your neighbor what an empty calorie is."
* "Discuss empty calories in the cafeteria, vending machines, or your lunch."
* "What does counting your heart or breathing rate tell you?"

Take It Home

* "Explain to your family what an empty calorie is."
* "Avoid eating empty calories in front of the TV."
* "See if your family can avoid eating empty calories for the weekend."

ASSESSMENT

* **Performance check:** Observe students successfully moving to music during the fitness activity and the video routines.
* **Comprehension check:** Responses to the Comprehension Check questions and Reflection and Review questions serve as a check for student understanding.

Lesson Plan 2.1

OVERVIEW

In this lesson, students will practice the Wellness Week 2 video routine and have an opportunity to create and add new movements to the routine.

NASPE STANDARDS

* **Grades 3-5:** 1A, 1B, 2A, 2D, 4A, 4B, 4C, 5A, 5B, 5E, 5H, 5J, 6B, 6D, 6F
* **Grade 6:** 1D, 1F, 2G, 2I, 4J, 5G, 5M, 6I, 6J

(See appendix B for details.)

OBJECTIVES

Students will

* move to the beat of the music using a variety of locomotor movements,
* monitor the intensity of their activity by taking their heart rate and breathing rate,
* explain what *FITT* stands for in the FITT formula, and
* explain the overload principle.

EQUIPMENT

* CD player and 45/15 interval music (music CD tracks 5 and 7)
* TV, DVD player, and DVD 2 (Activity Routines)
* 4 hula hoops
* 40 to 60 different-colored beanbags (orange, green, red, blue, purple, yellow, brown, and black)
* Paper and pencil for each student (sixth grade variation)

RESOURCES

 General

At-a-Glance PE Lesson Plan card

G3: Physical Activity Pyramid for Kids

 Wellness Week 2 → 3-6 Resources

Moving to Music task cards

Week 2 signs file with the following signs:

* Choose activity from the pyramid. Do vigorous activity from steps 2 and 3!
* To be fit, you must think FITT!
* Avoid empty calories! Calories with few nutrients are empty calories.
* Athletes have healthy and strong hearts!

CHANTS

Leader: "The heart is a muscle . . ."

Students: ". . . that allows me to hustle!"

> ⭐ **teacher tip** • • •
> You may not get through the whole lesson the first time through. Decide which part of the lesson is most important for your students to experience.

DELIVERING THE LESSON

1. Instant Activity: Athletes in Motion

Introduction

"When I say 'Play,' show me some athletes in motion. Try to show me some sports that demand good cardiorespiratory fitness. These athletes have strong heart muscles."

Activity

Students perform a locomotor movement in the designated area. On your signal, they freeze in open space and create a statue of an athlete in motion. Guess what activity the athlete is performing; for instance, it might be kicking a soccer ball, swimming, or skating. Change the locomotor skills frequently, and encourage students to be still, as if they were made of cement or ice.

Extensions

* Have students move like athletes during the locomotion phase of the activity. This might require zigzagging, running a pattern, or moving and creating shapes.

> **teacher tip** • • •
> Start with locomotor movements with a lower intensity (e.g., sliding and galloping), and build to more intense locomotor movements (e.g., skipping and running).

* Have students freeze on different numbers of body parts.
* Have students freeze at different levels (low, high).
* Have older students perform the athlete's action in slow motion instead of freezing.

2. Fitness Activity: Moving to Music

> **review** • • •
> Point out a few student statues and ask students at what step of the Physical Activity Pyramid for Kids they would place that activity (probably step 2 or 3). Review the FITT formula for that step.

Introduction

"This week we will be working on activities from the second and third steps of the Physical Activity Pyramid for Kids. What can you tell me about activities at the second and third steps of the pyramid?" (Answers include that they are vigorous activities, they increase heart rate and breathing rate, and they improve cardiorespiratory fitness.) "*Cardio* is a Latin word that means 'heart.' When we work at steps 2 and 3 of the pyramid, we build our heart muscle and our cardiorespiratory fitness. Cardiorespiratory fitness helps us play longer at activities like skipping rope, mountain biking, and skating. Let's try coordinating our movement to music and work for the whole time the music is going in order to build our cardiorespiratory fitness."

Activity

Students will move to music in different ways, with and without a partner. Use the ideas on the Moving to Music task cards. Have students spread out in the activity area. Play some interval music (use track 7 on the music CD) and see if students can clap to the music, stomp to the music, or walk to the music. You may have to have them watch you first. Once they have the idea, introduce the activities on the Moving to Music task cards. When the music stops, have students stop and count their heartbeats or the number of times they breathe.

During a music stoppage (or over several stoppages), explain the FITT formula acronym, using the "To be fit, you must think FITT!" sign and the Physical Activity Pyramid for Kids sign.

* **Frequency:** How many times per week?
* **Intensity:** How hard? (Measured using heart rate or breathing rate.)
* **Time:** How long?
* **Type:** What activity or step of the pyramid?

Introduce the overload principle (i.e., in order to build fitness you need to do more than before), and explain that you can increase any of the first three letters of the formula (e.g., frequency, time, or intensity) to overload and build cardiorespiratory fitness, muscle fitness, or flexibility.

Grade Variations

Sixth grade: Have students count their heartbeats or breaths for 15 seconds and then figure out how many breaths or beats per minute that equates to. Have students log the intensity of their activity at various times throughout the lesson (paper and pencil). Have them determine their maximum, minimum, and average heart rate based on five measurements throughout the lesson.

Refinements

* Observe students' movements to music. Help students find the beat.
* Introduce the idea of counting "1, 2, 3 4, 1, 2, 3, 4" to the music.

Extensions

* Have students count the beat in another language.
* Have students clap on beats 1 and 3 or 2 and 4.
* Have students come up with an idea for moving to the music.
* Have students work in larger groups, moving to the music.
* Have students come up with a short routine, moving to the music.

Moving to Music activities teach about FITT.

3. Lesson Focus: Video Routine Variations

Introduction

"Last class we practiced the video routine you are performing in your classroom. Today we are going to use our creativity and make up some new moves for the routine."

? comprehension check • • •
* "What movements got your heart beating fast? Can you explain why this happens?"
* "What other changes in your body can you sense that let you know you are challenging your body?"

✪ teacher tip • • •
If your school has heart rate monitors, this would be a good week to introduce them to the class. Be sure to teach students that heart rate informs them about their activity intensity, the *I* in the FITT formula.

Activity

Practice the grade-specific video routine using the following steps.

1. Insert DVD 2 and play the video routine that is appropriate for your class:
   - Third grade: Go Aerobics Go
   - Fourth grade: Latin Aerobics
   - Fifth grade: Tinikling
   - Sixth grade: Salsaerobics

2. Have the students follow along with the routine. Observe students performing the routine and take note of the movements that give them trouble.

? comprehension check •••
Ask students to explain what the video messages are trying to tell them. Reinforce the message by using some of your own examples or having students share examples.

3. Before going through the routine again, provide a demonstration and help students with any movements that are giving them trouble. Provide tips that will help them succeed.

4. Break the students into 16 pairs, 8 groups, or 4 groups using a grouping strategy of your choice (see page 25). These group sizes allow you to pair groups together to make an even number of fewer (and larger) groups as the activity progresses.

5. Instruct the students that you will play the video routine, and their job is to make up new movements for the routine that are in time with the music.

6. Play the video routine for your class, and visit the student groups to see the movements they are trying.

7. At the end of the routine, highlight a few moves that students came up with.

8. Have each group get with another group (e.g., 16 pairs become 8 groups) and play the music again. Have the two groups share their moves with each other.

9. Allow some time for the groups to combine their moves, and play the video routine so they can practice. Visit the new groups to see how they are combining their movements.

10. Repeat steps 8 and 9 until you have two large groups or the whole class working together with new movements.

👁 observation •••
Observe student groups to see if they are working well with others in a cooperative activity.

11. Encourage students to share their new moves with their classroom teachers.

↻ review •••
Review the important behaviors associated with working cooperatively with others, or ask the students to identify and provide an example of these behaviors (e.g., listening; sharing thoughts, feelings, and equipment; providing encouragement; and making sure everyone feels included). Give examples of what this might sound or look like in the class.

4. Culminating Activity: Soda Swarm

Introduction

"Soda and sweets give us a lot of calories but few vitamins. This is why we say that soda and sweets have *empty calories*. Who can tell me what a calorie is? Right, calories are the energy in food that fuels our movement. We need calories, but we want to eat foods that have calories and vitamins. We should only eat or drink foods with empty calories once in a while. This is why we call them *treats.* In this game we are trying to get as many healthy foods as we can and few treats."

Activity

Break the class into groups of four using a grouping strategy of your choice (see page 25). Groups get together at four separate hula hoops that are spread equidistant apart in the gym or activity area. Inside each hula hoop, place 10 to 15 beanbags of various colors. When the music starts (use music CD track 5), each team tries to get as many healthy foods as possible (orange, green, red, blue, and purple beanbags) while avoiding the empty-calorie sweets (brown, black, or yellow beanbags). Specify how students move and introduce the following rules:

* Players can only carry one beanbag at a time.
* They take an empty-calorie beanbag from their hoop or anyone else's hoop and drop it off at another hoop. No one wants empty calories.
* After dropping off an empty-calorie beanbag, they can take a healthy-food beanbag back to their hoop.
* No throwing beanbags.
* Healthy beanbags are worth 1 point, and empty calories are worth −2 points.
* The first team sitting back at its hoop when the music stops gets 4 bonus points.

Grade Variations

* Third grade: Skip, gallop, or slide for safety. If moving safely, students may begin to run.
* Fourth through sixth grades: Allow students to run if they can control their bodies.

Refinements

* Ensure students move using the teacher-designated locomotor movements.
* Have teams take a minute to decide on a strategy. Share strategy ideas such as delivering empty calories to teams with lots of beanbags or dividing responsibilities (some members deliver empty calories, some collect healthy foods).

Extensions

* Have students transfer the beanbag by balancing it on the head, shoulder, or foot. If they drop the beanbag, they must go back to where they got it.
* Have students report their scores in a language other than English.
* Have students take a 15-second heart rate after each game. Start the first game with locomotor movements that are less intense (e.g., walking), and progressively increase the intensity (e.g., slide, skip, run). Reinforce the concept of intensity using this approach.

CLOSURE ROUTINE

Compliments

Have some students share compliments about their classmates.

Reflection and Review

* "What was the message in the video routine today? What does it mean to you?"

* "What do the letters *FITT* stand for in the FITT formula?"

* "What is the overload principle?"

* "What could we measure to determine whether we are overloading our cardio-respiratory system?"

* "Explain to your neighbor what an empty calorie is."

Take It Home

* "Explain to a family member what an empty calorie is."

* "Avoid eating empty calories in front of the TV. Can you avoid empty calories for one school week?"

ASSESSMENT

* **Performance check:** Observe students successfully moving to music during the fitness activity and the video routines.

* **Comprehension check:** Responses to the Comprehension Check questions and Reflection and Review questions serve as a check for student understanding.

2.2 Lesson Plan

OVERVIEW

In this lesson, students practice the Fitnessgram PACER test.

NASPE STANDARDS

* **Grades 3-5:** 1C, 2A, 2E, 4A, 4B, 4C, 4G, 4H, 4M, 5A, 5E, 5F, 5J, 6A
* **Grade 6:** 1D, 1E, 1F, 2G, 3H, 4J, 4K, 5F, 5K, 6J

(See appendix B for details.)

OBJECTIVES

Students will

* move to music using a variety of dance steps and movement patterns,
* be able to monitor exercise intensity using their heart rate, and
* assess and interpret their cardiorespiratory fitness using the PACER test.

EQUIPMENT

* CD player, 45/15 interval music (music CD tracks 5-7), continuous music (music CD tracks 9-11), and the fitness assessment track (music CD track 14)
* 8 cones
* Stage counter (e.g., volleyball scoring flip chart)
* 6 beanbags or balls (2 red, 2 yellow, and 2 green)
* 2 nets, a ball, and sport equipment (varies by sport)
* Pencils
* Pinnies (two different colors)

RESOURCES

 General

At-a-Glance PE Lesson Plan card
G3: Physical Activity Pyramid for Kids

 Wellness Week 2 → 3-6 Resources

Moving to Music activity cards

Fitnessgram PACER self-assessment worksheet

Week 2 signs file with the following signs:

* Choose activity from the pyramid. Do vigorous activity from steps 2 and 3!
* To be fit, you must think FITT!

- Avoid empty calories! Calories with few nutrients are empty calories.
- Athletes have healthy and strong hearts!

CHANTS

Leader: "I'm a witness . . ."

Students: ". . . to my fitness!"

> ★ **teacher tip • • •**
> You may not get through the whole lesson the first time through. Decide which part of the lesson is most important for your students to experience.

DELIVERING THE LESSON

1. Instant Activity: Tempo Tag

Introduction

"We have talked about drinking and eating fewer foods with empty calories like soda and sweets. Did you know that foods that have lots of fat, like french fries, donuts, and ice cream, also have lots of calories? I know these foods are tasty, but eating too much of them is bad for your heart. In fact, heart disease is often the result of eating too much fatty food, like donuts, red meat, and french fries. People who have heart disease often have heart attacks. Can anyone explain what that is? In this tag game you want to avoid the yellow fatty foods because they slow you down and make you move like a slug. You also want to avoid the red heart attacks because they stop you in your tracks."

Activity

Designate two students with green beanbags, two students with yellow beanbags, and two students with red beanbags. (You can also use balls of those colors.) Specify the locomotor movement, and on your signal, have students move in the designated area. The object is for students to try to keep moving for the whole activity.

If students are tagged by the high-fat foods (yellow beanbags), they become sluggish and must slow to a slow walk. If students get tagged by a heart stopper (red beanbags), they must freeze in place. The high-fat foods and the heart stoppers try to get everyone frozen.

The goers (green beanbags) can return the sluggish students to full speed. Frozen students need to be touched once by a goer to get to a sluggish pace and twice by two different goers to get back to full speed. If goers are tagged by high-fat foods or heart stoppers, they must balance on one leg (i.e., stork stand) for a count of five "vegetables."

Extensions

* Have students tagged by the high-fat foods (yellow beanbags) move in slow motion instead of doing a slow walk.

* Have frozen students freeze in an athletic pose or balance on one foot.

* Shrink or expand the playing area to challenge the taggers.

2. Fitness Activity: Moving to Music

Introduction

"Today we are going to continue practicing movements to music. When we are moving to music, we are moving to a musical signal. We need to use our ears to pace ourselves to this musical signal."

 comprehension check • • •
- "Can you describe some activities that require moving to signals?" (100m dash, drag racing)
- "How will you know how hard you are working?"
- "What letter in the FITT formula relates to how hard we are working?" (intensity)

Activity

Students will move to music in different ways, with and without a partner. Use the ideas on the Moving to Music task cards. Have students spread out in the activity area. Play some interval music (use tracks 5, 6, or 7 on the music CD) and see if students can clap to the music, stomp to the music, or walk to the music. You may have to have them watch you first. Once they have the idea, introduce the activities on the Moving to Music task cards. When the music stops, have students stop and count their heartbeats or the number of times they breathe.

Refinement

Observe students moving to the beat. Help students who are having trouble to find the beat.

Extensions

* Have students count the beat in another language.

* Have students move to the music using sport movements.

* Have students come up with a short routine, moving to the music.

(?) comprehension check • • •
- "In the breaks, how did you count your heartbeats?"
- "How did you count your breathing rate?"
- "Who can tell me how to convert that to beats or breaths per minute?"

3. Lesson Focus: PACER Practice

Introduction

"Who can tell me what cardiorespiratory fitness is?" (It's the health of the heart and blood vessels that distribute blood to the working muscles.) "Why is cardiorespiratory fitness important? Running is a great way to build cardiorespiratory fitness. How do we know if we have good cardiorespiratory fitness? Well, today we are going to practice a test that measures our cardiorespiratory fitness. The test we will use is called the PACER test, and it requires us to practice our pacing. Pacing is like moving to music. You need to control your speed and match it to something like a signal, another person, or a clock. Let's practice controlling our running speed using a test of cardiorespiratory fitness called the PACER."

Activity

Measure and mark two end lines 20 meters apart. Place some cones along each end line to make the lines more prominent. Put on the PACER music (music CD track 14) and have students line up along one of the designated lines. When the voice on the CD says "Start," students jog to the other line and wait. When they hear the beep, they jog back to the other line. Have students continue doing this for 10 to 15 lengths. Once students begin jogging, remind them to change directions on the beep. Encourage students to try to time their running so that they make it across the floor to the other line on or before the beep. Don't worry if they don't. Students don't get eliminated; they just turn and run when they hear the beep.

Refinements

* Stop the music if students get too far off pace. Start the music again and work on pacing (getting to the other side at the same time as the beep).

* Try to get the whole group moving together, just like moving to music.

* Have students estimate their maximum heart rate: Students aged 11 or 12 use 200 for their estimate; students aged 10 use 201; and students aged 8 or 9 use 202. Students can also use the formula $208 - (0.7 \times age)$ to calculate their maximum heart rate. Have students record their 15-second pulse rate at the end of the PACER, and have them calculate what percentage of their estimated maximum heart rate they reached during the PACER. Ask students if they reached the target zone heart rate of 130 to 180 beats per minute.

(↺) review • • •
Ask students if they remember what the overload principle is. Review how in order to build fitness, you need to do more than before. You can overload cardiorespiratory fitness by increasing the first three letters of the FITT formula—the *F*, the *I*, or the *T*.

Second Time Through

If you are teaching this lesson a second time, you may want to introduce the following activities.

Introduction

"Today we are going to perform the PACER test. Who can tell me what the PACER test is measuring? Remember that you need to control your speed. The PACER starts slow and gradually gets faster. Let's see how many stages you can do."

Activity

Have students pair up with someone they trust. One person performs the PACER while the other encourages and scores. Provide each student pair with a pencil and two Fitnessgram PACER self-assessment worksheets. Put on the PACER music and start all students along a line in the gym. Explain to students that, in the early stages, they only need to jog or walk slowly so that they arrive at the other line when the next beep sounds. Move with the students to show them the pacing. The second time you run the test, the pairs switch roles.

The first time students fail to reach the line before the beep, they reverse direction immediately and try to get back on pace. The second time they fail to reach the line before the beep, the test is over.

Students can record their PACER scores on the Fitnessgram PACER worksheet. Use the PACER chart to determine whether or not they reached the healthy fitness zone. You will need to explain to students what the healthy fitness zone is (a level of fitness associated with good health) and how they can improve their cardiorespiratory fitness to get in the healthy fitness zone (activities from steps 2 and 3 of the Physical Activity Pyramid for Kids using the FITT formula).

For more information, see the Fitnessgram test administration manual at www.fitnessgram.net/FG-Ch5-27-34.pdf.

 comprehension check · · ·
- "What sports require good cardiorespiratory fitness?"
- "What activities could you do to build cardiorespiratory fitness?"
- "What does it mean to score in the healthy fitness zone?"

PACER Lap Range for Healthy Fitness Zone

Age in years	Boys' lap range	Girls' lap range
5-9	Participation in run. Lap count standards not recommended.	Participation in run. Lap count standards not recommended.
10	23-61	7-41
11	23-72	15-41
12	32-72	15-41
13	41-83	23-51
14	41-83	23-51

Adapted from The Cooper Institute, 2005, *Fitnessgram test administration manual* (Champaign, IL: Human Kinetics).

4. Culminating Activity: Small-Sided Sports

Introduction

"We've been working on our cardiorespiratory fitness and activities from the second and third steps of the Physical Activity Pyramid for Kids. You have been practicing different moves to music and working on your cardiorespiratory fitness. Let's see if you can apply your movement skills and fitness to a sport game."

Activity

Break the class into two teams using a grouping strategy of your choice (see page 25). Have each team put on different-colored pinnies and line up along a sideline of the activity area. The first four players on each sideline move into the activity area. On your signal (music CD tracks 9-11), start the small-sided game. After 60 to 90 seconds, have the next four players on the sideline enter the area while the previous players head to the end of the line. Players on the sidelines are standing, encouraging their team, and keeping the ball in play. Sport variations include soccer, basketball, handball, speedball, ultimate (also called ultimate Frisbee), and floor hockey.

> ↻ **review** • • •
>
> "Even though we are playing a game that has two teams competing, I want to see supportive behavior and encouraging words among players on the same team and on different teams. Can someone give me an example of something you could say to encourage a player on the other team?"

Refinements

* Observe students to make sure they are in control of their bodies.
* Encourage all students to work hard for the time that they are on the court. Their hearts should be beating rapidly when their shift is over.
* Have teams take a minute to discuss strategy.
* Share strategy ideas such as passing backward when they can't move forward; making short, successful passes; and communicating with teammates.

Extensions

* Have students check their heart rate and breathing rate when their shift is over. Is their heart beating faster than at the end of last shift?
* Specify that every member on the court must touch the ball before scoring.
* Specify that two passes must be made to the sideline players before scoring.
* Have students play without saying anything. Ask them how that affects the game.
* Have sideline players make up a cheer that incorporates clapping together or moving together in unison.

CLOSURE ROUTINE

Compliments

Have some students share compliments about their classmates.

Reflection and Review

* "Give me an example of a high-calorie food that we should eat only once in a while."
* "What does it mean to pace yourself?"
* "What does the PACER test measure?"
* "What is the healthy fitness zone?"
* "At what steps of the Physical Activity Pyramid for Kids do we need to be active to improve cardiorespiratory fitness?"
* "Why is pacing so important in sport?"
* "What senses are important for playing sports?"
* "How does it feel to be encouraged by others? Discouraged by others?"

Take It Home

* "Practice your sport skills with a family member or friend."
* "The next time you play sports, take time to encourage members of your own team and the other team. Find something nice to say about your opponents."

ASSESSMENT

* **Performance check:** Observe students successfully executing the pyramid circuit movements, moving to music, pacing themselves during the PACER test, and encouraging teammates and opponents during the small-sided games.

* **Comprehension check:** Responses to the Comprehension Check questions and Reflection and Review questions serve as a check for student understanding.

Observe PACER performance and offer help with pacing.

Lesson Plan 2.3

OVERVIEW

In this lesson, students will practice a variety of sport skills at different stations.

NASPE STANDARDS

* **Grades 3-5:** 1C, 2A, 2C, 2E, 3B, 4A, 4B, 4C, 4I, 4L, 5A, 5E, 5G, 5I, 5J, 6E, 6F
* **Grade 6:** 1D, 1E, 1F, 2G, 2H, 2I, 4J, 5F, 5G, 5K, 5L, 6I, 6J, 6K

(See appendix B for details.)

OBJECTIVES

Students will

* practice the basic skills for several sports,
* demonstrate respect and kindness for their classmates by encouraging them during activity, and
* be able to correct errors in sport skills when given feedback and detect errors in skill performance and make corrections.

EQUIPMENT

* CD player, 45/15 interval music (music CD tracks 5-8), and continuous music (music CD tracks 9-11)
* Equipment for Sport Skills Circuit (depends on activities chosen)
* 6 beanbags or balls (2 red, 2 yellow, and 2 green)
* 2 nets, a ball, and sport equipment (varies by sport chosen)
* Pinnies (two different colors)

RESOURCES

 General

At-a-Glance PE Lesson Plan card

G3: Physical Activity Pyramid for Kids

 Wellness Week 2 → 3-6 Resources

Moving to Music activity cards

Sport Skills activity cards

Week 2 signs file with the following signs:

* Choose activity from the pyramid. Do vigorous activity from steps 2 and 3!
* Athletes have healthy and strong hearts!
* Expect respect . . .
* Practice your skills. You have to work at the basics to realize greatness.

CHANTS

Leader: "The heart is a muscle . . ."

Students: ". . . that allows me to hustle!"

> ⭐ **teacher tip** • • •
> You may not get through the whole lesson the first time through. Decide which part of the lesson is most important for your students to experience.

DELIVERING THE LESSON

1. Instant Activity: Tempo Tag

Introduction

"We have talked about drinking and eating fewer foods with empty calories like soda and sweets. Did you know that foods that have lots of fat, like french fries, donuts, and ice cream, also have lots of calories? I know these foods are tasty, but eating too much of them is bad for your heart. In fact, heart disease is often the result of eating too much fatty food, like donuts, red meat, and french fries. People who have heart disease often have heart attacks. Can anyone explain what that is? In this tag game you want to avoid the yellow fatty foods because they slow you down and make you move like a slug. You also want to avoid the red heart attacks because they stop you in your tracks."

Activity

Designate two students with green beanbags, two students with yellow beanbags, and two students with red beanbags. (You can also use balls of those colors.) Specify the locomotor movement, and on your signal, have students move in the designated area. The object is for students to try to keep moving for the whole activity.

If students are tagged by the high-fat foods (yellow beanbags), they become sluggish and must slow to a slow walk. If students get tagged by a heart stopper (red beanbags), they must freeze in place. The high-fat foods and the heart stoppers try to get everyone frozen.

The goers (green beanbags) can return the sluggish students to full speed. Frozen students need to be touched once by a goer to get to a sluggish pace and twice by two different goers to get back to full speed. If goers are tagged by high-fat foods or heart stoppers, they must balance on one leg (i.e., stork stand) for a count of five "vegetables."

Extensions

✳ Have students tagged by the high-fat foods (yellow beanbags) move in slow motion instead of doing a slow walk.

✳ Have frozen students freeze in an athletic pose or balance on one foot.

✳ Shrink or expand the playing area to challenge the taggers.

2. Fitness Activity: Moving to Music

Introduction

"You have been getting very good at moving to music. Practice has really paid off. Today I am going to challenge you to move to the music for longer than you have before. Pick up the beat and start moving as soon as you can. Try to move to the beat for the whole time the music is playing."

Activity

Students will move to music in different ways, with and without a partner. Use the ideas on the Moving to Music task cards and solicit some ideas from students. Use a longer-interval music track (music CD track 5, 6, 7, or 8).

Refinement

Observe students moving to the beat. Help students who are having trouble finding the beat.

Extensions

✳ Have students count the beat in a language other than English.

✳ Have students move to the music using sport movements.

✳ Have students come up with a short routine for moving to the music.

 comprehension check • • •

• "Can you describe some activities that require moving to signals?" (100m dash, drag racing)

• "How will you know how hard you are working?"

• "What letter in the FITT formula relates to how hard we are working?" (I = intensity)

• "In the breaks, how will you count your heartbeats? Your breathing rate?"

• "Who can tell me how to convert that to beats or breaths per minute?"

• "What do beats per minute and breaths per minute tell us about activity? Can you relate your answer to the FITT formula?" (intensity or how hard we are working)

3. Lesson Focus: Sport Skills Circuit

Introduction

"What kinds of activities are found at steps 2 and 3 of the Physical Activity Pyramid for Kids? That's right, vigorous aerobics and vigorous sports and recreation. Today we are going to practice some basic skills that are used in most sports. Practicing the basics gives us a good foundation to learn more advanced skills. The best figure skaters, rock climbers, and football players have learned the basics in their sports. When learning the basics, we want to focus on moving in control. This might mean you will have to move slowly to start. Let's get to it!"

Activity

Split the class into four groups using a grouping strategy of your choice (see page 25). Have each group move to a station and look at the signs. When the music starts, the students will perform the activities at each sign. See Sport Skills activity cards for the activities.

> **review** • • •
> Explain to students that everyone has different abilities and skill levels. Some people are good at piano, some at soccer. Some people can sing, some people are math stars, and others are soccer stars. Remind students that they need to be supportive of each other by encouraging everyone to do their best. Everyone's best is different, and that is OK.

Refinements

Observe students at the various stations. Provide feedback to help them perform the skills correctly.

Extensions

* Have students count how many successful repetitions of a skill they can do at a station.

* Have students count the number of successful repetitions in a language other than English.

> **observation** • • •
> Observe students' body language and verbal communication. Look for positive body language and encouragement. Model this behavior for your students.

4. Culminating Activity: Small-Sided Sports

Introduction

"We've been working on our cardiorespiratory fitness and activities from the second and third steps of the Physical Activity Pyramid for Kids. You have been practicing different moves to music and working on your cardiorespiratory fitness. Let's see if you can apply your movement skills and fitness to a sport game."

Activity

Break the class into two teams using a grouping strategy of your choice (see page 25). Have each team put on different-colored pinnies and line up along a sideline of the activity area. The first four players on each sideline move into the activity area.

On your signal (music CD tracks 9-11), start the small-sided game. After 60 to 90 seconds, have the next four players on the sideline enter the area while the previous players head to the end of the line. Players on the sidelines are standing, encouraging their team, and keeping the ball in play. Sport variations include soccer, basketball, handball, speedball, ultimate (also called ultimate Frisbee), and floor hockey.

review • • •

"Even though we are playing a game that has two teams competing, I want to see supportive behavior and encouraging words among players on the same team and on different teams. Can someone give me an example of something you could say to encourage a player on the other team?"

comprehension check • • •

• Have students explain the overload principle. Encourage them to apply the overload principle by working harder on each shift in the small-sided games.

• Check to see if students can describe how they will determine how hard (intensity) they are working (heart rate, breathing rate, and body temperature increase).

Refinements

Encourage students to work hard when they are on the court. Their hearts should be beating rapidly when their shift is over.

Extensions

✳ Have each team come up with a cheer for their opposition.

✳ Have students check their heart rate and breathing rate when their shift is over. Is their heart beating faster than at the end of last shift?

CLOSURE ROUTINE

Compliments

Have some students share compliments about their opponents during the culminating activity.

Reflection and Review

✳ "What does it mean to pace yourself?"

✳ "What movement skills in moving to music did you use in the game?"

✳ "Why is pacing so important in sports?"

✳ "What senses are important for playing sports?"

✳ "At what steps of the Physical Activity Pyramid for Kids do we need to be active to improve cardiorespiratory fitness?"

✳ "How does it feel to be encouraged by others? Discouraged by others?"

Take It Home

✳ "Practice your sport skills with a family member or friend."

✳ "The next time you play sports, take time to encourage members of your own team and the other team. Find something nice to say about your opponents."

ASSESSMENT

✳ **Performance check:** Observe students successfully executing the basic sport skills, and listen to them encourage group members at each station.

✳ **Comprehension check:** Responses to the Comprehension Check questions and Reflection and Review questions serve as a check for student understanding.

The Sport Skills Circuit and Small-Sided Sports activities promote skill learning.

EXTRA ACTIVITIES AND RESOURCES

If your school has physical education more than three times per week, consider delivering some of the lesson plans a second time through or consider using some of the extra activities and resources in appendix A of this book (see page 245). You can also use some of the additional activities described in appendix A of the classroom guides. Ask your wellness coordinator for access to these guides.

WELLNESS WEEK 3

Fitness for Life Elementary School

These lesson plans provide students with a variety of experiences, including exploring activities from steps 4 and 5 of the Physical Activity Pyramid for Kids (e.g., yoga), moving to music, practicing the Fitnessgram muscle fitness and flexibility tests, and learning about fitness and nutrition concepts such as the importance of a warm-up and cool-down, the FITT formula, the overload principle, and the role of protein in the diet. In Wellness Week 3, the activity theme is "muscle fitness and flexibility exercises," the nutrition theme for grades 3-5 is "protein power," and the nutrition theme for grade 6 is "protein is important." These themes are reinforced through activities, signs, and chants. Take time to look through the lesson plans for Wellness Week 3 and determine what objectives are most important and which activities you will use to meet those objectives. Table 3.3 summarizes the Wellness Week 3 activities for the physical education lesson plans.

For Wellness Week 3, the lesson plans include the following:

- A warm-up lesson plan to be used during the week before Wellness Week 3. The same basic warm-up lesson plan is used for grades 3 through 6, but the Lesson Focus (practicing the video routine) is different for each grade.

Table 3.3 Summary of Wellness Week 3 Activities

Lesson Plan	Instant Activity	Fitness Activity	Lesson Focus	Culminating Activity
Warm-Up 3 (week before Wellness Week 3)	Partner Pathways	Yoga Circuit	Video Routine Practice: 3: Tic Tac Toe 3 4: Tic Tac Toe 4 5: Tic Tac Toe 5 6: Tic Tac Toe 6	Cool-Down
3.1	Partner Pathways	Yoga Circuit	Video Routine Variations: 3: Tic Tac Toe 3 4: Tic Tac Toe 4 5: Tic Tac Toe 5 6: Tic Tac Toe 6	Cool-Down
3.2	Body Shapes	Yoga Circuit	Muscle Fitness and Flexibility	Cool-Down
3.3	Body Shapes	Yoga Circuit	Power Yoga	Food Frenzy

- Three lesson plans (3.1, 3.2, and 3.3) to be used during Wellness Week 3. The same basic lesson plan is used for grades 3 through 6, with grade-specific variations, refinements, and extensions for some of the activities.

- Extra activity ideas for schools that have physical education class more than three days a week are provided in appendix A.

Eat Well Wednesday

Each Wednesday, known as Eat Well Wednesday, all teachers and staff are encouraged to emphasize nutrition. The wellness coordinator might plan special schoolwide events. During Wellness Week 3, the nutrition event is a yogurt bar in the cafeteria. If you have a physical education lesson on Eat Well Wednesday, place an emphasis on nutrition signs and messages.

Get Fit Friday

Each Friday, known as Get Fit Friday, a schoolwide event focusing on physical activity will be planned. (If your school participates in this event, your wellness coordinator will provide you with more details.) The Get Fit Friday activities are called TEAM Time activities (TEAM stands for Together Everyone Achieves More). During Wellness Week 3, this activity is called Little Kids Lead. Your wellness coordinator and students from kindergarten, first grade, and second grade will lead all students in three activities. First, kindergarten students will lead an activity called We Get Fit; then first-grade students will lead an activity called CYIM Fit; and finally, second-grade students will lead an activity called Wave It. These activities will have been learned in physical education or in the classroom earlier in the week.

Newsletter

The CD-ROM contains a newsletter for use during Wellness Week 3. It is recommended that your school's wellness coordinator edit and distribute the newsletter. Alternatively, you (or the classroom teachers) can do it. Just open the appropriate file, follow the instructions to edit and customize the newsletter, and send printed copies home with students or send them electronically via e-mail. Remind students to talk to their families about Wellness Week and the information in the newsletter.

 **Wellness Week 3 → Newsletter**

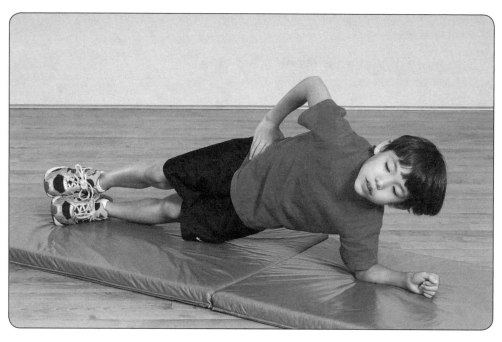

The activity theme for Wellness Week 3 is muscle fitness and flexibility exercises (steps 4 and 5 of the Physical Activity Pyramid for Kids).

Warm-Up Lesson Plan 3

OVERVIEW

In this lesson, conducted during the week before Wellness Week 3, students will learn the grade-specific video routine that they will perform in their classroom during Wellness Week 3. You can aid the classroom teachers by teaching these routines in advance to make it easier for both students and teachers and to increase the chances that the classroom teachers will do the video routines in their classrooms.

NASPE STANDARDS

* **Grades 3-5:** 1A, 1B, 2E, 4D, 4E, 4H, 5B, 6A
* **Grade 6:** 1D, 1F, 2G, 2H, 3G, 4J, 4M, 5F, 5L, 6J

(See appendix B for details.)

OBJECTIVES

Students will

* explain the importance of a warm-up and cool-down,
* demonstrate a variety of yoga poses (asanas), and
* practice moving to music and moving together with their classmates.

EQUIPMENT

* CD player and 30/15 interval music (music CD track 3)
* TV, DVD player, and DVD 1 (Instructional Routines)
* 6 to 10 cones
* Soft mats for yoga and cool-down activities (optional)

RESOURCES

 General

At-a-Glance PE Lesson Plan card

G3: Physical Activity Pyramid for Kids

Wellness Week 3 → 3-6 Resources

Yoga Circuit activity cards

Week 3 signs file with the following signs:

- Choose activity from the pyramid. Do muscle fitness exercises (step 4) and flexibility exercises (step 5)!
- Before you hustle, warm up your muscles! To avoid injury during activity, it is important to warm up your muscles.

CHANTS

Leader: "Namaste." (Pronounced *nam-a-stay;* it means "The light in me honors the light in you.")

Students: "Namaste."

> ⭐ **teacher tip** • • •
> You may not get through the whole lesson the first time through. Decide which part of the lesson is most important for your students to experience.

DELIVERING THE LESSON

1. Instant Activity: Partner Pathways

Introduction

"Today we are going to work on flexibility and muscle fitness. Can anyone tell me what flexibility is? Right, it's the ability of your body parts to move in a variety of directions. To become more flexible, you need to stretch, but you cannot stretch cold muscles. Cold muscles don't stretch as far as warm muscles. Let's warm up our muscles to prepare for our yoga routine."

Activity

Have students get with a partner using a grouping technique of your choice (see page 25). Specify a locomotor movement (e.g., slide, run, skip) and, on your signal, have one partner lead while the other follows. Freeze students, specify a new locomotor movement, and specify a movement pathway. Options include curved lines, straight lines, zigzags, triangular lines, and so on.

Refinements

- ✳ Make sure all students move in space without touching others.
- ✳ Have students match their partner's movements as closely as possible.

Extensions

- ✳ Have students move at different distances from their partner (e.g., near and far).

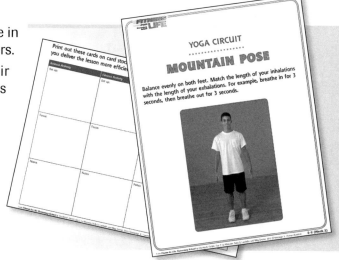

✳ Encourage students to move at different heights (e.g., low and high).

✳ Encourage students to change their speed and have their partner match their speed.

2. Fitness Activity: Yoga Circuit

Introduction

"Yoga is an individual activity that has been done for thousands of years. It's a great activity for building flexibility and muscle fitness. It can also help us relax and quiet our minds. Yoga poses are called *asanas,* and we will be performing several asanas today. Your focus should be on forming stable poses that you can hold for the length of the station. Also, pay attention to the thoughts that come into your mind during the poses."

Activity

Place 6 to 10 Yoga Circuit activity cards on cones to create stations. You may want to supply soft mats at each. Break the class into 6 to 10 groups using a grouping strategy of your choice (see page 25). Place a group at each yoga station. Have them read the card and slowly move into the pose when the music starts (use music CD track 3). When the music stops, have students move quietly to the next station and start getting into the pose.

Refinements

✳ Instruct students to remain quiet during the whole session and concentrate on stable poses.

✳ Encourage students to readjust their poses to make them more stable and comfortable.

> **? comprehension check** • • •
> "What are some reasons for warming up our muscles before activity?" (increasing range of motion, preparing them for activity by increasing blood flow, protection from injury)

> **↺ review** • • •
> "Remember the Physical Activity Pyramid for Kids? Muscle fitness exercises are at step 4 and flexibility exercises are at step 5. Notice that the FITT formula is different from moderate physical activities at step 1, vigorous aerobics at step 2, and vigorous sports and recreation at step 3."

Grade Variations

Sixth grade: Have students use a mirror or work with partners to create precise poses. Have students focus on the accurate position of the body to create precise poses. You can have them record their strengths and weaknesses for each pose so they can focus their practice and monitor their improvement over the week.

3-6 • WEEK 3
WARM-UP 3

> **↻ review •••**
> Explain to students that everyone has different body shapes, abilities, and skill levels. Yoga is an individual activity and not a competition. Students should work slowly into the poses (asanas) and avoid pushing their bodies to pain or discomfort. Everyone's level of flexibility and muscle fitness is different, and that is OK.

3. Lesson Focus: Video Routine Practice

Introduction

"Next week is Wellness Week 3. During Wellness Week 3, we will be learning about physical activity, fitness, and healthy nutrition. Today we are going to practice the video routine you will be performing in your classroom during Wellness Week 3. This video routine is fun and will challenge you to move to music."

Activity

Introduce and practice the grade-specific video routine using the following steps.

1. Insert DVD 1 and play the instructional routine that is appropriate for your class:
   - Third grade: Tic Tac Toe 3
   - Fourth grade: Tic Tac Toe 4
   - Fifth grade: Tic Tac Toe 5
   - Sixth grade: Tic Tac Toe 6

> **✦ teacher tip •••**
> The Tic Tac Toe video routines show three dancers performing and two tic-tac-toe boards in the background that provide cues for student movements. Encourage students to watch the dancers' movements first. Once they see the dancers' movements, they may want to watch the boards to cue their own movements. Encourage your students to choose one or the other. Watching dancers' movements and the board cues at the same time is not the best strategy.

2. Have the students follow along with the routine. Observe students performing the routine and take note of the movements that give them trouble.
3. Before going through the routine again, provide a demonstration and help students with any movements that are giving them trouble. Provide tips that will help them succeed.
4. Play the routine again and compliment students on any improvements.
5. Remind students that next week is Wellness Week 3, and they will perform this routine every day in their classrooms next week.

Refinements

Observe the students' movements and listen to the reciting of the words. Have students focus on staying with the music and moving together.

4. Culminating Activity: Cool-Down

Introduction

"Just as it is important to warm up your muscles before you stretch or compete, it is equally important to cool down after activity. Cool-downs help your muscles recover from activity by removing waste products that build up during exercise and by preventing blood from pooling in leg muscles."

Activity

Have students walk around the area quietly. Have them freeze. Honor them with a "Namaste" and perform the following cool-down sequence to music (use music CD track 3).

1. "Standing in place, stretch as high as you can, and relax."
2. "Swing your arms and upper body gently back and forth, letting your body guide the movements."
3. "Give yourself a hug, swing your arms out wide, and swing them back to hug yourself, switching the top arm each time."
4. "Standing in place, stretch as high as you can, and relax."
5. "Move to the ground, lie on your back, hug your knees to your chest, and then extend them as long as you can." (repeat)
6. "Lie quietly on your back with your eyes closed and pay attention to your thoughts."

Extensions

✳ Add in some of your own or students' cool-down activities.
✳ Invite students to bring in some cool-down (mellow) music.

CLOSURE ROUTINE

Compliments

Have some students share compliments about their classmates.

Reflection and Review

✳ "At what step of the Physical Activity Pyramid for Kids would you place yoga?"
✳ "What new sensations did you feel when performing the yoga poses?"
✳ "Share your favorite pose with your neighbor."
✳ "How did yoga make you feel?"
✳ "What thoughts came into your mind during quiet relaxation?"

Take It Home

✳ "Perform some yoga poses during commercial breaks with your family members."
✳ "Yoga can be done almost anywhere with no equipment. Warm your muscles up and perform yoga in your favorite place. Honor your favorite place with a 'Namaste.'"

ASSESSMENT

✳ **Performance check:** Observe students successfully executing the yoga circuit movements and moving to music during the video routines.
✳ **Comprehension check:** Responses to the Comprehension Check questions and Reflection and Review questions serve as a check for student understanding.

Flexibility exercises are on step 5 of the Physical Activity Pyramid for Kids.

3 WELLNESS WEEK

3.1 Lesson Plan

OVERVIEW

In this lesson, students will practice the Wellness Week 2 video routine and have an opportunity to create and add new movements to the routine. Students will also practice yoga poses.

NASPE STANDARDS

* **Grades 3-5:** 1A, 1B, 2E, 4D, 4E, 4I, 4L, 5A, 5B, 5E, 5F, 5H, 6A, 6B, 6D, 6E, 6F
* **Grade 6:** 1D, 1F, 2G, 2H, 2I, 3G, 3I, 4J, 5F, 5G, 5L, 6I, 6J, 6K

(See appendix B for details.)

OBJECTIVES

Students will

* explain the importance of a warm-up and cool-down,
* work cooperatively to create a dance routine to music, and
* practice and refine a variety of yoga poses (asanas).

EQUIPMENT

* CD player and 30/15 interval music (music CD track 3)
* TV, DVD player, and DVD 2 (Activity Routines)
* 6 to 10 cones
* Soft mats for yoga and cool-down activities (optional)

RESOURCES

 General

At-a-Glance PE Lesson Plan card

G3: Physical Activity Pyramid for Kids

 Wellness Week 3 → 3-6 Resources

Yoga Circuit activity cards

Week 3 signs file with the following signs:

* Choose activity from the pyramid. Do muscle fitness exercises (step 4) and flexibility exercises (step 5)!
* Before you hustle, warm up your muscles! To avoid injury during activity, it is important to warm up your muscles.

CHANTS

Leader: "Namaste."

Students: "Namaste."

DELIVERING THE LESSON

1. Instant Activity: Partner Pathways

Introduction

"Today we are going to continue working on flexibility and muscle fitness activities. At what steps of the Physical Activity Pyramid for Kids are these activities? Last time we defined *flexibility* as the ability of our body parts to move in a variety of directions. To be more specific, it is the range of motion that a body part has. Can someone show me a body part that has a large range of motion?

"Now, who can tell me what muscle fitness is? Muscle fitness is two things—muscular endurance and strength. Muscular endurance is the ability of a muscle to work for a long time. A good example is shoveling. You don't have to lift a lot of weight, but you might have to shovel hundreds of scoops. Strength is the ability of a muscle to move heavy weights. A good example is moving furniture. You need a lot of strength to move a fridge, but you probably only have to move it for a short time. Flexibility and muscular endurance and strength activities should not be performed with cold muscles. So, let's warm up our muscles to prepare for our yoga routine."

Activity

Have students get with a partner using a grouping technique of your choice (see page 25). Specify a locomotor movement (e.g., slide, run, skip) and, on your signal, have

one partner lead while the other follows. Freeze students, specify a new locomotor movement, and specify a movement pathway. Options include curved lines, straight lines, zigzags, triangular lines, and so on.

Refinements

* Make sure all students move in space without touching others.
* Have students match their partner's movements as closely as possible.

> **review** • • •
>
> "Do you remember the overload principle? This is a training principle that tells us we need to do more than before in order to increase fitness. What activities could we do to overload our bodies and build flexibility? Muscular endurance? Strength?" Have students provide activity examples for each part of fitness and link the activities to the Physical Activity Pyramid for Kids.

Extensions

* Have students move at different distances from their partner (e.g., near and far).
* Encourage students to move at different heights (e.g., low and high).
* Encourage students to change their speed and have their partner match their speed.

2. Fitness Activity: Yoga Circuit

Introduction

"Yoga is an individual activity that has been done for thousands of years. It's a great activity for building flexibility and muscle fitness. It can also help us relax and quiet our minds. Yoga poses are called *asanas,* and we will be performing several asanas today. Your focus should be on forming stable poses that you can hold for the length of the station. Also, pay attention to the thoughts that come into your mind during the poses."

Activity

Place 6 to 10 Yoga Circuit activity cards on cones to create stations. You may want to supply soft mats at each. Break the class into 6 to 10 groups using a grouping strategy of your choice (see page 25). Place a group at each yoga station. Have them read the card and slowly move into the pose when the music starts (use music CD track 3). When the music stops, have students move quietly to the next station and start getting into the pose.

> **review** • • •
>
> "Remember, yoga is not a competition. Work on improving your ability to make stable and accurate poses. Match the pictures on the activity cards."

Refinements

* Instruct students to remain quiet during the whole session and concentrate on stable poses.
* Encourage students to readjust their poses to make them more stable and comfortable.

Extensions

* Have students create yoga activity cards. Have them identify the name of the pose and the muscles that it targets.

* Sixth grade: Have students use a mirror or work with partners to create precise poses. Have students focus on the accurate position of body to create precise poses. You can have them record strengths and weaknesses of each pose so they can focus their practice and monitor their improvement over the week.

3. Lesson Focus: Video Routine Variations

Introduction

"Last class we practiced the video routine you are performing in your classroom. Today we are going to use our creativity and make up some new moves for the routine."

Activity

Practice the grade-specific video routine using the following steps.

1. Insert DVD 2 and play the video routine that is appropriate for your class:
   - Third grade: Tic Tac Toe 3
   - Fourth grade: Tic Tac Toe 4
   - Fifth grade: Tic Tac Toe 5
   - Sixth grade: Tic Tac Toe 6

2. Have the students follow along with the routine. Observe students performing the routine and take note of the movements that give them trouble.

> **(?) comprehension check • • •**
> Ask students to explain what the video messages are trying to tell them. Reinforce the message by using some of your own examples or having students share examples.

3. Before going through the routine again, provide a demonstration and help students with any movements that are giving them trouble. Provide tips that will help them succeed.

4. Break the students into 16 pairs, 8 groups, or 4 groups using a grouping strategy of your choice (see page 25). These group sizes allow you to pair groups together to make an even number of fewer (and larger) groups as the activity progresses.

5. Instruct the students that you will play the video routine, and their job is to make up new movements for the routine that are in time with the music.

6. Play the video routine for your class, and visit the student groups to see the movements they are trying.

7. At the end of the routine, highlight a few moves that students came up with.

8. Have each group get with another group (e.g., 16 pairs become 8 groups) and play the music again. Have the two groups share their moves with each other.

9. Allow some time for the groups to combine their moves, and play the video routine so they can practice. Visit the new groups to see how they are combining their movements.

> **(◎) observation • • •**
> Observe student groups to see if they are working well with others in a cooperative activity.

> **teacher tip • • •**
> Explain the importance of working with others. Identify the important elements of working with others, such as listening; sharing thoughts, feelings, and equipment; providing encouragement; and making sure everyone feels included. Provide examples of what this might sound or look like in the class.

10. Repeat steps 8 and 9 until you have two large groups or the whole class working together with new movements.

11. Encourage students to share their new moves with their classroom teachers.

4. Culminating Activity: Cool-Down

Introduction

"Just as it is important to warm up your muscles before you stretch or compete, it is equally important to cool down after activity. Cool-downs help your muscles recover from activity."

> **?** **comprehension check • • •**
> "Who can tell me why we perform a cool-down activity?"

Activity

Have students walk around the area quietly. Have them freeze. Honor them with a "Namaste" and perform the following cool-down sequence (soft music is nice for this).

1. "Standing in place, stretch as high as you can, and relax."
2. "Swing your arms and upper body gently back and forth, letting your body guide the movements."
3. "Give yourself a hug, swing your arms out wide, and swing them back to hug yourself, switching the top arm each time."
4. "Standing in place, stretch as high as you can, and relax."
5. "Move to the ground, lie on your back, hug your knees to your chest, and then extend them as long as you can." (repeat)
6. "Lie quietly on your back with your eyes closed and pay attention to your thoughts."

Extensions

✳ Add in some of your own or students' cool-down activities.
✳ Invite students to supply some cool-down music.

CLOSURE ROUTINE

Compliments

Have some students share compliments about their classmates.

Reflection and Review

* "Who can tell me why we perform a warm-up?"

* "Who can tell me why we perform a cool-down?"

* "What new sensations did you feel when performing the yoga poses?"

* "Share your favorite pose with your neighbor."

* "How did yoga make you feel?"

* "What thoughts came into your mind during quiet relaxation?"

* "How did holding the poses longer affect you?"

Take It Home

* "Perform some yoga poses during commercial breaks with your family members."

* "Yoga can be done almost anywhere with no equipment. Warm your muscles up and perform yoga in your favorite place. Honor your favorite place with a 'Namaste.'"

ASSESSMENT

* **Performance check:** Observe students executing the yoga poses correctly, moving to music, and working cooperatively with each other.

* **Comprehension check:** Responses to the Comprehension Check questions and Reflection and Review questions serve as a check for student understanding.

Yoga poses require flexibility and muscle fitness.

3.2 Lesson Plan

OVERVIEW

In this lesson, students will have an opportunity to warm up, perform yoga poses, and explore the various Fitnessgram muscle fitness and flexibility self-assessments.

NASPE STANDARDS

* **Grades 3-5:** 2E, 2F, 3B, 4C, 4D, 4E, 4G, 4H, 4I, 5A, 5E, 6A, 6D
* **Grade 6:** 1D, 2G, 2H, 2I, 3G, 3H, 3I, 4J, 4K, 4L, 4M, 5F, 5L, 6I, 6J

(See appendix B for details.)

OBJECTIVES

Students will

* demonstrate a variety of yoga poses (asanas),
* practice the Fitnessgram muscle fitness and flexibility tests, and
* be able to explain the overload principle and how to manipulate the FITT formula to apply this principle.

EQUIPMENT

* CD player, 30/15 interval music (music CD track 3), and fitness assessment track (music CD track 15)
* Sit-and-reach measuring stations (see the Fitnessgram page of the **FFL: Elementary** Web site at www.fitnessforlife.org for details)
* Tape and a measuring tape for curl-up station
* Soft mats for curl-up station, yoga, and cool-down activities (optional)
* Pencils

RESOURCES

 General

At-a-Glance PE Lesson Plan card

G3: Physical Activity Pyramid for Kids

 Wellness Week 3 → 3-6 Resources

Yoga Circuit activity cards

Fitnessgram muscle fitness and flexibility self-assessment worksheet

Week 3 signs file with the following signs:

- Choose activity from the pyramid. Do muscle fitness exercises (step 4) and flexibility exercises (step 5)!
- Before you hustle, warm up your muscles! To avoid injury during activity, it is important to warm up your muscles.

CHANTS

Leader: "Muscles need more!"

Students: "More than before!"

> ⭐ **teacher tip** • • •
> You may not get through the whole lesson the first time through. Decide which part of the lesson is most important for your students to experience.

DELIVERING THE LESSON

1. Instant Activity: Body Shapes

Introduction

"Today we are going to practice some tests of muscle fitness and flexibility. However, before we do anything, we need to warm up our muscles. Let's warm our muscles by moving and making shapes with our bodies."

Activity

Have students move in the designated area using a specified locomotor movement. Freeze the students and have them make a shape with their bodies while standing (e.g., stork, rocket, bird, plane). Have them hold this position for at least five seconds. Specify a new locomotor movement and a new shape upon freezing (e.g., letter, fruit, insect). Point out interesting shapes and challenge students to be creative.

Refinements

- ✳ Make sure all students move in space without touching others.
- ✳ Have them be as still as possible when they make their shapes.

Extensions

✳ Encourage students to make their shapes at different heights (e.g., low and high).

✳ Encourage students to make tall and small shapes using their bodies.

✳ Have students identify their shapes in languages other than English.

 comprehension check • • •

- "Why is it important to warm up your muscles?"
- "What are the two kinds of muscle fitness?" (muscular endurance and strength)
- "Who can explain the difference between the two?"

2. Fitness Activity: Yoga Circuit

Introduction

"Today I am going to challenge you to work a little longer at each yoga station. What part of the FITT formula am I manipulating?" (Time.) "What training principle does this relate to?" (Overload.) "Let's build some muscular endurance and flexibility at the stations today."

Activity

Place 6 to 10 Yoga Circuit activity cards on cones to create stations. You may want to supply soft mats at each. Break the class into 6 to 10 groups using a grouping strategy of your choice (see page 25). Place a group at each yoga station. Have them read the card and slowly move into the pose when the music starts (use music CD track 3). When the music stops, have students move quietly to the next station and start getting into the pose.

Refinements

✳ Move around the area and help students improve their poses by giving specific feedback.

✳ Encourage students to hold their poses for the full time.

✳ Instruct students to remain quiet during the whole session and concentrate on stable poses.

✳ Encourage students to readjust their poses to make them more stable and comfortable.

Extension

✳ Place two similar poses at each station and allow students to transition between poses.

✳ Sixth grade: Have students use a mirror or work with partners to create precise poses. Have students focus on the accurate position of the body to create precise poses. You can have them record their strengths and weaknesses for each pose so they can focus their practice and monitor their improvement over the week.

3. Lesson Focus: Muscle Fitness and Flexibility

Introduction

"How do you know if you have enough flexibility or muscle fitness for good health? That's right, we have to measure our flexibility or muscle fitness with a test. Students all over the United States take Fitnessgram tests to see if their fitness is in the healthy fitness zone. Can anyone remember what the healthy fitness zone is? It's the amount of flexibility, muscular fitness, or cardiorespiratory fitness you need for good health. Today we are going to practice some of the tests that can assess our muscle fitness and flexibility."

Activity

Walk students through the various stations and demonstrate each Fitnessgram muscle fitness and flexibility self-assessment activity. Provide each student with a Fitnessgram muscle fitness and flexibility self-assessment worksheet and a pencil. Have students partner up with someone they trust. Place three or four pairs at each of the five stations: back-saver sit-and-reach, 90-degree push-ups, curl-ups, trunk lift, and shoulder stretch. Move students through each station using start and stop signals of your choice. Detailed instructions for the setup and administration of these tests are available at the Fitnessgram page of the **FFL: Elementary** Web site at www. fitnessforlife.org.

 review • • •

"Who can explain what *private* or *personal* means? Fitness assessments are personal and private information. It is not OK to share someone else's personal fitness scores without permission. Demonstrate integrity and trustworthiness by keeping your partner's fitness scores private."

Second Time Through

If you are teaching this lesson a second time, you may want to introduce the following activities.

Introduction

"Last class we practiced some tests that can assess our muscle fitness and flexibility. Once we know our fitness levels and what our favorite activities are, we can determine if we need to improve our fitness. In order to improve our muscle fitness and flexibility, we have to overload our muscles with flexibility or muscle fitness activities (i.e., we have to do more than before). Let's learn how to score our own fitness tests so we can decide what parts of fitness we want to work on."

Activities

Walk students through the various stations and demonstrate each activity. Have students partner up with someone they trust. Place three or four pairs at each of the five stations: back-saver sit-and-reach, 90-degree push-ups, curl-ups, trunk lift, and shoulder stretch. Detailed instructions for the setup and administration of these tests are available at the Fitnessgram page of the **FFL: Elementary** Web site at www. fitnessforlife.org.

4. Culminating Activity: Cool-Down

Introduction

"Thanks for working so hard on your fitness tests. Let's perform a cool-down to help your muscles recover from your activity."

Activity

Have students walk around the area quietly. Have them freeze. Honor them with a "Namaste" and perform the following cool-down sequence (soft music is nice for this).

1. "Standing in place, stretch as high as you can, and relax."
2. "Swing your arms and upper body gently back and forth, letting your body guide the movements."
3. "Give yourself a hug, swing your arms out wide, and swing them back to hug yourself, switching the top arm each time."
4. "Standing in place, stretch as high as you can, and relax."
5. "Move to the ground, lie on your back, hug your knees to your chest, and then extend them as long as you can." (repeat)
6. "Lie quietly on your back with your eyes closed and pay attention to your thoughts."

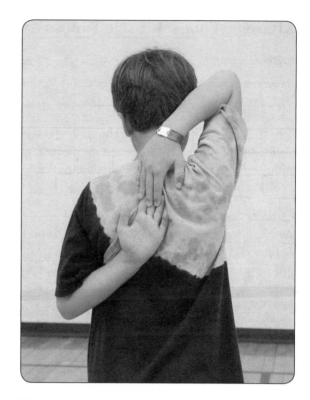

The zipper stretch is a flexibility test for the shoulders that can be done at home.

Extension

Add in some of your own or the students' cool-down activities.

CLOSURE ROUTINE

Compliments

Have some students share compliments about their classmates.

Reflection and Review

* "What Fitnessgram test did you like to perform?"
* "Can someone tell me what the shoulder test measures? Other tests?"
* "What type of fitness does your favorite activity require?"
* "Did you improve any of your muscle fitness or flexibility scores?"
* "Which score is more important for your favorite activity?"
* "What thoughts came into your mind during quiet relaxation?"

Take It Home

* "Show some family members one of the tests you performed today and see how they do. The shoulder stretch and push-ups can be done anywhere."

* "Yoga can be done almost anywhere with no equipment. Warm your muscles up and perform yoga in your favorite place. Honor your favorite place with a 'Namaste.'"

ASSESSMENT

* **Performance check:** Observe students successfully executing the Fitnessgram self-assessments tests and scoring them properly.

* **Comprehension check:** Responses to the Comprehension Check questions and Reflection and Review questions serve as a check for student understanding.

3 WELLNESS WEEK

3.3 Lesson Plan

OVERVIEW

In this lesson, students engage in muscle fitness activities and yoga poses in a circuit.

NASPE STANDARDS

* **Grades 3-5:** 1C, 2E, 3B, 4A, 4C, 4D, 4I, 4L, 6D
* **Grade 6:** 1D, 2G, 2H, 2I, 3G, 3I, 4J, 5F, 5L, 6K

(See appendix B for details.)

OBJECTIVES

Students will

* be active for at least 50 percent of class time,
* demonstrate a variety of yoga poses (asanas) and muscle fitness poses, and
* identify foods that provide the body with protein.

EQUIPMENT AND RESOURCES

* CD player, 30/15 interval music (music CD track 3), 30/30 interval music (music CD track 4), and 45/15 interval music (music CD tracks 5, 6, 7, or 8)
* Soft mats for yoga and cool-down activities (optional)
* 10 to 12 cones
* Pinny for each student (scarves or flag football flags work, too)

RESOURCES

 General

At-a-Glance PE Lesson Plan card

G3: Physical Activity Pyramid for Kids

G4: MyPyramid for Kids

 Wellness Week 3 → 3-6 Resources

Yoga Circuit activity cards

Muscle Fitness Poses activity cards

Week 3 signs file with the following signs:

- Choose activity from the pyramid. Do muscle fitness exercises (step 4) and flexibility exercises (step 5)!
- Before you hustle, warm up your muscles! To avoid injury during activity, it is important to warm up your muscles.
- Fruits, veggies, eggs, and beans make you strong, moving machines . . .

CHANTS

Leader: "Fruits, veggies, eggs, and beans . . ."

Students: ". . . make us strong moving machines!"

> ⭐ **teacher tip • • •**
> You may not get through the whole lesson the first time through. Decide which part of the lesson is most important for your students to experience.

DELIVERING THE LESSON

1. Instant Activity: Body Shapes

Introduction

"Let's warm up our muscles by moving and making shapes with our bodies."

Activity

Have students move in the designated area using a specified locomotor movement. Freeze the students and have them make a shape with their bodies while standing (e.g., stork, rocket, bird, plane). Have them hold this position for at least five seconds. Specify a new locomotor movement and a new shape upon freezing (e.g., letter, fruit, insect). Point out interesting shapes and challenge students to be creative.

Refinements

Make sure all students move in space without touching others.

Extensions

- ✳ Have students come up with themes for making body shapes.
- ✳ Use different languages to identify the themes and objects.
- ✳ Have students follow a leader or a partner and match the shape.

2. Fitness Activity: Yoga Circuit

Introduction

"Let's continue working on our flexibility and balance with our yoga circuit. As you move through the circuit today, try to tune in to how your body is feeling."

Activity

Place 6 to 10 Yoga Circuit activity cards on cones to create stations. You may want to supply soft mats at each. Break the class into 6 to 10 groups using a grouping strategy of your choice (see page 25). Place a group at each yoga station. Have them read the card and slowly move into the pose when the music starts (use music CD track 3). When the music stops, have students move quietly to the next station and start getting into the pose.

3-6 • WEEK 3
LESSON PLAN 3.3

Refinements

✳ Move around the area and help students improve their poses by giving specific feedback.

✳ Encourage students to hold their poses for the full time.

✳ Instruct students to remain quiet during the whole session and concentrate on stable poses.

✳ Encourage students to readjust their poses to make them more stable and comfortable.

Extensions

✳ Place two similar poses at each station and allow students to transition between poses.

✳ Sixth grade: Have students use a mirror or work with partners to create precise poses. Have students focus on the accurate position of the body to create precise poses. You can have them record their strengths and weaknesses for each pose so they can focus their practice and monitor their improvement over the week.

3. Lesson Focus: Power Yoga

Introduction

"Today we are going to power up our yoga routine by adding some muscle fitness poses to each station. I am going to challenge you to hold the poses for the whole time at each station. Let's get to it."

Activity

Break the class into 6 to 10 groups using a grouping strategy of your choice (see page 25). Place groups at various yoga stations that have a Yoga Circuit activity card and a Muscle Fitness Poses activity card on cones. Have students slowly move into a pose of their choice when the music starts (use music CD track 4). When the music stops, have students move quietly to the next station and start getting into the pose.

> **interdisciplinary** • • •
> This is a good opportunity to have students create a Muscle Fitness Poses activity card. They would need to draw or capture an image, write out the instructions, identify the muscle groups targeted, and present the card to the class. You could incorporate student activity cards into the lesson.

Refinements

* Instruct students to remain quiet during the whole session and concentrate on stable poses.
* Encourage students to readjust their poses to make them more stable and comfortable.

Extensions

* Use a longer music interval (use music CD tracks 5, 6, 7, or 8) to challenge students.
* Have students transition smoothly from the asana to the muscle fitness pose.

Power yoga can build both muscle fitness and flexibility.

* Sixth grade: Place three or four activity cards at each station and encourage students to move through the poses in any order they choose. The goal is to be fluent and precise. They should be able to find a smooth transition between the three or four poses. Observe them working and making corrections to improve transitions.

4. Culminating Activity: Food Frenzy

Introduction

"Your body needs healthy foods every day. We have already talked about eating sweets, eating fatty foods, and drinking sodas only once in a while because they have lots of calories but very few vitamins. We have also talked about the importance of getting at least 5 fruits and veggies each day because they have lots of vitamins. We have not talked about protein, though. Protein is in drinks like milk and foods like chicken and fish. Protein is also found in beans, nuts, and eggs. Protein is important for building structures in our body like muscles and hair. Some might call protein a power food. In this game, you are trying to gather as many fruits, veggies, and protein as possible."

Activity

Provide each student with a pinny (or flag football flag). Have students lightly tuck the pinny into their shorts on the right hip. More of the pinny should be showing than is tucked. On your signal, students move in the designated space using a specified locomotor movement and try to collect as many healthy foods (pinnies) as possible by pulling them out of another student's shorts. When students take a pinny from another student, they must place it in their shorts. Thus, they will have multiple pinnies hanging out of their shorts.

You can give different colors more or less value (e.g., today is protein power day—red pinnies are protein and they are worth 2; or today is green vegetable day—green pinnies are worth 3). Use music intervals (45/15) and start over (i.e., everyone has a pinny).

 teacher tip • • •
This could be an excellent time to go over the food groups identified by MyPyramid.

Second Time Through

If you are teaching this lesson a second time, you may want to introduce the following activities.

Introduction

"Last class we reviewed the importance of fruits and veggies and we introduced protein. What are some protein foods? Why are they important? Let's play Food Frenzy, and I will make some fun changes to the rules."

Refinements

* Observe students moving using the specified locomotor movement, even when under pressure.
* Observe students playing respectfully and keeping body contact to a minimum.

Extensions

* Allow third- and fourth-grade students to run if they are controlling their bodies.

* Change the size of the space (smaller means more dodging, bigger means more running).

* On a few pinnies, staple mystery messages related to healthy eating, such as the following:

  * "This is a donut, and it has hidden fat that slows you down; in the next game, you can only walk."

  * "This is a watermelon, and it has water to help keep your body temperature low so you can continue moving fast; in the next game, you can run."

> **teacher tip** • • •
> Leave some time for a cool-down. Use instructions from the cool-down for lesson 3.2 on page 205.

CLOSURE ROUTINE

Compliment

Have some students share compliments about their classmates.

Reflection and Review

* "What kinds of foods provide our bodies with protein?"

* "Why is protein important for a healthy body?"

* "Share your favorite protein food with your neighbor."

* "What activity challenged your muscles the most?"

* "What happens to your muscles when you work them harder than before?"

* "What kinds of foods help you build muscles?" (fruits, veggies, foods with protein)

Take It Home

* "Have a family member guide you through the fridge and identify all the high-protein foods. Read food labels if you are not sure."

* "Perform some yoga or muscle endurance poses during commercial breaks. Have your family members perform them with you."

ASSESSMENT

* **Performance check:** Observe students successfully performing the asanas and muscle fitness poses.

* **Comprehension check:** Responses to the Comprehension Check questions and Reflection and Review questions serve as a check for student understanding.

EXTRA ACTIVITIES AND RESOURCES

If your school has physical education more than three times per week, consider delivering some of the lesson plans a second time through or using some of the extra activities and resources in appendix A of this book (see page 245). You can also use some of the additional activities described in appendix A of the classroom guides. Ask your wellness coordinator for access to these guides.

WELLNESS WEEK 4

Fitness for Life Elementary School

These lesson plans provide students with a variety of experiences, including exploring activities while manipulating the senses (e.g., sight, hearing), moving to music, estimating body mass index, and learning about the importance of physical activity for maintaining energy balance. In Wellness Week 4, the activity theme is "integration (energy balance)," the nutrition theme for grades 3-5 is "balance energy in (food) with energy out (exercise)," and the nutrition theme for grade 6 is "balance calories." These themes are reinforced through activities, signs, and chants. A secondary theme is building a healthy body with a healthy mind. Take time to look through the lesson plans for Wellness Week 4 and determine what objectives are most important and which activities you will use to meet those objectives. Table 3.4 summarizes the Wellness Week 4 activities for the physical education lesson plans.

For Wellness Week 4, the lesson plans include the following:

- A warm-up lesson plan to be used during the week before Wellness Week 4. The same basic warm-up lesson plan is used for grades 3 through 6, but the Lesson Focus (practicing the video routine) is different for each grade.

- Three lesson plans (4.1, 4.2, and 4.3) to be used during Wellness Week 4. The same basic lesson plan is used for grades 3 through 6, with grade-specific variations, refinements, and extensions for some of the activities.

Table 3.4 Summary of Wellness Week 4 Activities

Lesson Plan	Instant Activity	Fitness Activity	Lesson Focus	Culminating Activity
Warm-Up 4 (week before Wellness Week 4)	Pirate Fitness	Sensational Circuit	Video Routine Practice: 3: Jumpnastics 4: Keep on Clapping 5: Fit Funk 6: Harvest Time	Water Fight
4.1	Pirate Fitness	Sensational Circuit	Video Routine Variations: 3: Jumpnastics 4: Keep On Clapping 5: Fit Funk 6: Harvest Time	Water Fight
4.2	Pirate Fitness	Sensational Circuit	BMI Practice	Water Fight
4.3	Pirate Fitness	Sensational Circuit	Sensational Small-Sided Games	Water Fight

- Extra activity ideas for schools that have physical education class more than three days a week are provided in appendix A.

Eat Well Wednesday

Each Wednesday, known as Eat Well Wednesday, all teachers and staff are encouraged to emphasize nutrition. The wellness coordinator might plan special schoolwide events. During Wellness Week 4, the nutrition event is a fruit and vegetable bar with bottled water in the cafeteria. If you have a physical education lesson on Eat Well Wednesday, place an emphasis on nutrition signs and messages.

Get Fit Friday

Each Friday, known as Get Fit Friday, a schoolwide event focusing on physical activity will be planned. (If your school participates in this event, your wellness coordinator will provide you with more details.) The Get Fit Friday activities are called TEAM Time activities (TEAM stands for Together Everyone Achieves More). During Wellness Week 4, this activity is called Mid Kids Lead. Your wellness coordinator will teach several third- and fourth-grade students how to do the routine ahead of time so that they can help lead. Then the coordinator and the selected students will lead the TEAM Time activity at the beginning of the school day. All students in the school will congregate in the gym, multipurpose room, or outside so that they can participate together. The activity includes a warm-up, a Hawaiian Surfing routine, and a cool-down. If time allows, you can teach these activities in advance to make it easier for students to perform them during TEAM Time. A video and script are provided on the DVD that accompanies the *Guide for Wellness Coordinators*.

ACES Day

In 1984, Len Saunders created a program called Project ACES (All Children Exercising Simultaneously). May is National Physical Fitness Month, and the first week in May is National Physical Education Week. Each year in the first week of May, children throughout the world participate in Project ACES by doing exercise at the same time on the same day. The children in your school can participate by performing the TEAM Time activity on ACES Day at the designated time. More information is available at http://lensaunders.com/aces/aces.html.

Newsletter

The CD-ROM contains a newsletter for use during Wellness Week 4. It is recommended that your school's wellness coordinator edit and distribute the newsletter. Alternatively, you (or the classroom teachers) can do it. Just open the appropriate file, follow the instructions to edit and customize the newsletter, and send printed copies home with students or send them electronically via e-mail. Remind students to talk to their families about Wellness Week and the information in the newsletter.

 Wellness Week 4 → Newsletter

The activity theme for Wellness Week 4 is integration (energy balance).

Warm-Up Lesson Plan 4

OVERVIEW

In this lesson, conducted during the week before Wellness Week 4, students will practice the grade-specific video routine that they will perform in their classroom during Wellness Week 4. You can aid the classroom teachers by teaching these routines in advance to make it easier for both students and teachers and to increase the chances that the classroom teachers will do the video routines in their classrooms.

NASPE STANDARDS

* **Grades 3-5:** 1A, 1B, 1C, 2A, 4C, 4I, 5A, 5B, 5E, 5I, 6D
* **Grade 6:** 1D, 1F, 2G, 5K, 6I, 6J

(See appendix B for details.)

OBJECTIVES

Students will

* provide examples of how senses are important for skill performance,
* practice moving to music, and
* explain the importance of hydration and sweating in physical activity.

EQUIPMENT

* CD player, 45/15 interval music (music CD track 8), and continuous music (music CD track12)
* TV, DVD player, and DVD 1 (Instructional Routines)
* 6 cones
* Ear protection (3-4 pairs)
* 4 eye patches
* 6 to 10 plastic (or wooden) bowling pins
* 3 tennis balls
* 6 basketballs
* 3 balloons
* Juggling scarves (or plastic bags)
* 10 beanbags
* 3 large balls
* 3 hula hoops
* 30 balls for throwing
* 30 Frisbees or small cones (optional)

RESOURCES

 General

At-a-Glance PE Lesson Plan card

G3: Physical Activity Pyramid for Kids

 Wellness Week 4 → 3-6 Resources

Pirate Fitness task cards

Sensational Circuit activity cards

Week 4 signs file with the following signs:

- Use your senses—build your brain . . .
- When activity makes you hotter, go for some water!

CHANTS

Leader: "When you play and when you train . . ."

Students: ". . . moving makes me use my brain!"

DELIVERING THE LESSON

1. Instant Activity: Pirate Fitness

teacher tip • • •
You may not get through the whole lesson the first time through. Decide which part of the lesson is most important for your students to experience.

Introduction

"Pretend you are on a pirate ship. I am the captain. You must obey the captain! You need to work hard on my ship so that you don't get tossed overboard."

Activity

Call out directions for the students to follow. You will need to explain the different commands and parts of the boat (e.g., port, starboard, stern, and bow). You can also specify locomotor movements. Commands are on the Pirate Fitness task cards.

? comprehension check • • •
- "What are some body reactions that tell you that you have warmed up?" (breathing hard, heart rate, sweat or body heat)
- "What are some ways you could cool your body?" (water, sweating)
- "How does water help cool our bodies?" (evaporation of sweat cools the body)

Refinements

✳ Have students move without touching others.
✳ Make sure all students hold Submarine, Walk the Plank, and Crow's Nest for five "cannonballs" (five seconds).

Extensions

✳ Have students use a different locomotor movement.
✳ Have students come up with new pirate movements or boat parts that require activity.

2. Fitness Activity: Sensational Circuit

Introduction

"We use many of our senses when we participate in physical activities. What are the five senses? Senses picked up by the eyes, nose, ears, body, and tongue need to be interpreted by the brain. This means that when we use our senses, we use our brains. Let's try a physical activity circuit that challenges our senses."

Activity

Break the class into six groups using a grouping strategy of your choice (see page 25). Demonstrate the activities at each station. Place groups at the Sensational Circuit stations with activity cards on cones. When the music starts (use music CD track 8), students try the activities at their station. When the music stops, have students put the equipment back where they found it and move quietly to the next station.

interdisciplinary • • •
This is a great opportunity to introduce the biology of the senses (i.e., how they work). This is also a great opportunity to discuss the challenges that people with disabilities face when participating in physical activities. Encourage students to share ideas about how to be more inclusive and accommodating of people with disabilities when participating in physical activity.

3-6 • WEEK 4
WARM-UP 4

Refinements

* Encourage students to try the different activities and practice to get better.
* Sixth grade: Have students record the number of successful attempts at each station with and without senses compromised. Have them compare their scores when their left and right eyes are compromised. Which eye is dominant?

3. Lesson Focus: Video Routine Practice

Introduction

"Next week is Wellness Week 4. During Wellness Week 4, we will be learning about physical activity, fitness, and healthy nutrition. Today we are going to practice the video routine you will be performing in your classroom during Wellness Week 4. This video routine is fun and will challenge you to move to music."

Activity

Introduce and practice the grade-specific video routine using the following steps.

1. Insert DVD 1 and play the instructional routine that is appropriate for your class:
   * Third grade: Jumpnastics
   * Fourth grade: Keep on Clapping
   * Fifth grade: Fit Funk
   * Sixth grade: Harvest Time
2. Have the students follow along with the routine. Observe students performing the routine and take note of the movements that give them trouble.
3. Before going through the routine again, provide a demonstration and help students with any movements that are giving them trouble. Provide tips that will help them succeed.
4. Play the routine again and compliment students on any improvements.
5. Remind students that next week is Wellness Week 4, and they will perform this routine every day in their classrooms next week.

Refinements

Observe the students' movements and listen to the reciting of the words. Have students focus on staying with the music and moving together.

4. Culminating Activity: Water Fight

Introduction

"When you are active, your body sweats. Why do we sweat? That's right, to keep our body temperature down. If you lose a lot of body water through sweating, you can become dehydrated. This means you have lost a lot of body water. When you are dehydrated, you will not be able to run as fast, jump as high, or move for as long as someone who is hydrated. So, remember to rehydrate your body with water after physical activity."

Activity

Set up three large balls (exercise balls or large playground balls) inside three hula hoops in the middle of the gym (see figure). Place numerous smaller throwing balls on two straight lines equidistant (about 10-15 ft, or 3-4.5 m) and on opposite sides of the large balls. To help the balls stay in place, put them inside Frisbees or on top of small cones. Finally, place two cones well behind the throwing lines to mark a starting line for each team.

Break the class into two teams using a grouping strategy of your choice (see page 25). Have teams line up along their starting line (marked by the cones; see figure). On your signal (e.g., "Water fight!", music CD track 12), students run and grab balls (water) on their throwing line and try to knock (squirt) the large balls across the other team's throwing line. A point is scored for each large ball that crosses the other team's throwing line. Students must follow these rules:

* No going over the throwing line

* No throwing at an opponent

* No touching the large (scoring) balls with any body parts (only balls)

> ↻ **review** • • •
> Discuss the importance of playing by the rules. When the rules are broken, the game is ruined for others. Also, remind students to encourage each other and opponents during the game. Ask students to provide an example of how they could encourage their teammates and their opponents during the game.

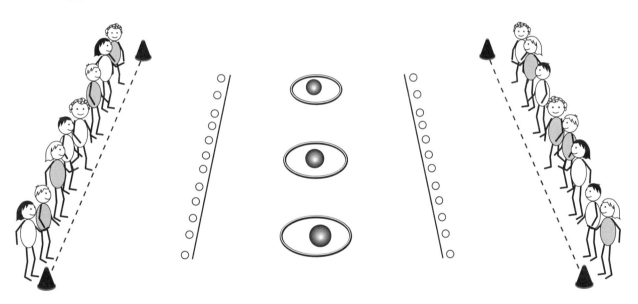

Extensions

* Have teams start in different positions (e.g., plank, crab walk, balancing, on back).

* Have teams get balls using different locomotor movements.

* Introduce new scoring balls.

> 👁 **observation** • • •
> Observe students playing and make sure all are following the rules.

CLOSURE ROUTINE

Compliments

Have some students share compliments about their classmates.

Reflection and Review

✳ "How did limiting your senses affect your performance?"

✳ "Did you have to rely on different senses?"

✳ "What is the most important sense for your sport or activity?"

✳ "Which station was the hardest? Why?"

✳ "Why is it important to be hydrated?"

✳ "What do we call the back of a boat? Front? Right side? Left side?"

✳ "What sensations help during the water fight? Why?"

✳ "How do we modify sports for people who have sense disabilities?"

✳ "Share your favorite sensation with your neighbor."

Take It Home

✳ "Challenge family members to try some of the activities with and without all of their senses."

✳ "Have a family member help you find out about an activity that can be modified for people who have lost one of their senses."

ASSESSMENT

✳ **Performance check:** Observe students participating in the Sensational Circuit, successfully moving to music during the video routines, and playing by the rules in Water Fight.

✳ **Comprehension check:** Responses to the Comprehension Check questions and Reflection and Review questions serve as a check for student understanding.

Allowing students to create physical activities can be motivating.

Lesson Plan **4.1**

OVERVIEW

In this lesson, students will practice the video routine and have an opportunity to create and add new movements to the routine.

NASPE STANDARDS

* **Grades 3-5:** 1A, 1B, 1C, 4A, 4C, 4I, 5A, 5B, 5E, 5G, 5I, 6B, 6D, 6F
* **Grade 6:** 1D, 1F, 2G, 5G, 5K, 6I, 6J

(See appendix B for details.)

OBJECTIVES

Students will

* provide examples of how senses are important for skill performance,
* work cooperatively in groups to create a dance routine,
* explain why we sweat and how water helps us be physically active, and
* identify some physical activity inclusion strategies for people with disabilities.

EQUIPMENT

* CD player, 45/15 interval music (music CD track 8), and continuous music (music CD track 12)
* TV, DVD player, and DVD 2 (Activity Routines)
* 6 cones
* Ear protection (3-4 pairs)
* 4 eye patches
* 6 to 10 plastic (or wooden) bowling pins
* 3 tennis balls
* 6 basketballs
* 3 balloons
* Juggling scarves (or plastic bags)
* 10 beanbags
* 3 large balls
* 3 hula hoops
* 30 balls for throwing
* 30 Frisbee or small cones (optional)

RESOURCES

 General

At-a-Glance PE Lesson Plan card
G3: Physical Activity Pyramid for Kids

 Wellness Week 4 → 3-6 Resources

Pirate Fitness task cards
Sensational Circuit activity cards
Week 4 signs file with the following signs:
- Use your senses—build your brain . . .
- When activity makes you hotter, go for some water!

CHANTS

Leader: "When you play and when you train . . ."
Students: ". . . moving makes me use my brain!"

DELIVERING THE LESSON

teacher tip • • •
You may not get through the whole lesson the first time through. Decide which part of the lesson is most important for your students to experience.

1. Instant Activity: Pirate Fitness

Introduction

"Pretend you are on a pirate ship. I am the captain. You must obey the captain! You need to work hard on my ship so that you don't get tossed overboard."

Activity

Call out directions for the students to follow. You will need to explain the different commands and parts of the boat (e.g., port, starboard, stern, and bow). You can also specify locomotor movements. Commands are on the Pirate Fitness task cards.

comprehension check • • •
- "What senses are you using during this activity?"
- "What body signals let you know that you are warmed up?"

Refinements

✳ Have students move without touching others.

✳ Make sure all students hold Submarine, Walk the Plank, and Crow's Nest for five "cannonballs" (five seconds).

Extensions

✳ Have students use a different locomotor movement.

✳ Have students come up with new pirate movements or boat parts that require activity.

review • • •
Review how water helps us keep our body from getting too hot. Being hydrated allows us to sweat. Sweat evaporates and cools our body. A good example is when you go swimming and get out of the water. When the wind hits your wet body, it causes the water to evaporate, and this cools your body.

2. Fitness Activity: Sensational Circuit

Introduction

"We use many of our senses when we participate in physical activities. What are the five senses? Senses picked up by the eyes, nose, ears, body, and tongue need to be interpreted by the brain. This means that when we use our senses, we use our brains. Let's try a physical activity circuit that challenges our senses."

Activity

Break the class into six groups using a grouping strategy of your choice (see page 25). Demonstrate the activities at each station. Place groups at the Sensational Circuit stations with activity cards on cones. When the music starts (use music CD track 8), students try the activities at their station. When the music stops, have students put the equipment back where they found it and move quietly to the next station.

3-6 • WEEK 4 LESSON PLAN 4.1

interdisciplinary • • •

- This is a great opportunity to introduce the biology of the senses (i.e., how they work).

- Students could use their language arts skills to write a story or a poem sharing how physical activity makes them feel. The written work could provide a rich description of the senses used during activity and the feelings associated with participation.

Refinements

✳ Encourage students to try the different activities and practice to get better.

✳ Sixth grade: Have students record the number of successful attempts at each station with and without senses compromised. Have them compare their scores when their left and right eyes are compromised. Which eye is dominant?

teacher tip • • •

This is a great opportunity to discuss the challenges that people with disabilities face when participating in physical activities. Encourage students to share ideas about how to be more inclusive and accommodating of people with disabilities when participating in physical activity.

The Pirate Fitness activity challenges students' cardiovascular and muscular fitness.

Second Time Through

If you are teaching this lesson a second time, you may want to introduce the following activities.

Introduction

"Last time we explored a circuit that challenged our senses. What are the five senses? We are going to try that circuit again. This time I want you to try to improve your performance when your senses are challenged. Remember that when we use our senses, we use our brains."

Refinement

Encourage students to try the different activities and practice to get better.

Extensions

✳ Incorporate some yoga and muscle fitness stations. Have students perform with eyes open and closed.

✳ Incorporate your own ideas or student ideas.

✳ Teach students the Spanish names of the senses (e.g., sight = *vista*, hearing = *oiga*).

3. Lesson Focus: Video Routine Variations

Introduction

"Last class we practiced the video routine you are performing in your classroom. Today we are going to use our creativity and make up some new moves for the routine."

Activity

Practice the grade-specific video routine using the following steps.

1. Insert DVD 2 and play the video routine that is appropriate for your class:
   - Third grade: Jumpnastics
   - Fourth grade: Keep on Clapping
   - Fifth grade: Fit Funk
   - Sixth grade: Harvest Time

2. Have the students follow along with the routine. Observe students performing the routine and take note of the movements that give them trouble.

? comprehension check • • •
Ask students to explain what the video messages are trying to tell them. Reinforce the message by using some of your own examples or having students share examples.

3. Before going through the routine again, provide a demonstration and help students with any movements that are giving them trouble. Provide tips that will help them succeed.

4. Break the students into 16 pairs, 8 groups, or 4 groups using a grouping strategy of your choice (see page 25). These group sizes allow you to pair groups together to make an even number of fewer (and larger) groups as the activity progresses.

5. Instruct the students that you will play the video routine, and their job is to make up new movements for the routine that are in time with the music.

6. Play the video routine for your class, and visit the student groups to see the movements they are trying.

7. At the end of the routine, highlight a few moves that students came up with.

observation • • •
Observe student groups to see if they are working well with others in a cooperative activity.

8. Have each group get with another group (e.g., 16 pairs become 8 groups) and play the music again. Have the two groups share their moves with each other.

9. Allow some time for the groups to combine their moves, and play the video routine so they can practice. Visit the new groups to see how they are combining their movements.

10. Repeat steps 8 and 9 until you have two large groups or the whole class working together with new movements.

11. Encourage students to share their new moves with their classroom teachers.

teacher tip • • •
Explain the importance of working with others. Identify the important elements of working with others, such as listening; sharing thoughts, feelings, and equipment; providing encouragement; and making sure everyone feels included. Provide examples of what this might sound or look like in the class.

4. Culminating Activity: Water Fight

Introduction

"When you are active, your body sweats. Why do we sweat? That's right, to keep our body temperature down. If you lose a lot of body water through sweating, you can become dehydrated. This means you have lost a lot of body water. When you are dehydrated, you will not be able to run as fast, jump as high, or move for as long as someone who is hydrated. So, remember to rehydrate your body with water after physical activity."

Activity

Set up three large balls (exercise balls or large playground balls) inside three hula hoops in the middle of the gym (see figure). Place numerous smaller throwing balls on two straight lines equidistant (about 10-15 ft, or 3-4.5 m) and on opposite sides of the large balls. To help the balls stay in place, put them inside Frisbees or on top of small cones. Finally, place two cones well behind the throwing lines to mark a starting line for each team.

Break the class into two teams using a grouping strategy of your choice (see page 25). Have teams line up along their starting line (marked by the cones; see figure). On your signal (e.g., "Water fight!", music CD track 12), students run and grab balls (water) on their throwing line and try to knock (squirt) the large balls across the other team's throwing line. A point is scored for each large ball that crosses the other team's throwing line. Students must follow these rules:

* No going over the throwing line
* No throwing at an opponent
* No touching the large (scoring) balls with any body parts (only balls)

> **review** • • •
> Discuss the importance of playing by the rules. When the rules are broken, the game is ruined for others. Also, remind students to encourage each other and opponents during the game. Ask students to provide an example of how they could encourage their teammates and their opponents during the game.

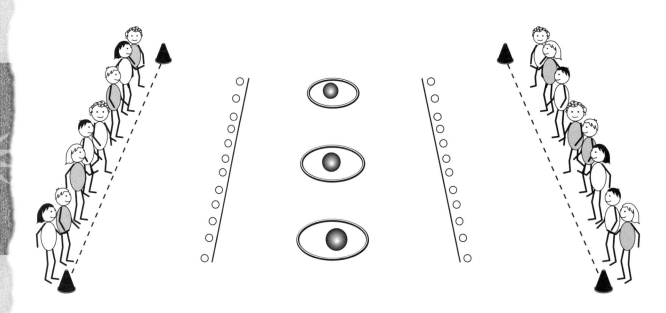

Refinement

Observe students playing and make sure all are following the rules.

Extensions

* Have teams start in different positions (e.g., plank, crab walk, balancing, on back).
* Have teams get balls using different locomotor movements.
* Introduce new scoring balls.

CLOSURE ROUTINE

Compliments

Have some students share compliments about their classmates.

Reflection and Review

* "How did limiting your senses affect your performance?"
* "Did you have to rely on different senses?" (explore proprioception)
* "What is the most important sense for your sport or activity?"
* "Which station was the hardest? Why?"
* "Why is it important to be hydrated?"
* "What do we call the back of a boat? Front? Right side? Left side?"
* "What sensations help during the water fight? Why?"
* "How do we modify sports for people who have sense disabilities?"
* "Share your favorite sensation with your neighbor."

Take It Home

* "Challenge family members to try some of the activities with and without all of their senses."
* "Have a family member help you find out about an activity that can be modified for people who have lost one of their senses."

ASSESSMENT

* **Performance check:** Observe students successfully moving to music during the video routines and following the rules during Water Fight.
* **Comprehension check:** Responses to the Comprehension Check questions and Reflection and Review questions serve as a check for student understanding.

4.2 Lesson Plan

OVERVIEW

The focus of this lesson is for students to learn how to self-assess their body mass index (BMI).

NASPE STANDARDS

  * **Grades 3-5:** 1C, 2E, 4H, 4I, 5I, 5J, 6A
  * **Grade 6:** 1D, 2G, 3G, 4J, 4K, 5K, 6J

(See appendix B for details.)

OBJECTIVES

Students will

  * identify positive feelings they get from participating in physical activity,
  * practice the Fitnessgram self-assessment for determining BMI, and
  * describe how physical activity helps maintain a healthy body weight.

EQUIPMENT

  * CD player, 45/15 interval music (music CD track 8), and continuous music (music CD track 12)
  * 6 cones
  * Ear protection (3-4 pairs)
  * 4 eye patches
  * 6 to 10 plastic (or wooden) bowling pins
  * 3 tennis balls
  * 6 basketballs
  * 3 balloons
  * Juggling scarves (or plastic bags)
  * 10 beanbags
  * 3 large balls
  * 3 hula hoops
  * 30 balls for throwing
  * 30 Frisbees or small cones (optional)
  * Optional: measuring tapes (or stadiometers) for height, scales for measuring weight, pencils and paper, calculators

RESOURCES

 General

At-a-Glance PE Lesson Plan card

G3: Physical Activity Pyramid for Kids

 Wellness Week 4 → 3-6 Resources

Pirate Fitness task cards

Sensational Circuit activity cards

Fitnessgram BMI self-assessment worksheet

BMI poster

Week 4 signs file with the following signs:

- Use your senses—build your brain . . .
- When activity makes you hotter, go for some water!
- Balance calories in (food) with calories out (activity)!

CHANTS

Leader: "When you play and when you train . . ."

Students: ". . . moving makes me use my brain!"

 teacher tip • • •
You may not get through the whole lesson the first time through. Decide which part of the lesson is most important for your students to experience.

DELIVERING THE LESSON

1. Instant Activity: Pirate Fitness

Introduction

"Pretend you are on a pirate ship. I am the captain. You must obey the captain! You need to work hard on my ship so that you don't get tossed overboard."

Activity

Call out directions for the students to follow. You will need to explain the different commands and parts of the boat (e.g., port, starboard, stern, and bow). You can also specify locomotor movements. Commands are on the Pirate Fitness task cards.

? comprehension check • • •
"What are some good feelings we get from participating in physical activity?"

Refinements

* Have students move without touching others.

* Make sure all students hold Submarine, Walk the Plank, and Crow's Nest for five "cannonballs" (five seconds).

3-6 • WEEK 4
LESSON PLAN 4.2

Extensions

✳ Have students use a different locomotor movement.

✳ Have students come up with new pirate movements or boat parts that require activity.

✳ Encourage classroom teachers to have students create and decorate paper pirate hats.

2. Fitness Activity: Sensational Circuit

Introduction

"We use many of our senses when we participate in physical activities. Identify your favorite physical activity and describe some of the senses that the activity requires. Remember that the brain has to interpret the sensations it receives through the sense organs. This means that when we use our senses, we use our brains. Let's try a physical activity circuit that challenges our senses."

Activity

Break the class into six groups using a grouping strategy of your choice (see page 25). Demonstrate the activities at each station. Place groups at the Sensational Circuit stations with activity cards on cones. When the music starts (use music CD track 8), students try the activities at their station. When the music stops, have students put the equipment back where they found it and move quietly to the next station.

Refinements

* Encourage students to try the different activities and practice to get better.

* Sixth grade: Have students record the number of successful attempts at each station with and without senses compromised. Have them compare their scores when their left and right eyes are compromised. Which eye is dominant?

> **⊗ interdisciplinary • • •**
> This is a great opportunity to introduce the biology of the senses (i.e., how they work). This is also a great opportunity to discuss the challenges that people with disabilities face when participating in physical activities. Encourage students to share ideas about how to be more inclusive and accommodating of people with disabilities when participating in physical activity.

3. Lesson Focus: BMI Practice

Introduction

"People come in all shapes and sizes. Some sizes and shapes are healthier than others. We can find out if our body is a healthy weight by figuring out our body mass index, or BMI. When we measure BMI, we are looking at our height and our weight. We are asking the question, 'Are we a healthy weight for our height?' Today we are going to find out the answer to that question. However, instead of measuring height and weight, we are going to estimate our height and weight. Who can tell me what *estimate* means? Right—we are going to make a guess based on some things we know. Today we are going to need to understand heights and weights to make a good guess."

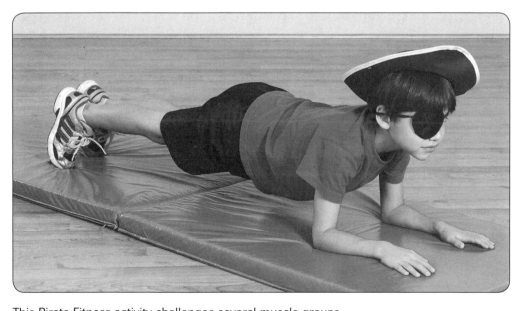

This Pirate Fitness activity challenges several muscle groups.

Activity

Have students pair up with a trusted partner and get their Fitnessgram BMI self-assessment worksheet and a pencil. Have students estimate their heights and weights together. Go around and calculate their estimated BMI (BMI = 703 × [pounds / inches^2]) by completing the following steps:

1. Multiply a student's estimated height in inches by itself (square it).
2. Divide a student's estimated weight in pounds by square inches (number from step 1).
3. Multiply the number from step 2 by 703 to get the student's estimated BMI.

review • • •
Review the concept of private and personal information. Remind students that they do not have to share their personal information. Tell students that whatever their BMI is, the important step is to continue being active.

Gather students around a BMI poster and explain the age-specific BMI categories. Have students put their name on their Fitnessgram BMI self-assessment worksheet and collect the papers so students have them for the next class. Explain how physical activity helps maintain a healthy body weight because it does the following:

* Burns calories (energy from food). Show the sign about balancing calories in with calories out.
* Builds muscle. Muscle is the engine of the body. The bigger the engine we have, the more calories we burn at rest and during activity.

Extension for Sixth Grade

Introduction

"Last time we estimated our body mass index. Can someone explain what BMI measures? Today we are going to measure our BMI."

Activity

Set up several stations where students can measure their height with a trusted friend. Also, set up a station where you can measure students' weight. Demonstrate how to

comprehension check • • •
• "What does it mean to be overweight or obese?"

• "What is one way that people become overweight or obese?" Explain the concept of balancing energy in with energy out.

• "If you are overweight or obese, what should you do? That's right, get off your seat and move your feet!"

• "If someone is in the overweight or obese range for BMI, what kinds of activities would be helpful?"

• "At what step of the pyramid should someone who is overweight or obese be performing activities?" (All activities—muscle fitness builds muscle that helps expend calories at rest, and vigorous aerobics and vigorous sports and recreation expend more calories in a short time.)

measure height and have students try to measure this with a partner or small group. Have students write down their height on their paper from the last class. Students bring you the paper and you help them perform their own weight measurement. Calculate BMI for the students using their measured height and weight, and discuss their results using the BMI poster.

Reflection and Review

✳ "How close was your estimated BMI to your measured BMI?"

✳ "Put up your hand if your estimated BMI was higher than your measured BMI."

✳ "Put up your hand if your estimated BMI was lower than your measured BMI."

✳ "If you are overweight or obese, what should you do? That's right, get off your seat and move your feet!"

4. Culminating Activity: Water Fight

Introduction

"When you are active, your body sweats. Why do we sweat? That's right, to keep our body temperature down. If you lose a lot of body water through sweating, you can become dehydrated. This means you have lost a lot of body water. When you are dehydrated, you will not be able to run as fast, jump as high, or move for as long as someone who is hydrated. So, remember to rehydrate your body with water after physical activity."

Activity

Set up three large balls (exercise balls or large playground balls) inside three hula hoops in the middle of the gym (see figure). Place numerous smaller throwing balls on two straight lines equidistant (about 10-15 ft, or 3-4.5 m) and on opposite sides of the large balls. To help the balls stay in place, put them inside Frisbees or on top of small cones. Finally, place two cones well behind the throwing lines to mark a starting line for each team.

    Break the class into two teams using a grouping strategy of your choice (see page 25). Have teams line up along their starting line (marked by the cones; see figure). On your signal (e.g., "Water fight!", music CD track 12), students run and grab balls

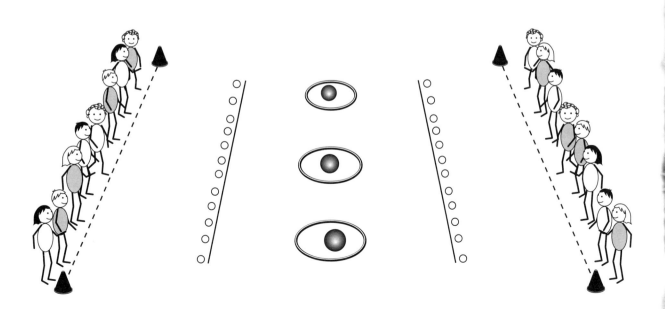

(water) on their throwing line and try to knock (squirt) the large balls across the other team's throwing line. A point is scored for each large ball that crosses the other team's throwing line. Students must follow these rules:

* No going over the throwing line
* No throwing at an opponent
* No touching the large (scoring) balls with any body parts (only balls)

> ⟳ **review** • • •
> Discuss the importance of playing by the rules. When the rules are broken, the game is ruined for others. Also, remind students to encourage each other and opponents during the game. Ask students to provide an example of how they could encourage their teammates and their opponents during the game.

Refinement

Observe students playing and make sure all are following the rules.

Extensions

* Have teams start in different positions (e.g., plank, crab walk, balancing, on back).
* Have teams get balls using different locomotor movements.
* Introduce new scoring balls.

CLOSURE ROUTINE

Compliments

Have some students share compliments about their classmates.

Reflection and Review

* "What are we measuring when we figure out our BMI?"
* "How does having a high BMI affect physical activity or sport performance?"
* "What athletes have overweight or obese BMIs? Why?"
* "What athletes have normal BMIs?"
* "What should you do if you have a BMI in the overweight or obese category?"

Take It Home

* "Burn some calories outside doing your favorite activities."
* "Encourage a family member to engage in some brain-boosting, calorie-burning physical activity."

ASSESSMENT

* **Performance check:** Observe students moving to the correct boat parts and performing Sensational Circuit activities correctly.
* **Comprehension check:** Responses to the Comprehension Check questions and Reflection and Review questions serve as a check for student understanding.

Lesson Plan 4.3

OVERVIEW

In this lesson, students will engage in an activity circuit and a small-sided game that manipulates the senses.

NASPE STANDARDS

* **Grades 3-5:** 1C, 3D, 4A, 4C, 5A, 5C, 5E, 5J, 6A
* **Grade 6:** 1D, 1E, 2G, 4J, 5F, 5G, 5K, 6I, 6J

(See appendix B for details.)

OBJECTIVES

Students will

* be active for at least 50 percent of class time,
* describe how senses are important for skill performance, and
* explain why we sweat and how water helps us be physically active.

EQUIPMENT

* CD player, 45/15 interval music (music CD track 8), and continuous music (music CD tracks 9-11)
* 6 cones
* Ear protection (3-4 pairs)
* 4 eye patches
* 6 to 10 plastic bowling pins (or wooden)
* 3 tennis balls
* 6 basketballs
* 3 balloons
* Juggling scarves (or plastic bags)
* 10 beanbags
* 3 large balls
* 3 hula hoops
* 30 balls for throwing
* 30 Frisbees or small cones (optional)
* Small-sided sport equipment (varies depending on sport chosen)
* Pencils
* Pinnies (two different colors)

RESOURCES

 General

At-a-Glance PE Lesson Plan card

G3: Physical Activity Pyramid for Kids

 Wellness Week 4 → 3-6 Resources

Pirate Fitness task cards

Sensational Circuit activity cards

Week 4 signs file with the following signs:

- Use your senses—build your brain . . .
- When activity makes you hotter, go for some water!
- Balance calories in (food) with calories out (activity)!

CHANTS

Leader: "When you play and when you train . . ."

Students: ". . . moving makes me use my brain!"

> **teacher tip** • • •
>
> You may not get through the whole lesson the first time through. Decide which part of the lesson is most important for your students to experience.

DELIVERING THE LESSON

1. Instant Activity: Pirate Fitness

Introduction

"Pretend you are on a pirate ship. I am the captain. You must obey the captain! You need to work hard on my ship so that you don't get tossed overboard."

Activity

Call out directions for the students to follow. You will need to explain the different commands and parts of the boat (e.g., port, starboard, stern, and bow). You can also specify locomotor movements. Commands are on the Pirate Fitness task cards.

> **?** **comprehension check** • • •
>
> • "What does BMI stand for?"
>
> • "How does physical activity help us maintain a healthy weight?"

Refinements

* Have students move without touching others.
* Make sure all students hold Submarine, Walk the Plank, and Crow's Nest for five "cannonballs" (five seconds).

Extensions

* Have students use a different locomotor movement.
* Have students come up with new pirate movements or boat parts that require activity.
* Encourage classroom teachers to have students create and decorate paper pirate hats.

2. Fitness Activity: Sensational Circuit

Introduction

"Remember that the brain has to interpret the sensations it receives through the sense organs. This means that when we use our senses, we use our brains. Let's try a physical activity circuit that challenges our senses."

Activity

Break the class into six groups using a grouping strategy of your choice (see page 25). Demonstrate the activities at each station. Place groups at the Sensational Circuit stations with activity cards on cones. When the music starts (use music CD track 8), students try the activities at their station. When the music stops, have students put the equipment back where they found it and move quietly to the next station.

interdisciplinary • • •
This is a great opportunity to introduce the biology of the senses (i.e., how they work). This is also a great opportunity to discuss the challenges that people with disabilities face when participating in physical activities. Encourage students to share ideas about how to be more inclusive and accommodating of people with disabilities when participating in physical activity.

Refinements

✳ Encourage students to try the different activities and practice to get better.

✳ Sixth grade: Have students record the number of successful attempts at each station with and without senses compromised. Have them compare their scores when their left and right eyes are compromised. Which eye is dominant?

3. Lesson Focus: Sensational Small-Sided Games

Introduction

"We use many senses to participate in sports and other physical activities. Today we are going to play some small-sided games, and I will introduce some rules that will limit how many senses you can use during the game. Remember that the brain has to interpret the sensations it receives through the sense organs. This means that when we use our senses, we use our brains."

Activity

Break the class into two teams using a grouping strategy of your choice (see page 25). Have each team put on different-colored pinnies and line up along a sideline of the activity area. The first four players on each sideline move into the activity area. On your signal or the start of the music (use music CD tracks 9-11), have the students start the small-sided game. After 60 to 90 seconds, have the next four players on the sideline enter the area and the previous players head to the end of the line. Players on the sidelines are standing, encouraging their team and keeping the ball in play. You can choose from several sports (e.g., soccer, basketball, handball, speedball, ultimate [also called ultimate Frisbee], floor hockey).

review • • •
Revisit the idea of supporting and encouraging teammates and opponents during competition. Remind students that they all have different abilities and specialized skills, and it is important to be supportive of all teammates.

Allow the students to play one shift using all the senses. Then manipulate the senses:

✳ Do not allow anyone to make a sound.

✳ Only allow players on the sideline to talk.

✳ Allow players to use two words (yes and no).

✳ Allow players to use one sound to communicate.

✳ Remove the pinnies from all the players and do not allow anyone to make a sound.

Refinements

✳ Observe students to make sure they are in control of their bodies.

✳ Encourage all students to work hard while they are on the court. Their hearts should be beating rapidly when their shift is over.

✳ Have teams take a minute to discuss strategy.

✳ Share strategy ideas such as passing backward when you can't move forward; making short, successful passes; and communicating with teammates.

Extensions

✳ Have students check their heart rate and breathing rate when their shift is over. Is their heart beating faster than at the end of the last shift?

✳ Specify that every member on the court must touch the ball before scoring.

✳ Specify that two passes must be made to the sideline players before scoring.

✳ Have sideline players make up a cheer that incorporates clapping together or moving together in unison.

4. Culminating Activity: Water Fight

Introduction

"When you are active, your body sweats. Why do we sweat? That's right, to keep our body temperature down. If you lose a lot of body water through sweating, you can become dehydrated. This means you have lost a lot of body water. When you are dehydrated, you will not be able to run as fast, jump as high, or move for as long as someone who is hydrated. So, remember to rehydrate your body with water after physical activity."

Activity

Set up three large balls (exercise balls or large playground balls) inside three hula hoops in the middle of the gym (see figure). Place numerous smaller throwing balls on two straight lines equidistant (about 10-15 ft, or 3-4.5 m) and on opposite sides of the large balls. To help the balls stay in place, put them inside Frisbees or on top of small cones. Finally, place two cones well behind the throwing lines to mark a starting line for each team.

Break the class into two teams using a grouping strategy of your choice (see page 25). Have teams line up along their starting line (marked by the cones; see figure). On your signal (e.g., "Water fight!", music CD track 12), students run and grab balls (water) on their throwing line and try to knock (squirt) the large balls across the other team's throwing line. A point is scored for each large ball that crosses the other team's throwing line. Students must follow these rules:

✳ No going over the throwing line

✳ No throwing at an opponent

✳ No touching the large (scoring) balls with any body parts (only balls)

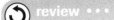 **review** • • •
Discuss the importance of playing by the rules. When the rules are broken, the game is ruined for others. Also, remind students to encourage each other and opponents during the game. Ask students to provide an example of how they could encourage their teammates and their opponents during the game.

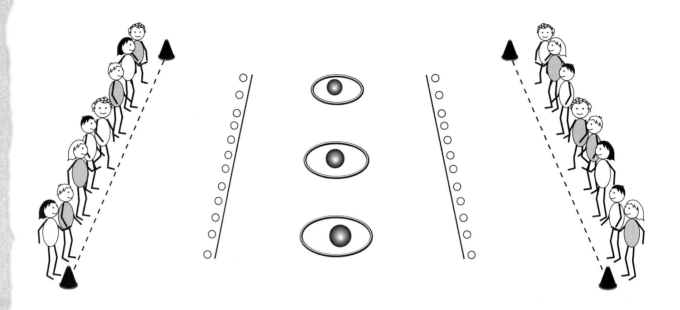

Refinements

Observe students playing and make sure all are following the rules.

Extensions

* Have teams start in different positions (e.g., plank, crab walk, balancing, on back).
* Have teams get balls using different locomotor movements.
* Introduce new scoring balls.

CLOSURE ROUTINE

Compliments

Have some students share compliments about their classmates.

Reflection and Review

* "Describe how limiting your senses affected the game."
* "What was your favorite sensational situation?"
* "Describe why you are sweating."
* "Share one thing that you learned from the Sensational Circuit or Sensational Small-Sided Games."

Take It Home

* "Participate in an activity with a family member and limit the senses you can use."
* "Participate in a physical activity with a family member that makes you sweat. When you are finished, drink a glass of cold water and discuss the sensations you feel."

Throwing at targets requires the integration of several senses.

ASSESSMENT

✳ **Performance check:** Observe students successfully executing the Sensational Circuit activities and following the rules for the Sensational Small-Sided Games.

✳ **Comprehension check:** Responses to the Comprehension Check questions and Reflection and Review questions serve as a check for student understanding.

EXTRA ACTIVITIES AND RESOURCES

If your school has physical education more than three times per week, consider delivering some of the lesson plans a second time through or using some of the extra activities and resources in appendix A of this book (see page 245). You can also use some of the additional activities described in appendix A of the classroom guides. Ask your wellness coordinator for access to these guides.

APPENDIX

A

Extra Activities and Resources

This section identifies some specific lesson plans and general resources that will help you reinforce the physical activity, health-related fitness, and nutrition concepts presented in the **Fitness for Life: Elementary School** program. These resources are organized by grade (K-2 or 3-6) and Wellness Week (1, 2, 3, and 4) for your convenience. Full references for the resources are provided on page 255. Note: A third edition of the *Physical Best Activity Guide* for elementary school is currently in the works. When it is released you will be able to find even more good activities to incorporate into Wellness Weeks. Also be sure to check the **Fitness for Life** Web site (www.fitnessforlife.org) for updates.

Wellness Week 1: K-2

Resource	Description	General concept
Physical Best Activity Guide: Elementary Level (NASPE, 2005)	Lesson 3.1, p. 23: Red Light, Green Light	Nutrition for activity
Physical Best Activity Guide: Elementary Level (NASPE, 2005)	Lesson 3.6, p. 34: On Your "Spot," Get Set, Go!	Warm-up and cool-down
PE Central (www.pecentral.org)	A Web site with numerous resources for physical educators, including elementary PE lesson plans	N/A

Wellness Week 1: 3-6

Resource	Description	General concept
Physical Best Activity Guide: Elementary Level (NASPE, 2005)	Lesson 6.4, p. 138: Everyday Activities	Health benefits
Physical Best Activity Guide: Elementary Level (NASPE, 2005)	Lesson 6.9, p. 149: Metabolism Medley	Physical Activity Pyramid for Kids
Pedometer Power (Pangrazi, Beighle, & Sidman, 2007)	Lessons using pedometers	Using technology in physical education Using pedometers to promote activity
PE Central (www.pecentral.org)	A Web site with numerous resources for physical educators, including elementary PE lesson plans	N/A

Wellness Week 2: K-2

Resource	Description	General concept
Physical Best Activity Guide: Elementary Level (NASPE, 2005)	Lesson 3.4, p. 30: Artery Avengers	Health benefits
Physical Best Activity Guide: Elementary Level (NASPE, 2005)	Lesson 3.14, p. 51: Healthy Heart Tag	Health benefits
Complete Guide to Sport Education (Seidentop, Hastie, & Van Der Mars, 2004)	Helps teachers present sport, dance, adventure, and fitness lessons in ways that positively affect their students and prepare them to be physically active and healthy as adults.	N/A

Wellness Week 2: 3-6

Resource	Description	General concept
Physical Best Activity Guide: Elementary Level (NASPE, 2005)	Lesson 3.2, p. 25: Taking Your Heart Rate	Aerobic fitness
Physical Best Activity Guide: Elementary Level (NASPE, 2005)	Lesson 3.11, p. 45: Jumping Frenzy	FITT formula
Complete Guide to Sport Education (Seidentop, Hastie, & Van Der Mars, 2004)	Helps teachers present sport, dance, adventure, and fitness lessons in ways that positively affect their students and prepare them to be physically active and healthy as adults.	N/A

Wellness Week 3: K-2

Resource	Description	General concept
Physical Best Activity Guide: Elementary Level (NASPE, 2005)	Lesson 4.7, p. 79: Statue, Statue	Muscle fitness
Physical Best Activity Guide: Elementary Level (NASPE, 2005)	Lesson 5.1, p. 104: Human Alphabet Stretch	Flexibility
Teaching Yoga for Life (Tummers, 2009)	A guide to teaching safe and developmentally appropriate yoga in the schools. Includes lesson and unit plans for yoga.	Health and flexibility

Wellness Week 3: 3-6

Resource	Description	General concept
Physical Best Activity Guide: Elementary Level (NASPE, 2005)	Lesson 4.2, p. 67: Muscle Hustle	Muscle fitness
Physical Best Activity Guide: Elementary Level (NASPE, 2005)	Lesson 5.6, p. 114: Mirror and Match	Flexibility
Youth Strength Training (Faigenbaum & Westcott, 2009)	An excellent guide for designing efficient, enjoyable, and productive programs for kids of varying abilities in elementary school (ages 7-10), middle school (11-14), and high school (15-18).	Muscle fitness

Wellness Week 4: K-2

Resource	Description	General concept
Physical Best Activity Guide: Elementary Level (NASPE, 2005)	Lesson 6.1, p. 132: Maintaining Balance	Energy balance
Physical Best Activity Guide: Elementary Level (NASPE, 2005)	Lesson 6.6, p. 142: Nutrition Hunt	Nutrition
PBS Teachers (www.pbs.org/teachers/)	Free health and fitness resources for teachers	Health and fitness

Wellness Week 4: 3-6

Resource	Description	General concept
Physical Best Activity Guide: Elementary Level (NASPE, 2005)	Lesson 6.9, p. 149: Metabolism Medley	Energy balance
Physical Best Activity Guide: Elementary Level (NASPE, 2005)	Lesson 7.9, p. 175: Everyday and Sometimes Foods	Nutrition
Eat Well & Keep Moving (Cheung et al., 2007)	This skill-building approach to motivating upper-elementary students to eat better and stay active began as a joint research project between the Harvard School of Public Health and Baltimore Public Schools.	Nutrition and activity

APPENDIX B

NASPE Standards

NASPE standards (NASPE, 2004) guided the development of the lesson objectives for each of the **FFL: Elementary** PE lesson plans. This appendix contains a list of the selected NASPE standards and a brief description of performance outcomes that are addressed in the **FFL: Elementary** lesson plans. They are grouped by NASPE grade-level groupings (K-2, 3-5, 6-8) and content standards (1-6). The standards and performance outcomes are adapted from NASPE, 2004, *Moving into the future: National standards for physical education*, 2nd ed. (Reston, VA: Author).

Grades K-2

NASPE standards are grouped by the following grade levels: K-2, 3-5, 6-8, and 9-12. NASPE standards and performance outcomes used in creating the **FFL: Elementary** program for the K-2 grade levels are presented here.

Standard 1: Motor Skills and Movement Patterns

Children are active and enjoy learning and mastering new skills. Children achieve mature forms of movement patterns, including more mature patterns using various body parts.
Performance outcomes:

- A: Performs simple dance steps.
- B: Demonstrates clear contrast between fast and slow movements—keeping tempo.
- C: Demonstrates a smooth transition between locomotor skills in time to music.
- D: Discovers how to balance on different body parts.

- E: Performs more mature movement patterns using various body parts.
- F: Enjoys learning new activities and skills.

Standard 2: Movement Concepts, Principles, Strategies, and Tactics Applied to Learning and Performance

Children mature in cognitive abilities associated with movement. They learn to apply concepts to movements and to identify correct form in movement performances.
Performance outcomes:

- A: Identifies body planes (front, back, side).
- B: Identifies various body parts (knee, foot, arm, palm).
- C: States short-term effects of physical activity on heart and lungs.
- D: Explains that appropriate practice improves performance.
- E: Uses knowledge in movement situations.

Standard 3: Participates Regularly in Physical Activity

Children participate for pleasure and have fun while being active. They perform locomotor and nonlocomotor activities and use them during free time. They recognize the temporary and lasting effects of activity on the body and choose to perform activities that benefit health.
Performance outcomes:

- A: Engages in moderate to vigorous physical activity on an intermittent basis.

- B: Engages in a variety of locomotor activities (hopping, walking, jumping).
- C: Has fun while being active.
- D: Learns locomotor and nonlocomotor activities and uses them in free time.
- E: Knows several health benefits of physical activity.

Standard 4: Achieves and Maintains Health-Enhancing Physical Fitness

Children engage in activities that enhance health-related fitness and enjoy them. They recognize factors associated with moderate to vigorous activity (e.g., sweating, fast heart rate, heavy breathing). Students have basic knowledge about and understand the five parts of health-related fitness.

Performance outcomes:

- A: Demonstrates sufficient muscular strength to be able to bear body weight.
- B: Engages in a series of locomotor activities (e.g., timed segments of hopping, walking, and so on) without easily tiring.
- C: Recognizes physical responses to activity associated with fitness.
- D: Participates in a variety of games that increase breathing and heart rate.
- E: Sustains activity for increasingly longer periods of time while participating in various activities in physical education.
- F: Recognizes that health-related physical fitness consists of several different parts.

Standard 5: Exhibits Responsible Personal and Social Behavior and Respect for Others in Activity

Children discover the joy of playing with friends makes activities fun. They know safe practices and know how to apply rules. They use successful interpersonal communication during group activity. They appreciate cooperation in learning skills and cooperate, share, and work together to solve problems or meet a challenge.

Performance outcomes:

- A: Practices specific skills as assigned until the teacher signals the end of practice.
- B: Follows directions given to the class for an all-class activity.
- C: Shows compassion for others by helping them.
- D: Works in diverse group settings without interfering with others.
- E: Enjoys participating alone and in groups while exploring movement tasks.
- F: Accepts all playmates without regard to personal differences (e.g., ethnicity, gender, disability).
- G: Displays consideration of others while participating.
- H: Demonstrates the elements of socially acceptable conflict resolution during class activity.
- I: Shares and works well with other children in activity settings.

Standard 6: Values Physical Activity for Health, Enjoyment, Challenge, Self-Expression, and Social Interaction

Children are active and enjoy participating. They meet challenges of new movements and skills. They feel joy when they achieve competence and begin to function as a member of a group and use cooperation in activity.

Performance outcomes:

- A: Exhibits both verbal and nonverbal indicators of enjoyment.
- B: Willingly tries new movements and skills.
- C: Continues to participate when not successful on the first try.
- D: Identifies several activities that are enjoyable.
- E: Expresses personal feelings on progress while learning a new skill.
- F: Enjoys activity involvement and achieving motor skills.
- G: Functions well with other children in group activities.

Grades 3-6

NASPE standards are grouped by the following grade levels: K-2, 3-5, 6-8, and 9-12. The performance outcomes used in creating the **FFL: Elementary** program for grades 3-5 are listed below and are based on the grades 3-5 NASPE standards. The grade 6 performance outcomes are based on selected standards appropriate for grade 6 from the grades 6-8 NASPE standards. The standards and performance outcomes for grades 3-6 are listed here.

Standard 1: Motor Skills and Movement Patterns

Grades 3-6: Older children develop more mature fundamental motor skills for pleasurable movement experiences. They demonstrate locomotor, nonlocomotor, and manipulative skills and use these skills in a variety of environments and in various combinations.

Performance outcomes:

- A: Performs basic dance steps (e.g., tinikling).
- B: Demonstrates correct pattern for dance steps (e.g., polka).
- C: Uses skills in various combinations.
- D: Demonstrates advanced (mature) movement patterns.
- E: Demonstrates tactics (grade 6).
- F: Performs a variety of dances (grade 6).

Standard 2: Movement Concepts, Principles, Strategies, and Tactics Applied to Learning and Performance

Grades 3-5: Older children comprehend more complex concepts and principles and apply them in activity. They use feedback to correct their performances and can transfer concepts and principles from one activity for use in another.

Grade 6: Children exhibit complex discipline-specific knowledge; can apply principles related to practice and conditioning in activity; and can apply movement concepts, principles, and strategies. They can correct personal errors and describe principles of training that improve fitness.

Performance outcomes:

- A: Describes how heart rate is used to monitor exercise intensity.
- B: Explains the necessity of transferring weight from the back leg to the front leg during any action that propels an object forward.
- C: Explains how appropriate practice improves performance.
- D: Identifies physical and psychological benefits that result from long-term participation in physical activity.
- E: Can correct errors when given feedback (grade 6).
- F: Applies movement concepts, principles, and strategies (grade 6).
- G: Exhibits specific knowledge (grade 6).
- H: Can detect personal errors (grade 6).
- I: Describes and applies fitness principles (grade 6).

Standard 3: Participates Regularly in Physical Activity

Grades 3-5: Older children use conscious decision making to choose enjoyable activities that have health benefits. They can be active for longer periods and can identify opportunities for being active in a variety of settings. They use movement concepts to sustain enjoyable activity and regulate it.

Grade 6: Children participate in activities independently, set goals based on needs and interests, and apply practices and training principles. They participate in a broad range of activities and maintain an activity log.

Performance outcomes:

- A: Chooses activities that are enjoyable, and knows their benefits (grade 6).
- B: Participates for longer periods of time (grade 6).
- C: Chooses to participate in moderate to vigorous physical activity.

- D: Chooses to participate in structured and purposeful activity.
- E: Monitors physical activity.
- F: Maintains a physical activity log for two or three days.
- G: Participates independently (grade 6).
- H: Sets personal goals based on needs and interests (grade 6).
- I: Applies and practices activity principles (grade 6).
- J: Participates in a range of activities and maintains a log (grade 6).

Standard 4: Achieves and Maintains Health-Enhancing Physical Fitness

Grades 3-5: Older children participate in activity to improve fitness and can participate for a longer time without tiring. They do activity for health-related fitness and use physical indicators to monitor and make adjustments in activity. They take and learn about fitness tests as well as learn to interpret results with assistance.

Grade 6: Children participate in many activities without fatigue, know the components of and participate in activities for many parts of health-related fitness, and know the physical signs of exertion (e.g., heart rate, fast breathing, sweating). They can assess health-related fitness and interpret the results, set goals and monitor progress, and apply principles of training (overload, threshold, specificity).

Performance outcomes:

- A: Participates in selected activities to promote health-related fitness.
- B: Engages in activity that promotes cardiorespiratory fitness.
- C: Recognizes physical responses to activity associated with fitness.
- D: Participates in activities that build strength.
- E: Can explain consequences of poor flexibility.
- F: Maintains heart rate in target zone in aerobic activity.

- G: Meets age- and gender-specific health-related fitness standards.
- H: Identifies strengths and weaknesses on Fitnessgram tests.
- I: Participates in many activities.
- J: Knows parts of health-related fitness and participates in activities that promote them (grade 6).
- K: Can assess health-related fitness and interpret results (grades 5-6).
- L: Applies fitness principles (grade 6).
- M: Sets goals and monitors progress (grade 6).

Standard 5: Exhibits Responsible Personal and Social Behavior and Respect for Others in Activity

Grades 3-5: Older children are active and learn to work independently in groups and enjoy diversity in activity settings. They follow rules, safe practices, procedures, and etiquette. They continue to develop communication and cooperative skills. They continue to develop cultural and ethnic awareness and appreciate differences in others.

Grade 6: Children recognize the role of activity in understanding diversity, respect differences of others, and can move beyond just following rules to reflect on ethical behavior in cooperative and competitive activities. They work with greater independence, develop the ability to resolve conflicts, and use time wisely.

Performance outcomes:

- A: Cooperates with other in taking turns and sharing.
- B: Works productively with others in dance sequences.
- C: Accepts teacher's decisions without negative reactions.
- D: Takes responsibility for personal actions and does not blame others.
- E: Shows ability to communicate (grade 6).
- F: Works independently (grades 5-6).
- G: Recognizes and appreciates similarities and differences of activity choices in peers.

- H: Respects views of peers in discussion of differences in dances.
- I: Demonstrates respect for peers with disabilities.
- J: Encourages others and refrains from put-down statements.
- K: Uses ethical behavior in activity and cooperates in competition beyond following rules (grade 6).
- L: Works with greater independence and uses time wisely (grade 6).
- M: Helps resolve conflicts (grade 6).

Standard 6: Values Physical Activity for Health, Enjoyment, Challenge, Self-Expression, and Social Interaction

Grades 3-5: Older children can identify fun activities and are challenged by new skills and activities. They can associate good practice with learning of skills. They choose appropriate activities for their ability levels and engage in activity with students of differing abilities.

Grade 6: Children interact well in social situations, respect others and their abilities, and build self-confidence and self-esteem through improved performance resulting from practice.

Performance outcomes:

- A: Identifies positive feelings associated with participation in activity.
- B: Chooses to participate in group physical activities.
- C: Understands that skill competency aids enjoyment and regular participation.
- D: Interacts with others and helps others in activity.
- E: Selects and practices a skill that needs improvement.
- F: Develops a dance sequence that is enjoyable.
- G: Defends the benefits of activity.
- H: Identifies fun activities.
- I: Interacts well in social situations (grade 6).
- J: Respects others and their abilities (grade 6).
- K: Builds self-confidence through activity and improvement from practice (grade 6).

REFERENCES AND SUGGESTED RESOURCES

Cheung, L.W.Y., Dart, H., Kalin, S., & Gortmaker, S. (2007). *Eat Well & Keep Moving: An interdisciplinary curriculum for teaching upper elementary school nutrition and physical activity.* 2nd ed. Champaign, IL: Human Kinetics.

Faigenbaum, A., & Westcott, W. (2009). *Youth strength training.* Champaign, IL: Human Kinetics.

Graham, G. (2008). *Teaching children physical education.* 3rd ed. Champaign, IL: Human Kinetics.

Hillman, C.H., Buck, S.M., Themanson, J.R., Pontifex, M.B., & Castelli, D. (2009a). Aerobic fitness and cognitive development: Event-related brain potential and task performance indices of executive control in preadolescent children. *Developmental Psychology, 45,* 114-129.

Hillman, C.H., Pontifex, M.B., Raine, L.B., Castelli, D.M., Hall, E.E., & Kramer, A.F. (2009b). The effect of acute treadmill walking on cognitive control and academic achievement in preadolescent children. *Neuroscience, 159,* 1044-1054.

Le Masurier, G.C., & Corbin, C.B. (2006). Top 10 reasons for quality physical education. *Journal of Physical Education Recreation and Dance, 77*(6), 44-53.

National Association for Sport and Physical Education (NASPE). (2004). *Moving into the future: National standards for physical education.* 2nd ed. Reston, VA: Author.

National Association for Sport and Physical Education (NASPE). (2005). *Physical Best activity guide: Elementary level.* 2nd ed. Champaign, IL: Human Kinetics.

Ogden, C.L., Carroll, M.D., & Flegal, K.M. (2008). High body mass index for age among US children and adolescents, 2003-2006. *Journal of the American Medical Association, 299*(20), 2401-2405.

Pangrazi, R.P., Beighle, A., & Sidman, C. (2007). *Pedometer power.* 2nd ed. Champaign, IL: Human Kinetics.

Ratey, J.J. (2008). *SPARK: The revolutionary new science of exercise and the brain.* New York: Little, Brown.

Seidentop, D., Hastie, P., & Van Der Mars, H. (2004). *Complete guide to sport education.* Champaign, IL: Human Kinetics.

Smith, N.J., & Lounsbery, M. (2009). Promoting physical education: The link to academic achievement. *Journal of Physical Education, Recreation and Dance, 80*(1), 39-43.

Tummers, N.E. (2009). *Teaching yoga for life.* Champaign, IL: Human Kinetics.

United States Department of Health and Human Services (USDHHS). (2008). 2008 physical activity guidelines for Americans: Be active, healthy, and happy. Washington, DC: Author. www.health.gov/paguidelines/guidelines/default.aspx.

ABOUT THE AUTHORS

Charles B. "Chuck" Corbin, PhD, is currently professor emeritus in the department of exercise and wellness at Arizona State University. He has published more than 200 journal articles and is the senior author of, sole author of, contributor to, or editor of more than 80 books, including the 5th edition of *Fitness for Life* (winner of the TAA's Texty Award), the 14th edition of *Concepts of Physical Fitness* (winner of the TAA's McGuffey Award), and the 7th edition of *Concepts of Fitness and Wellness*. His books are the most widely adopted high school and college texts in fitness and wellness. Dr. Corbin is internationally recognized as an expert in physical activity, health and wellness promotion, and youth physical fitness. He has presented keynote addresses at more than 40 state AHPERD conventions, made major addresses in more than 15 countries, and presented numerous named lectures (Cureton, ACSM; Hanna, Sargent, and Distinguished Scholar, NAKPEHE; Prince Phillip, British PEA; and Weiss and Alliance Scholar, AAHPERD). He is past president and fellow of AAKPE, fellow in the NASHPERDP, an ACSM fellow, and a lifetime member of AAHPERD. Among his awards are the Healthy American Fitness Leaders Award (President's Council on Physical Fitness and Sports—PCPFS, National Jaycees), AAHPERD Honor Award, Physical Fitness Council Honor Award, the COPEC Hanson Award, and the Distinguished Service Award of the PCPFS. Dr. Corbin was named the Alliance Scholar by AAHPERD and the Distinguished Scholar of NAKPEHE. He is a member of the Fitnessgram Advisory Board and was the first chair of the science board of the PCPFS and the NASPE Hall of Fame. In 2009 Dr. Corbin was chosen for the Gulick Award, the highest award of AAHPERD.

Guy Le Masurier, PhD, is a professor of physical education at Vancouver Island University, where he teaches courses in pedagogy, research methods, and nutrition for health and sport. Dr. Le Masurier is coauthor of the award-winning book *Fitness for Life: Middle School* (winner of the TAA's Texty Award) and has edited and contributed to several books, including the 5th edition of *Fitness for Life* and the *Physical Best Activity Guide*. He has published numerous articles related to youth physical activity and physical education and served as a coauthor on the *NASPE Physical Activity Guidelines for Children*. Dr. Le Masurier has delivered over 30 research and professional presentations at national and regional meetings and currently serves as the Epidemiology section editor for *Research Quarterly for Exercise and Sport* as well as the Health Foundations section editor for the *International Journal of Physical Education*. Dr. Le Masurier is the creator of the Walk Everyday Live Longer (WELL) program, a pedometer-based physical activity program used by the Arizona Department of Health Services. Dr. Le Masurier is a member of AAHPERD, NASPE, and ACSM. He lives with his wife on Protection Island in British Columbia, where they serve their community as volunteer firefighters. Guy is thankful for his morning kayak commutes.

Dolly D. Lambdin, EdD, is a senior lecturer in the department of kinesiology and health education at the University of Texas at Austin, where she teaches undergraduate courses in children's movement and methods of teaching as well as graduate courses in analysis of teaching and technology application in physical education.

Dr. Lambdin taught elementary physical education in public and private schools for 16 years and taught preservice teachers for 33 years at the university level. During much of that time, she taught simultaneously at both levels, a situation that required her to spend part of each day meeting the teaching and research demands of academia while tackling the daily adventure of teaching 5- to 14-year-olds. In addition, she has supervised over 100 student teachers, and as a result has been able to visit classes and learn from scores of wonderful cooperating teachers in the schools.

Dr. Lambdin has served as the president of NASPE (2004-05) and on the NASPE board of directors for two three-year terms. She has also served on numerous local, state, and national committees, including the writing teams for the Texas Essential Knowledge and Skills in Physical Education, the NASPE Beginning Teacher Standards, the Texas Beginning Teacher Standards, and the NASPE Appropriate Practices Revision. Dr. Lambdin has been honored as the Texas AHPERD Outstanding College and University Physical Educator of the Year.

Meg Greiner, MEd, is a national board-certified elementary physical education teacher at Independence Elementary School in Independence, Oregon. She has been teaching elementary physical education for 21 years and regularly receives student teachers and practicum students into her setting. Meg has received numerous national awards and accolades for her innovative physical education program and the development of TEAM Time, including the 2005 NASPE National Elementary Physical Education Teacher of the Year, 2005 *USA Today* All-USA Teacher Team, and the 2006 Disney Outstanding Specialist Teacher of the Year. Meg is currently working with NASPE as a Head Start Body Start trainer of trainers, serving on the AAHPERD Physical Best Committee, and presenting NASPE Pipeline Workshops all over the United States. She has served on the NASPE Council of Physical Education for Children and on the public relations committee. She has served as the physical education president for both Oregon and Northwest District AHPERDs. She also has served Oregon AHPERD in many capacities and has received the OAHPERD Honor Award.

CD/DVD INSTRUCTIONS

The **Fitness for Life: Elementary School** *Physical Education Lesson Plans* book contains two DVDs of videos, one CD-ROM of resources, and one CD of music. This section provides a brief overview of all four discs, along with technical details for accessing the CD-ROM. For details on how to use the contents of each disc, see "Using the Discs" on page 21.

Video DVDs

DVD 1 (Instructional Routines) and DVD 2 (Activity Routines) contain videos for physical educators to use with students. When you insert either disc in a DVD player, the screen displays a main menu of the routines for kindergarten through sixth grade. Select any grade to go to a submenu of that grade's routines for each Wellness Week. Table 1.3 (page 21) shows all the routines by grade and week.

Resources CD-ROM

The CD-ROM contains all the printable resources (as described starting on page 21) for use with the physical education lesson plans. This section explains the system requirements for using the disc and instructions for accessing its files.

System Requirements

You can use this CD-ROM on either a Windows®-based PC or a Macintosh computer. You will need Adobe® Reader® to view the PDF files.

Windows

- IBM PC compatible with Pentium processor
- Windows 98/2000/XP/Vista
- Adobe Reader 8.0
- Microsoft Word
- 4x CD-ROM drive

Macintosh

- Power Mac recommended
- System 10.4 or higher
- Adobe Reader
- Microsoft Word for Mac
- 4x CD-ROM drive

User Instructions

Follow the instructions for accessing the CD-ROM on a Windows-based PC or a Macintosh computer.

Windows

1. Insert the **Fitness for Life: Elementary School** *Physical Education Lesson Plans* CD-ROM. (Note: The CD-ROM must be present in the drive at all times.)
2. Select the "My Computer" icon from the desktop.
3. Select the CD-ROM drive.
4. Open the General folder or one of the Wellness Week folders to find the resource you wish to view. See the "00_Start.pdf" file for a complete list of the contents.

Macintosh

1. Insert the **Fitness for Life: Elementary School** *Physical Education Lesson Plans* CD-ROM. (Note: The CD-ROM must be present in the drive at all times.)
2. Double-click the CD icon located on the desktop.
3. Open the General folder or one of the Wellness Week folders to find the resource you wish to view. See the "00_Start.pdf" file for a complete list of the contents.

Music CD

The music CD contains 15 tracks for use with the physical education lesson plans. The lesson plans direct you when to play each track. For details about the music CD, see page 23.